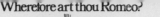

ERIC LYONS & SPAN

Edited by Barbara Simms

ERIC LYONS & SPAN

Edited by Barbara Simms

© Barbara Simms, 2006
Published by RIBA Publishing, 15 Bonhill Street, London EC2P 2EA

ISBN-10 1 85946 256 1
ISBN-13 978 1 85946 256 0

Stock Code 58648

The right of Barbara Simms to be identified as the Author of this Work have been asserted in accordance with the Copyright, Design and Patents Act 1988.

British Library Cataloguing in Publications Data
A catalogue record for this book is available from the British Library.

Publisher: Steven Cross
Commissioning Editor: Matthew Thompson
Managing Editor: Barbara Simms
Project Editor: Anna Walters
Copy Editor: Melanie Thompson
All images credited to Tim Crocker are © Tim Crocker. www.timcrocker.co.uk
Designed and typeset by Alison Oakley
Printed and bound by Cambridge University Press, Cambridge
Marketing: Indi Sihra

While every effort has been made to check the accuracy of the information given in this book, readers should always make their own checks. Neither the Authors nor the Publisher accept any responsibility for misstatements made in it or misunderstandings arising from it.

RIBA Publishing is part of RIBA Enterprises Ltd. www.ribaenterprises.com

Eric Lyons & Span was published with the support of the Paul Mellon Centre for Studies in British Art and CABE Space.

FOREWORD

I first encountered the work of Eric Lyons in the early 1970s as a student in Cambridge. John Meunier, then a young lecturer, gave one of his unmissable talks in which he unravelled the complex strands of current British architecture. John had a way of making a complicated world understandable and he spoke of an architectural spectrum in which he placed Archigram and its visions at one end and, separated by the mainstream, the work of Eric Lyons at the other. The talk was analytical rather than evaluating, as he rightly thought those conclusions were best left to history. Of course, it didn't stop us making up our own minds, and I think I was always more likely to be drawn to an architectural world in which true problems were solved and real buildings built, rather than inhabit a visionary world of theoretical fantasy.

Perhaps unsurprisingly, therefore, my second encounter was as an employee in Eric Lyons's office. In the idyllic setting of the Lyons's home, garden, and studio overlooking the River Mole at East Molesey, I began my first job. Although, as an office, it was far from democratic (we, in the drawing office, were placed in one space, whilst Eric Lyons and Ivor Cunningham drew energetically in another, which overlooked the foot of Eric's very beautiful garden), it was nevertheless a place where a young architect could learn and absorb a great deal. The office was very busy and Eric and Ivor both talked with an intense enthusiasm about their work.

In low-cost housing, the two of them were masters of the value of systematic repetition. This was never celebrated in the manner of some of their well-regarded (if over-heroic) contemporaries, but was used carefully to form elements incomplete in themselves but which, when placed together, would form a whole in which much more might be possible than by the simple sum of individual parts. They knew the value of a well-planted landscape and were unafraid of bringing buildings and landscape together in deliberately picturesque compositions to the benefit of both.

I was later able to test firsthand the success of their designs in my third encounter with their work. I was fortunate in the early eighties to buy a house in The Plantation at Blackheath. Whilst the houses were small (but even then affordable), I find it hard to imagine a more pleasant and safe place, so close to the city, in which to bring up young children. A shared garden setting made the making of friends easy and a sensible management structure helped to ensure the maintenance of not only the buildings and gardens but also the aims of the community.

Living closely with the work of Eric Lyons and Span, I am aware that it may never have grasped the imagination of the editors of fashionable architectural journals in the same way as some of Eric's more attention-seeking contemporaries. I cannot help feeling, however, that as the echoes of their 'loud' architecture fades, the qualities in his work, which has so manifestly touched the lives of so many, will cumulatively gain in its relative significance.

Graham Morrison
Allies and Morrison Architects

PREFACE

This book about the architect Eric Lyons and his main client Span Developments has taken some time to be completed – due primarily to the time taken to collect the vast amount of information available from a number of sources, whilst also carrying on the Eric Lyons Cunningham Metcalfe practice until my retirement in 2003. That, of course, is no excuse, as I could have started harvesting appropriate material much sooner after Eric died in 1980. Even before then, besides my own experiences of working with him since November 1955, there was information to be gathered from other members of his staff, consultants, clients and his friends. During the early to mid-1990s, I began to think seriously about a book on Eric Lyons and Span and approached a number of authors. I also started to carry out my own 'research', reading architectural magazines and the odd book, visiting the RIBA library, and contacting a number of people with knowledge of Eric Lyons and/or Span. I was able to visit and interview Geoffrey Townsend, the remaining member of the original Span Group, and a number of others and record their memories. Over the years, I have also been interviewed on the subject of Eric Lyons and Span by students and academics, many of whom were able to take advantage of the scope and extent of articles and drawings of our architecture and site layouts, as well as the planting of our schemes – in due course they sent me copies of their theses, which have added to this archive.

Eric Lyons had clear views on his approach to life, including where he lived and worked, and established his office as part of his living accommodation outside the Greater London area. To quote him: 'I have kept a small office going. I believe in small buildings. I think that good architecture comes from small groups working together. I married a small wife. Even if I don't totally believe that you can nourish life in small simple terms, it is a check against megalomania'. During my twenty-four years working with him Lyons employed over 130 staff, of which about 110 were architects and 'year out' students, two landscape architects and a couple of quantity surveyors. The minimum number (excluding support staff) was five in 1960, with a maximum of 15 in 1971. The total number of built Span jobs was 73, which included around 2,134 dwellings, whilst the number of built non-Span commissions was 38, including about 3,000 dwellings as well as five sheltered homes, three primary schools, a university building, a medical centre, a community hall, an office building, seven shops and the competition-winning development at the new leisure town of Vilamoura in Portugal.

Needless to say, Eric Lyons was deeply involved in all of the projects, as well as being on the RIBA Council for many years (1959-80), its President for two years (1975-77) and the first Chair of the Association of Consultant Architects (1973-75).

I am delighted that my many years of research, interviews and cataloguing of the plans and other archives in the office at Mill House, East Molesey, have formed the sure foundation on which this book is based, and that Eric Lyons's contribution to architecture and the quality of life has, at last, been fully acknowledged. In conclusion, I would like to quote a few words written in 1980 as part of an Association of Consultant Architects' brochure for the Eric Lyons Memorial Fund:

> As a modern architect and industrial designer, Eric wanted to put modern architecture within the financial and intellectual reach of the middle range of house buyers, and he did this through Span Developments Limited against all the worldly wisdom of housing experts. The creation of space within and without the dwelling fascinated him. His response to landscape was urban and he saw landscape design as an extension of architecture by other means and as a necessary component of urbanism.

Ivor Cunningham

EDITOR'S PREFACE

This book celebrates the achievement of Eric Lyons in the design of buildings and in their integration with their surroundings. Lyons was publicly recognised by many awards and also within his profession by his election as President of the Royal Institute of British Architects (RIBA) 1975-77. This book, and accompanying exhibition at the RIBA, is based on original drawings, models and photographs. Both are a showcase for Lyons's working life of nearly fifty years and, in a period of expanding house building, are a timely evaluation of a past example relevant to today's housing needs.

This comprehensive study of the work of Eric Lyons and Span has as its foundation the archive collected and catalogued over many years by Ivor Cunningham, architect and landscape architect in the Lyons practice. The ten chapters of the book, including the meticulously compiled and illustrated Gazetteer, bring together, as contributors, a group of academics, practitioners and Span enthusiasts. They have all been extraordinary in giving their time and expertise unstintingly. Kate Lyons, Eric's wife, has also generously given her time, her memories and the freedom of her home at Mill House to enable a full picture of Eric to be presented. The colour images used are largely the work of the architectural photographer, Tim Crocker, whose enthusiastic appreciation of Span has made a significant contribution to this authoritative publication.

The respect and affection which Eric Lyons commanded has been demonstrated time after time during the preparation of this book by the willingness of his family, friends and colleagues to provide information. Most importantly, thanks are due to the many Span residents, past and present, who have come forward with original documents, reminiscences and photographs, demonstrating their enjoyment of the Span way of life.

The publication of this book has been made possible by the support of the Paul Mellon Centre and CABE Space, whose confidence in the project is gratefully acknowledged. Thanks are also due to Matthew Thompson of RIBA Publishing whose enthusiasm and expertise has guided the book from concept to final form.

Barbara Simms
Managing Editor

CONTRIBUTORS

Madeleine Adams is an architect in practice and co-director of Research Design Architecture Ltd. She is a senior lecturer at the University of East London, and has taught at the University of Cambridge, University College London and the University of the West of England. She has a particular interest in current housing design and is involved in schemes ranging from the single dwelling to the large scale masterplanning for new communities. She lives in a T15 house in Blackheath.

Neil Bingham is an architectural and design historian. For more than twenty years he has been a curator of architectural drawings for the Royal Institute of British Architects and the Royal Academy of Arts, London. His best selling book is *Modern Retro: Living with Mid-Century Style*, with Andrew Weaving, which is in nine language co-editions. His latest book is *The New Boutique: Architecture and Design*. Neil is a regular contributor to *Blueprint*. He lives in an A3M-type Span house in Blackheath.

Patrick Ellard became interested in Span when his parents moved to New Ash Green in 1969. Inspired by the experience, he went on to study furniture design and the history of art and design, which led to a career in design education. He is currently senior lecturer in product design (Contextual Studies) at Ravensbourne College, Kent. Patrick has written widely on the early history of New Ash Green and was co-creator of the first Span website in 2000. He now lives in a perfectly preserved K1A bungalow in New Ash Green and is a consultant member of the Village's Amenity Committee.

Elain Harwood is a senior investigator with English Heritage, having for many years specialised in researching post-war buildings for listing. This resulted in *England, a Guide to Post-War Listed Buildings*, first published in 1999 and revised for Batsford in 2003. She is currently writing a book on English architecture between 1945 and 1975, *Space, Hope and Brutalism*, to be published by English Heritage and Yale University Press, and is completing a PhD at Bristol University on post-war architecture for theatre, music and the fine arts. Elain is also one of the editors of *Twentieth Century Architecture*, the Journal of the Twentieth Century Society.

Charlie MacKeith is a practising architect and co-director of Research Design Architecture Ltd. He studied architecture at Cambridge and Harvard universities and was a senior lecturer at the University of Manchester until 1994. Charlie was the project architect on the RIBA award winning Manchester Museum extension completed in 2003. His practice explores contemporary possibilities, but is often involved in the restoration of valued historic buildings. He is currently working on the refurbishment of a 1954 Festival of Britain housing project by Maxwell Fry and Jane Drew, and the restoration of a Grade 1 listed former Chapel in Lewisham. Charlie lives in a T15 house in Blackheath.

Alan Powers is Reader in Architecture and Cultural History at the University of Greenwich. He has written widely on 20th-century British architecture, art and design, including *Serge Chermayeff* (RIBA Publications, 2001), *Eric Ravilious, Imagined Realities* (Philip Wilson, 2003), *The Twentieth Century House in Britain* (Aurum, 2004) *Modern: the Modern Movement in Britain* (Merrell, 2005) and *Britain* in the series 'Modern Architectures in History' (Reaktion, 2006). He has also curated a number of exhibitions, most recently *Elegant Variation: the architecture of H. T. Cadbury-Brown RA*, at the Royal Academy, 2006.

Barbara Simms is a garden and landscape historian with a particular interest in the design, conservation and interpretation of landscapes of the 20th and 21st centuries. She is a lecturer in garden history at Birkbeck College (University of London) and Cambridge University Institute of Education. A former owner of a T8 house in Wimbledon, Barbara recently completed a dissertation on landscape conservation on Span estates at the Architectural Association. She is editor of *Garden History*, the Journal of the Garden History Society and is currently writing a book on the garden designer John Brookes, to be published by Conran Octopus in 2007.

Jan Woudstra trained as a landscape architect and historian. He initially worked for Travers Morgan in London and later set up his own practice, EDA Environmental Design Associates. In 1997 he completed his PhD, *Landscape for Living: Landscape theory and design of the Modern Movement*, at University College London. He has taught on a part-time basis on the course *Landscape Conservation and Change*, at the Architectural Association School of Architecture in London since 1988 and at the University of Sheffield, where he teaches landscape architecture and history, including modules on site planning for housing, since 1995.

CONTENTS

"There is a tendency to contain the architect, guide him,
control him, make sure he doesn't make a mistake. The
process is guaranteed to get rid of the bumps, and one
of my obsessions is that bumps matter. Like porridge,
bumps are good for you. They are the sign of man
whereas flatness is the sign of the machine."

Eric Lyons

The figure lies on his back, head bent forward, legs bunched up, arms entangled. He struggles within a closed space weighed down by the interring wall. The contorted form, a slim Atlas holding up his world, is *The Architect in Society* (Fig. 1.1). In 1959, this sculpture by Keith Godwin had been placed at the main entrance of Hallgate, marking the completion of these flats in Blackheath Park, southeast London: 'A bit obvious as a joke but we didn't want anyone to miss it', said Eric Lyons of the piece.[1] Getting the flats built had been a gruelling struggle for its architect and the development company Span, particularly over planning issues. The sculpture was a victory marker. No one who knew the story missed the point that the struggling figure represented Eric Lyons.

Like *The Architect in Society*, Eric Lyons was a fighter. He fought to build his designs, and he challenged changes others wanted to impose upon him. He clashed with central government and local authorities, planners and other architects. And when Lyons went to battle, he never did it quietly. He was motivated by the desire to free himself and other architects from what he viewed as the tyrannies of aesthetic and bureaucratic control.

Architecturally trained during the 1930s in the new modernism, Eric Lyons emerged after the Second World War into the heady atmosphere of social utopianism. The urgent need to rehouse a British population much displaced and living in poor conditions had accelerated building technology, based upon standardised and economical systems of construction. In his own architecture, Lyons embraced many of the prevailing rational approaches to design and

build, especially repetition of form and standardisation of parts, using them to create not only fine social housing, but exceptional speculative middle-income housing. But with a rebel's heart, he perceived the authoritarian ideology that such technology could engender: 'There is a tendency to contain the architect, guide him, control him, make sure he doesn't make a mistake. The process is guaranteed to get rid of the bumps, and one of my obsessions is that bumps matter. Like porridge, bumps are good for you. They are the sign of man whereas flatness is the sign of the machine'.[2]

Lyons argued for social justice through architecture and design. He was a brilliant conversationalist (if not perhaps, it was often remarked, a little one-sided), and spoke passionately with wit, humour and intelligence. His humane values came to be appreciated, his architecture admired. He won the respect of his architectural and professional peers, his opponents and the thousands of residents who live in his buildings (even if they might not be familiar with his identity). By the time he became President of the Royal Institute of British Architects (RIBA) in 1975, Eric Lyons had come to national and international recognition as a spokesperson for the 'architect in society'.

Eric Lyons's early life and training
Scepticism, tempered by a sharp wit that often accompanies it, was Eric Lyons's inheritance. His father, Benjamin Wolff Lyons (1877–1946), had fought in the First World War on the front lines around Ypres, taking part in the battle of Hill 60.[3] The experience had undermined his Jewish faith. Eric's younger sister, Rita, recalls

Fig 1.1 *The Architect in Society.* The sculpture by Keith Godwin placed at the entrance to Hallgate, Blackheath, in 1959.

Fig 1.2 Eric Lyons, in the centre, pulling his father's hair, with his sister Rita and cousin Cecil, c. 1920.

Fig 1.3 Eric's parents, Ben and Caroline Lyons, in the garden of the family home in Balham, c. 1935.

that their father had a strong influence on Eric, and in such matters of religion, Eric himself never practiced. Eric had been young when his father was away in the trenches. He was born 2 October 1912 in Highbury, north London, relocating with his mother Caroline (nee Emanuel) (1887–1974) to Brighton during the war, Rita having been born in 1914. When his father returned, the family moved back to London, living in the City for a time with Eric's maternal grandfather, an orange importer, before eventually settling in Balham,[4] south London, where Eric attended Rae Central School in nearby Clapham. With the addition of his brother Stanley, eleven years Eric's junior, the family was a close one. For a living Mr Lyons made soft-toys; he was creative and a problem solver – and a good amateur magician too. Eric often competed with his father in games and mathematical puzzles. There was a half-size snooker table in the home and the family also enjoyed playing different types of card games, especially poker. Everyone was fond of singing popular songs and the operettas of Gilbert and Sullivan, with Benjamin accompanying on one of the several instruments he played (Figs. 1.2 and 1.3).

Eric Lyons began his architectural training in May 1929, first as a pupil then articled clerk to the architect J. Stanley Beard in Baker Street, London.[5] In those early years he would have learnt office routine, how to survey sites and existing buildings, and worked on detail drawings. He also enrolled in the evening courses in architecture at the Regent Street Polytechnic, known for its good design and sensible approach to construction.[6] Graduating in 1932, he passed many of his courses with distinction.[7] After three years of articles with Beard, Lyons stayed on for a further year as a junior assistant. Beard was a cinema architect and cinema design was to become a speciality for the young Lyons over the next decade. In

January 1934, he moved on to the offices of William Edward Trent, cinema architect for the Gaumont–British Picture Corporation, as a junior draughtsman, then assistant.[8] This was followed by time with Leslie Kemp, yet another cinema architect, from January 1934 to April 1935.

With Gropius

On 12 February 1936, as he was recovering from chicken pox, the 23-year old Lyons received two offers of work in the post. One came from his former employer, W. E. Trent.[9] The other was from E. Maxwell Fry and demanded a prompt response: 'We shall expect to see you here at 9:30am tomorrow (Thursday) and should be glad if you could bring a tee-square with you'.[10] This was a position that Lyons must have pressed vigorously to obtain. Fry was a leading British architect, only in his mid-30s at the time, but having just completed a series of major buildings in the high modern style. And, if this was not incentive enough for Lyons to join his office, working alongside Fry was one of the most revered architects of the period – Walter Gropius.

As the founder of the Bauhaus in Weimar, Germany, in 1919, and architect of numerous modern movement masterpieces, Gropius had found himself under pressure to leave Germany in 1934 with the rise of Nazism. Max Fry had offered to be his architectural sponsor, for under British regulations émigré architects had to be associated with established local practitioners. Gropius worked with Fry until March 1937, when he moved to America to take up the Chair of Architecture at Harvard University. The final year that Gropius practiced with Fry coincided with Lyons's employment. Lyons was assigned to the project for Impington Village College, Cambridgeshire, a day school with facilities for adult evening classes. He undertook a survey of the site in October 1936 followed by drawing up the design plans.[11] Fry later recalled that in designing Impington 'it raised us all, Gropius and all my fellow workers, to a higher level of existence'.[12] Lyons became a disciple of Gropius, struck by his heartfelt approach to architecture; he found inspiration in his hero's beliefs in the architect as a leader in the arts, embracing technology but keeping control of it: 'You must come through with the fundaments',[13] was one of Gropius's maxims that Lyons liked to quote to his own young architects later in his career.[14]

Lyons's lively character in the Fry and Gropius office was fondly remembered by Jack Howe, whom Gropius would entrust with carrying through the Impington project after his departure for America. Howe recalled how Lyons was a fan of Groucho Marx, dressing up like the comedian for a party, a caper he often repeated when fancy dress was called for. Complete with large painted black moustache and cigar, Lyons bore an uncanny resemblance to Groucho, and knew all the wisecracks.[15] This lasting affinity made

Fig 1.4   Perspective drawing by Eric Lyons of Alhambra House, Charing Cross Road, London, designed by Andrew Mather and Harry Weedon, 1937.

Fig 1.5   Eric Lyons and Geoff Townsend, 1955.

Lyons sometimes break out into the snarling accents of Groucho at the most serious moments, be it over discussions about contract documents,[16] or when, for instance, at the height of his career in responding to a left-wing architect in a conference audience, he quipped 'I'm a Marxist too, you know – a Groucho Marxist'.[17]

After leaving Fry and Gropius, Lyons moved back into cinema design, joining as an architect's assistant to Andrew Mather. At the time, Mather was working with Harry W. Weedon, another respected name in British cinema architecture, creating their most well-known and finest building, the Odeon Leicester Square. Lyons, coming on to the team at the end of March 1937, arrived at the tail end of the job, just before the theatre's grand opening in November. His main assignment became Alhambra House, the large office block backing the Odeon on Charing Cross Road (Fig. 1.4).[18]

Leaving Mather's office in November 1938, Lyons stepped into a new life and career, although it was to be for a short period only, as the Second World War broke out less than a year later. Whilst at Regent Street Polytechnic, he had met fellow architectural student Geoff Townsend; the two of them now joined forces to design speculative houses in and around Twickenham and Whitton in southwest London. It was the beginning of what would become Span.

Lyons and Townsend

Geoffrey Paulson Townsend was just a year older than Lyons, born on 11 May 1911 in Twickenham.[19] He came from a family of artists. His father, William, was a decorative painter and a tutor at the Royal College of Needlework, and Ernest, his father's brother, was a highly-respected portrait painter in Derby, from where the family originated (Fig. 1.5). When very young, Ernest had started his career in architecture before turning his hand to painting. Even Geoff's mother, Beatrice (Biddy) Jones, was an art teacher. His father-in-law, however, was a stockbroker and Geoff was to be very influenced by his good business sense.

Astute and entrepreneurial, Geoff Townsend had left school when sixteen years old to take up carpentry. His first jobs were refurbishing sash window frames and other bits of buildings, working out of a shed in the garden of the family home. Within a few years, to learn about architectural practice, he had taken a position as a draughtsman to an architect in nearby Hounslow, who was designing speculative houses in the popular neo-Tudor style, sometimes turning round a set of drawings in two days. Absorbing this quick approach to building, Townsend, at the age of only twenty-one, used a small amount of family money to start designing and building small, terraced maisonette and semi-detached houses in Whitton and Twickenham. Having gained contacts with local sub-contractors, who were available to be on site quickly and worked fast, Townsend could execute a project in as little as six weeks. Meanwhile, he was honing his architectural skills by working three days a week as a draughtsman for the architect Robert Lutyens, the son of Sir Edwin Lutyens. Beginning in 1933, he also became an evening student at Regent Street Polytechnic, where he befriended Eric Lyons.

In 1938, Townsend set up a company called Modern Homes with offices in the converted Victorian baths known as Dome Buildings in The Quadrant, Richmond upon Thames, not far from Twickenham. It was here that Lyons joined him. Their first joint venture consisted of Lyons developing Townsend's basic designs for speculative houses, which included a group of maisonettes adjoining the Royal Military School of Music at Kneller Hall in Twickenham.

Instrumental in several of these schemes was a local Twickenham family company of builders, E. Gostling Builders Limited – a father with a trio of sons. The company was to become the constructional backbone throughout Eric Lyons's whole career, especially for the Span projects. Edward Gostling Junior had taken over the firm from his father, and his son Frank, who had joined him in 1927, had met Townsend in the same year when the firm was carrying out plumbing works and alterations to the Townsend's family home. Townsend had even drawn up a few house plans for the Gostlings. In 1936, Peter Gostling joined the company, as did Jack two years later.[20]

Building for victory

However, all these joint ventures dissolved when war was declared in late 1939. Lyons obtained a temporary position as senior draughtsman in March 1940 with the Trussed Concrete Steel Company, at a war wage of £3.0s.0d a week – a change from the £5.0s.0d he was making with Fry and Gropius. Working with this large company, known more informally as Truscon, brought Lyons into contact with civil and structural engineers standardising building techniques for quick results.

But after just less than a year, he fell back upon his cinema connections by going to work for Harry Weedon; this meant moving up to Weedon's office in Harborne, on the outskirts of Birmingham (Fig. 1.6).[21] Weedon, who besides cinemas had been building large industrial structures, was now specialising in air raid shelters, hostels and shadow factories (camouflaged buildings).[22] 'We would finish a place one day, stir up the ashes the following morning and put it up again', Lyons later recounted.[23] Whilst practicing in Weedon's office, he also worked up a few simple designs by Weedon, such as a stadium for Birmingham City Football Club, an optimistic exercise during those dark days. Everyone in his office found Weedon to be an aloof character of the old school, a

Fig 1.6   Eric at his drawing table, probably in Harry Weedon's office c. 1942.

Fig 1.7 Tecta armchair designed by Eric Lyons, 1946.

great authoritarian who did not allow general staff to enter his office unless he switched on a green light. Lyons, in a more senior capacity, however, had free access and John Sheldon, a fellow architect in the practice at the time, recalled that there were often loud arguments heard throughout the office from behind the closed door when Eric was in seeing their boss.[24]

Mill House

To keep himself intellectually attuned, Lyons attended classes in English Literature at the local Workers' Education Association. Here, one cold October evening in 1942, lounging bundled up against the chill of the unheated room in his coat, scarf and incongruous trilby hat, he met Kate Townsend – a twenty year old school teacher working in the deprived areas of Birmingham.[25] She took rooms in the house that Eric was renting with his friends, the engineer John Price and his wife Jean. In March 1944, Lyons and Kate married at the Registry Office in Birmingham, borrowing the fee from their friends who had come as witnesses. A few months later they moved down to London so that Lyons could rejoin Townsend, who had also been working during the war on the organisation of factories. In East Molesey, a ten-minute stroll south across the River Thames from Hampton Court Palace, Eric and Kate Lyons found rooms to rent in a large, late-Victorian villa later named Mill House. Imposing and turreted, the house stood hidden from the road, approached along the drive through a large stand of trees, an expansive lawn behind reaching down to the pretty banks of the River Mole. Mill House was to become the Lyons's family home and Eric's studio for the rest of his life.[26]

In those closing days of the war and when peace finally arrived, Eric Lyons and Geoff Townsend took almost anything in the form of work that came their way. Townsend had the contacts, especially among the local estate agents in the area; he found the properties, either virgin sites or, more usually during that immediate post-war period, a house or building bomb-damaged and in need of repairs, to be converted into flats or semi-demolished for almost totally new build. Townsend also fished for larger commissions from local authorities for public housing, which the government had authorised as high priority; these were substantial jobs. The Gostling brothers returned as invaluable allies as builders and, until he succumbed to multiple sclerosis, Townsend's brother, Philip, assisted with business matters, making valued connections in property transactions.

And Lyons did the designs. In those first few years, alongside the building works, Lyons entered the major competitions of the period, such as the Trades Union Congress Building.[27] Although rarely scoring a win, he found these exercises invaluable and would later encourage younger architects to try their hand at as many competitions as they had time to enter. During this period, however,

Fig 1.8   Leslie Bilsby, 1962.

designing exhibition stands proved more lucrative, and Lyons put together several for the McMurdo Instrument Company; he even designed a battery charger for them. For Celestion, a sister company of McMurdo, he produced an audio 'midget speaker'. However, his most successful enterprise was a range of bentwood furniture, called Tecta, manufactured by the Packet Furniture Limited. He first exhibited a table and two dining chairs in the range at the important *Britain Can Make It* exhibition held at the Victoria & Albert Museum in 1946.[28] There was also an armchair and lounge chair in the series, which he modified in 1949 (Fig. 1.7). The range was demountable, picking up on the latest post-war fashion for pieces that could be shipped flat-packed and assembled.[29] As an admirer of modern Scandinavian design, Lyons's furniture was inspired by chair designers such as the Dane Hans Wegner. There were also overtones in Lyons's pieces of the bentwood furniture by the Danish architect Arne Jacobsen, whom Lyons believed had gained a greater insight into building construction through designing furniture.[30]

Soon after the war, Lyons and Townsend took on staff. John Sheldon, who had worked under Lyons in Weedon's office, appears to have been the first, arriving in November 1945 and staying until 1949 when he left to join the 1951 Festival of Britain team. When he first met Lyons, Sheldon had taken a dislike to him, but finding him clear-headed and a strong and stimulating personality, he ended up such an admirer that, half a century later, looking back over his own successful career, he acknowledged that Lyons had not only been his greatest influence, but those years at the end of the 1940s had been the best of his life.[31] Sheldon's heartfelt tribute spoke for many of the more than one hundred architects over the next thirty-five years who passed through Eric Lyons's office.

The architect acting as property developer had been a common practice in Britain, especially during the Georgian period, but by the mid-19th century was viewed as a conflict of interests. As Geoff Townsend found himself clearly on the developing side of his partnership with Lyons, he resigned from the RIBA in 1953 and set up a development partnership with Henry Cushman, a mortgage agent for the Alliance Building Society. Townsend and Cushman were to run several companies under various names – Townsman Investments, Bargood Estates, Hampton Cross – purchasing and developing sites.

What set Townsend apart from the vast majority of other developers was his great commitment to contemporary design, especially in the field of speculative housing. Being an architect himself, he nurtured the architects he worked alongside, particularly, of course, Eric Lyons. He understood that he had to put more, both financially and personally, into these projects to make them attractive to a middle-income buyer looking for modern quality. Townsend also took into consideration the continued well-being of the residents and buildings by introducing residents' associations – in other words, a community.

Leslie Bilsby and the emergence of Span

Oaklands, the block of flats completed in 1948 with its unique combination of generous landscaping, modern-styled building and residents' association, is considered the first Span development. These were the Span ideals, but as a name, Span did not enter the architectural lexicon until 1957, after the completion of Parkleys, Ham Common. Townsend, by this time, had joined up with another property developer, Leslie Bilsby, who was also to take an important role in the story of Span (Figs. 1.8 and 1.9). Townsend and Bilsby, along with Ernest Haynes acting as the financial agent on behalf of Royal London Insurance Company, formed Span Developments Ltd in 1957.[32] The name Span was chosen just because it sounded contemporary.[33]

Fig 1.9   Leslie Bilsby and Eric, 1962.

Fig 1.10   The drawing office in the corner turret of Mill House, 1956. From left to right: Ronald Jones, Geoffrey Scoble, Ivor Cunningham, John Malyan and John Kerss.

Townsend had been introduced to Leslie Bilsby in about 1952, when Bilsby had been supervising the making of built-in fittings for Lyons and Townsend's Cavendish Court in Richmond, Surrey. For that project, Bilsby was working with Geoffrey Dunn, who ran a furnishings store in Bromley, south London – one of the few suppliers during the post-war period specialising in modern interior objects, textiles and furniture.[34] Bilsby resided in Blackheath and was an enthusiastic supporter of contemporary architecture and design. He lived with his family in a Victorian house, which had been extensively redesigned by Patrick Gwynne, the architect who was to build a further two houses of extremely modern design for him in Blackheath in the late 1960s and 1970s.[35] Leslie Bilsby had worked for Patrick Gwynne in the late 1930s, supplying soft furnishings and contracting the built-in units from cabinetmakers in London's East End for the house Gwynne was building for his own family, The Homewood in Esher, Surrey. Around the same time, Bilsby was undertaking similar jobs for other up-and-coming early modern architects, such as Denys Lasdun and Ernö Goldfinger, who were creating their first major houses. After the war, Bilsby had met up with Charles Bernard Brown, an architect who designed neo-Georgian houses and restored older buildings in Blackheath. All this had led Bilsby to become a builder well-versed in manufacturers and contractors specialising in modern work of high quality. Extremely out-going, fond of throwing parties and with a finger in many pies,

Bilsby was to help swing numerous land deals for Span, beginning with The Priory at Blackheath.[36]

Mill House was the architectural centre of Span's operations. Lyons's offices occupied the rooms in and around the turreted corner of the house, with views through windows edged with green and red-leafed Virginia creeper. At first, the linoleum was a well-worn brown, the wooden furniture homemade and the heating from gas fires, which Lyons lit every morning.[37] Photographs of projects lined the corridor of the ground floor reception, along with an Antelope bench designed by Ernest Race. There were up to five architects and two secretaries working in the practice by 1956 (Fig. 1.10). Townsend and Lyons had separate offices.[38] Lyons furnished his with one wall in geometrically patterned wallpaper and contemporary lamps with spindly metal supports; his desk was a hardwood flush door resting on bent copper tubing supports; and his chair was one of his own-designed bentwood pieces.

In 1955-56, having purchased Mill House and with a growing family, Lyons had added a single-storey brick extension onto the west side of the house for extra bedrooms, a study, kitchen, covered terrace and a split-level living space of a dining area with a seating arrangement below. This open plan living space was stylishly furnished with such contemporary items as Arne Jacobsen chairs, a sharp-edged sofa, a sculptural paper lamp by Noguchi and big booming hi-fi speakers, no doubt of Lyons's design. The new addition had a distinctly stylish Scandinavian spirit, similar to Lyons's large exhibition submission shown in Halsingborg, Sweden, in the same year as the home extension was completed.[39]

Eric and Kate Lyons had four children by then, two boys and two girls, each born two years apart: first Richard in 1945, then Jane, Antony and finally Naomi (Figs. 1.11 and 1.12). The house was a lively one, especially with Kate's enthusiasm for the stage. Play-readings were a regular event, and became such a passion that Lyons built a rehearsal room beside the house in the 1960s for her to train other children. There was croquet on the lawn and a punt at the bottom of the garden for floating down the quiet waters of the River Mole. Guests were often invited to take part in events. The young Michael Manser, later himself to be President of the RIBA, and his wife José, were both writing for newspapers and journals in the late 1950s and remember that they thought themselves 'lucky' to be invited to Mill House: 'We felt that we had "arrived" although we were out of our milieu amongst all of the other important and older architects'.[40]

A growing practice
Up in the offices, three architects, who were to become important and long-standing members of staff and eventually partners in

Fig 1.11   Eric Lyons with Richard, Jane, Antony and Naomi on the new terrace, Mill House, 1957.

Fig 1.12   Kate and Eric Lyons on the terrace, Mill House, 1959.

the practice, had joined Lyons; Ivor Cunningham in 1955, Warner Baxter in 1959 and, a couple of years later, Gilbert Powell. Having first trained at Medway School of Art, Cunningham attended the Architectural Association, qualifying in 1951. He had then gone on to specialise in landscape, with a year's training at King's College, University of Durham, followed by a year in the landscape school at the agricultural university at Wageningen in the Netherlands and, finally, a year and a half with the well-known English landscape architects, Brenda Colvin and Sylvia Crowe. Just before starting with Lyons, he motored on his scooter to Stockholm for the summer, meeting up with Eric and Kate Lyons in Copenhagen to visit the nearby border city of Halsingborg at the southern tip of Sweden. At the H55 Exhibition (the largest industrial exhibition that had been held in Sweden since the famous Stockholm Exhibition of 1930) they toured the exhibit of Lyons's six-room show flat, based on a Parkleys example.

Cunningham not only became the principle landscape specialist in the firm, but closest to Lyons of all his working colleagues. They came to share an office, where they were often to be found working together hunched over the same drawing board, their ideas flowing fast, playing off each other, running their 6B or charcoal pencils across a drawing in tandem, knowing instinctively where the line would end.[41]

Warner Baxter had been working on private housing projects for the architects Leslie Gooday and Wycliffe Noble after finishing his training at Kingston Polytechnic. In Eric Lyons's office, Baxter was to oversee the working drawings for Span and other contracts, acting as the executive on building construction, mostly as job architect. He had an extremely pleasant and engaging manner when dealing with touchy contractors and local government officials, and technically he was very strong. Lyons said admiringly of Baxter that 'he always catches the brick just before it hits the ground'.[42]

Running the business side of the practice was Gilbert Powell, whom Lyons called 'our Martha', meaning that he was an efficient behind-the-scenes manager.[43] Although Powell had trained as an architect at Leicester University, he had gone on to become a quantity surveyor, probably because of his colour blindness. In the office he looked after administration, continuity of practice, method and cost control. He became a partner in 1962, leaving in 1971.

Lyons would try to do the rounds of the office daily, although in later years as the practice grew larger and his outside responsibilities time-consuming, he relied on his partners for everyday supervision. Kenneth Wood, who was in the office between 1953 and 1955 working on Parkleys, and then the Soviet Trade Delegation flats in Highgate, remembers that each fortnight the staff would adjourn to the nearby Albion public house, with everyone always having the same dish

– Welsh rarebit. Lyons would be very chatty and witty, then in the last half-hour switch to discussing the practice, an informal way of having a meeting.[44]

In the office, Lyons would often make preliminary pencil sketches of ideas, and then hand them over to members of staff to work up. As the number of completed projects grew, staff were able to lean upon previous detailing as examples. Lyons unassumingly said that he knew his limits when it came to his own drawing technique and that he 'had modest talent'. He found doing perspectives frustrating, but 'a reminder (sometimes a revelation) of what you're designing. If you find yourself forcing a perspective, there's something wrong with the design'.[45]

Completed in 1956, Parkleys was closely followed by a burst of estates in Blackheath, Twickenham and Teddington. All under the Span banner, these innovative housing schemes in beautiful landscape settings had, by the early 1960s, placed Eric Lyons in the front ranks of the younger generation of established British architects. His work stood as a stark contrast to the contemporary 'angry young men' generation of the likes of Alison and Peter Smithson. Lyons's designs, embodying the more humane aspects of domestic architecture, were a modern return to the ideals of 18th-century, speculative housing using the pattern book repetitive module. Lyons considered his designs to be not only their natural successors, but an advancement.[46]

Recognition for Lyons came not only in the form of substantial reviews of his Span work, but in articles about him in the daily newspapers and popular magazines like *Punch*, where he was called 'one of the most articulate, heretical, visionary and (here's the difference) commercially successful architects of the 1960s'.[47] In 1959, Eric Lyons was awarded the Order of the British Empire.

Voicing his opinion
If Lyons's architecture didn't look angry – unlike the concrete Brutalist style of much contemporary architecture – Lyons himself was angry. His main focus of resentment was the planning laws, which had so vexed him to commission Godwin's 1959 sculpture of *The Architect in Society*. The problem was that the shortages of the post-war period had necessitated building restrictions, especially on parts and materials; this was accepted as a fact of life for the period. However, more of a predicament for architects and developers like Lyons and Townsend had been the passing of the Town and Country Planning Act of 1947. The intention of this legislation (basically still in place today) was the much-needed consensus in co-ordinating comprehensive planning when rebuilding bombed-out towns and cities, and to help reorganise industry.

A consequence was that local authorities were bestowed the rights of approval, changes and refusal to all planned developments. Decisions devolved to officials such as planning officers, building inspectors and committees – members of whom were a mix of professionals and lay people. Even to the present day, the planning dilemma has been about getting the balance right. There are many factors to consider, from the need to cherish and retain structures of historic merit, to ensuring that a development is not detrimental to the well-being of the existing neighbourhood. Balancing these are the needs to keep industries financially stimulated and to allow the public to enhance their lives through changes in design. Almost all these factors are usually subjective. Lyons considered the majority of the town and country planning laws as democratic tyranny, a means of the architecturally ignorant to impose their uninformed views on the aesthetics and social requirements of any proposed building: 'I have never opposed the idea of planning. It is just that it is rarely relevant', he said.[48]

As their projects grew in size and scope, Lyons and Townsend fell ever more foul of the planning system. Their first big altercation came with Parkleys in the mid-1950s, followed soon after by the multiple of early Span schemes in Blackheath. Local preservationists, argued Lyons, wanted to 'embalm' the neighbourhoods and to plump only for the commonplace:[49] 'By accepting an "average", is to absolve oneself of all responsibility – opting out with a purely bureaucratic solution. Any society attempting to control change is a dangerous society'.[50]

In the case of Lyons's designs, although gently modern in style, but nevertheless modern when compared to the revivalist styles prevalent in British suburbs, the rejection was often one of stylistic prejudice. Lyons, like many architects before and since, felt provoked and he sometimes found a means of getting around the smaller setbacks. An all white exterior, for example, which in itself implied a modernist aesthetic, was typically disliked by anti-modernists. In such cases, Lyons used to submit a whole spectrum of white samples for approval; inevitably, the authorities chose the darkest, which was white nevertheless. It took many years and battles, but as he became more aware of the workings of the planning system, Lyons learnt the various tricks to help circumnavigate the dangerous waters. 'We are now at a stage', he ruefully remarked by 1968, 'of having a certain cunning: how to fake drawings, provide ambivalent information, accept irrelevant compromises'.[51] Nevertheless, Lyons and his business partners had to endure decades of going to appeal, which were expensive and time-consuming, and sometimes losing encounters.

To make his voice heard and try to change the situation, Eric Lyons successfully campaigned to become a member of the Council of the Royal Institute of British Architects. Although this appeared to be a case of joining a bureaucracy to fight bureaucracy, Lyons himself recognised the inherent dangers of turning into just another 'fat bureaucrat', a phrase he often intoned against his rivals.[52] He was

to make it one of his principal aims to change any such failings in officialdom and mismanagement within the RIBA. He believed that the RIBA stood for the improvement of social values as embedded in its Royal Charter of 1837, and was particularly fond of quoting the charter passage, a reflection of his own modern ideals in archaic language, stating architecture to be 'an art esteemed and encouraged in all enlightened nations, as tending greatly to promote the domestic convenience of citizens, and the public improvement and embellishment of towns and cities'.

Lyons first took his place on the RIBA Council in July 1959, under the Presidency of Sir Basil Spence, and served for almost thirty years. Right from the outset he made a full commitment, sitting on a host of committees, sub-committees and boards: Registration, Competitions, Public Relations, Exhibitions, Design and Planning. For a year previous to his election, it appears that he was involved with the Town and Country Planning and Housing Committee, taking part in a symposium in May 1958 entitled *Design Pays*, when architects, builders and clients had gathered to discuss how to better house design, especially through improved layouts.

His years at the RIBA brought Lyons into contact with the international community of architects and designers, from Arne Jacobsen to Charles Eames. Appreciating education as a key to the future, he acted as a critic for the RIBA prizes and scholarship programme, sometimes giving his very candid view on the lack of prize money being offered and the low standard of the student work presented.[53] Over the Christmas period of 1960, he delivered the holiday lecture to a packed-out theatre of young people. His amusing style of storytelling made his challenging topic of the modern house and its environment entertaining and, it was reported, the audience was 'left in no doubt about what he thought on such matters as housing density, green belts, gardens, lamp standards, the problem of the motor-car and much else'.[54]

During the early to mid-1960s, in conjunction with the RIBA, Lyons became very involved, and outspoken, over two major issues facing British architects. Both hinged upon centralised planning control, his great bugbear – one was the Parker Morris Report of 1961 which, by 1967, had created standards for local authority housing. The Parker Morris standards were to have an influence on the social housing that Lyons was then building, especially for the London County Council. The second issue, and more important for Lyons as it touched upon Span, was the revision to the Town and Country Planning Act, enacted in 1968, transferring even greater powers of regulation to central government and local authorities.[55] Lyons vigorously joined in RIBA committees and working parties, writing articles and addressing the membership on these issues. He was not completely opposed to the government policies and legislation, but

Fig 1.13 The drawing office, Mill House Studio, 1979.

rather saw in them the potential to stifle creativity and good design. He believed that legislative control was part of the trend towards industrialised standardisation, of closed systems short on flexibility and lacking compassion.

Lyons's own design practice, of course, epitomised the standardisation in house planning by the use of repetitive elements. The types he used so successfully for Span were grouped according to the various model floor plans, which he gave names like T1, T2, T2A, and so on. But – here was the difference – Lyons was continually experimenting with the repetitive typology 'to discover', he said, 'more satisfactory solutions: economic, aesthetic and functional'.[56] In the field of speculative housing he was not so tied down to the rules he had to adhere to when designing for local authorities. He could create a luxuriant landscape with more land given over to planting and communal spaces. 'You wouldn't think it had come out of the same office', he said of the public, as opposed

to his private work.[57] Lyons relished the idea that 'industrialised housing was a beautiful concept one *could* believe in – in the way one could believe in fairies'.[58]

Architects, as he saw it, were in danger of losing the power of their central position as designers to specialists who implemented standard packaging. At the RIBA Conference of 1966, held in Dublin, Lyons gave a key lecture debating whether architects were falling into the trap of managing without design. Were too many architects just running their offices whilst letting others do the designing? Were they shrouding their design talents from the client in order to stress their professional skills in administrating a project?[59]

The question of whether the technical aspects of building were stifling imagination had been a long-standing debate within the architectural community. But the issue was coming to a head with the increasing legislation applying standardisation in planning and building construction and the associated advances in technological parts and systems. The 1960s was the decade of a phenomenal number of packaged local authority housing, much of it high-rise, but it was also the years that Norman Foster and Richard Rogers were creating their first elegant essays in hi-tech using prefabricated components. Lyons's passionately-held view, that technology and the convenience of production had the potential of destroying the architectural profession and the lives of those who had to live with it, won him many supporters.

By the end of the 1960s, Eric Lyons was both an architectural and professional phenomenon. Between 1961 and 1968, his practice was awarded eleven Ministry of Housing and Local Government Medals, six Civic Trust Awards and a RIBA Award. Considering the disputes he had had with the authorities, Lyons joked that these honours 'should really have been medals for bravery'.[60] All the schemes but one were housing for Span, and the one that was not was an old peoples' home. In May 1968, the BBC broadcast a television documentary, hosted by Ian Nairn, called *The more we are together: Eric Lyons, the architect and suburbia*. The following month, in Portland, Oregon, Lyons was made an Honorary Fellow of the American Institute of Architects.

Mill House Studio

In 1964, Lyons had built an office studio next to Mill House, making two smaller additions over the next few years. The long drawing office for the staff had a double-height, sloping ceiling, lit by a clerestory window to give internal light but privacy to the family in the garden of the house (Fig. 1.13). Lyons and Ivor Cunningham were at the far end in their own drawing office, separated from the staff by the conference room; and Lyons also had his own separate private offices with a personal secretary. For the first four years, Mrs Eve Smith came in to serve tea, then Fred Molyneux joined as 'tea boy'. Molyneaux, who had fought in the First World War, wore dark trousers and a white double-breasted jacket; he allowed only a single biscuit.

One of the many staff who arrived in Mill House Studio in the 1960s was Preben Jakobsen, who was to spend almost the whole of the decade with Lyons, working on landscaping before leaving to establish his own highly successful practice. Jakobsen was Danish and had trained at the Royal Academy of Art in Copenhagen under the country's most famous landscape architect Carl Theodor Sørensen. He had come to England as a student attached to the Royal Botanic Gardens, Kew, and married his English girlfriend. He answered an advertisement in the *Architects' Journal* for a landscape specialist in Lyons's office and turned out to be an excellent plantsman, with a breadth of knowledge of plant names and properties, as well as knowing the art of combining texture and colour. Cunningham,

the chief landscaper of the practice, would generally design the scheme and then hand it over to Jakobsen for detailing. Jakobsen was instrumental in most of the Span projects of the period and only left the practice after New Ash Green came to an abrupt end.

Three other important figures that appeared in Lyons's architectural life at the end of the 1960s were connected to the World's End estate in the west end of Chelsea: John Metcalfe and J. T. (Jim) and Elizabeth (Betty) Cadbury-Brown. Metcalfe and Jim Cadbury-Brown entered into partnership with Lyons and Cunningham as the Eric Lyons Cadbury-Brown Group Partnership, working from a separate office in Neal Street, Covent Garden. Metcalfe had earlier worked for a short time with the Greater London Council, then with Farmer and Dark on industrial buildings. He had collaborated previously with Jim and Betty Cadbury-Brown on their design with Hugh Casson for the Royal College of Art, Kensington. Originally from the north of England, he had trained in architecture at King's College, University of Durham. Jim Cadbury-Brown was the older hand, a veteran of the 1951 Festival of Britain, having designed the Land of Britain Pavilion with the assistance of American-born and architecturally trained Betty, whom he married in 1953. Elegant and with gentlemanly reserve, he was in many ways the antithesis of the extrovert casualness of Eric. 'But we struck it off', recalls Cadbury-Brown, 'myself as very particular, Eric a wonderful raconteur and elaborator of stories'.[61] Cadbury-Brown believes he brought to the World's End project the more sculptural elements: 'Eric would have had a flat roof, I was able to bring out the balcony and so forth'. Betty's forté was her meticulous attention to detail and she created the majority of the working drawings.

In late 1969, Lyons travelled to Argentina to attend the Congress of the International Union of Architects. He flew on to Brasilia, the new capital of Brazil, 'thrilled (a rare architectural emotion) by the grandeur of the enterprise', surprised to find Oscar Niemeyer's 'superblocks so humane in scale and obviously working well'.[62]

But a few months later, in December, work started to deteriorate when Span was forced to pull out of New Ash Green for financial reasons. This was a terrible blow to Lyons, Townsend, Bilsby and all those involved in creating this Kent countryside village. There were, however, the other non-Span projects still underway, including World's End and the first phase of Vilamoura, a new seaside marina on Portugal's Algarve coast. But the heyday of Span had come to an abrupt end.

The collapse of Span was symptomatic of the emerging problems within the British economy. The energy crisis, triggered by the Arab–Israeli conflict, began in 1973 and, coupled with rising inflation and unemployment, brought the building industry and the architectural community into deep decline. It was an era of endless labour strikes.

Fig 1.14 Eric Lyons, 1975.

The state of architecture, moreover, in the general public's view, was nastily coloured by the proliferation of council estate buildings that were increasingly failing, both socially and structurally. The image of the architectural profession was further eroded in 1974 by the highly publicised indictment and gaoling of the architect John Poulson for corruption, having bribed civil servants for building contracts.

President of the Royal Institute of British Architects

In this difficult period, Eric Lyons took office at the RIBA, first as senior Vice-President 1973–75 and then, at the age of 62, as President, from July 1975 to July 1977 (Fig. 1.14).

The recession had hit the RIBA hard; finances were precarious and staffing was considered too heavy. As Vice-President, Lyons led a group to study how to re-order the Institute's affairs. The result was the Lyons Report, recommending the appointment of a chief executive, the simplification of the committee structure, streamlining of staff and better public relations. The RIBA accepted these proposals.[63]

Upon entering the Presidency, the cartoonist for the *Architects' Journal*, Louis Hellman, published his spoof of a neat little tile-hung Span building dated 1965, compared with an image dated 1975 showing Lyons standing stoically with his arms behind his back at the entrance to RIBA headquarters at 66 Portland Place (Fig. 1.15). The great building is in near ruin, plastered with such signboards which read 'ERILYON Ltd CORNER HOUSE' (a reference to the old Lyons Tea Houses), 'Under new management' and 'Grand staff reduction sale'. The title at the bottom of the cartoon reads 'exspansion'.[64] Hellman was to portray Lyons many times throughout his Presidency as a variety of omniscient figures – guru, Old Testament prophet, winged lion – always giving his opinions from upon high with god-like authority.

In other words, Lyons was perceived as a strong RIBA President, someone speaking out on the prevailing ills suffocating the architectural community. Although, as reported by one architectural editor, Lyons was 'not exactly reputed for his diplomacy when giving his views on architecture, or the state of the profession, or the future of the RIBA', this was seen by many as a positive value for getting the message out.[65] *The Times* reported that the choice of Lyons for RIBA President 'was made in full consciousness of his outspokenness and lack of diplomacy'.[66] Phrases like 'the RIBA's saviour' and the 'new hero' were also voiced.[67]

Lyons, himself, had great confidence in his own abilities and was strongly supported by the RIBA membership; nevertheless, he found it tough going. In his first council meeting sitting in the Presidential chair (he said that the uncomfortable chair was the

Fig 1.15   Cartoon by Louis Hellman caricaturing Eric Lyons as the new President of the RIBA standing in front of the large crumbling RIBA headquarters in 1975 contrasted with a 'modest' Span home of 1965.

worst part of the job), he was defeated by opposition council members who pushed their own candidate into his personally chosen inner circle within the policy committee.

At the RIBA, Lyons was supported skilfully by his staff and colleagues. The long standing Secretary of the RIBA, Patrick Harrison, guided him through the labyrinth of Institute affairs. His senior Vice-President, in line to be the next President, was Gordon Graham, whom Lyons lent upon, especially for his political acumen. Lyons had chosen Owen Luder, another future RIBA President, as his Honorary Treasurer. Although there was great trust between them, Luder felt that Lyons might have been a bit suspicious of

him professionally, 'perhaps I was too commercial'.[68] But Luder's approach to finance was straightforward so that, together with Lyons, who was a good businessman himself, they were able to pull the RIBA funds back on course by putting the RIBA companies in check. They were also very conscious of the public relations side of their posts and both went on media presentation courses.

As RIBA President, Lyons undertook the associated duties with his usual gusto. He ran council meetings firmly and efficiently. Touring the country, he visited architects in their offices, attended receptions given by members and local dignitaries, met with architectural students at their universities and polytechnics, and

Fig 1.16 Eric Lyons (centre front) leaving No. 10 Downing Street, with Patrick Harrison (right), after meeting with Prime Minister James Callaghan about the crisis in the building industry, June 1977.

inspected new buildings. He travelled outside Britain, taking his wife Kate to the Caribbean islands where they visited the local Institute of Architects in Barbados, Jamaica and Trinidad. In Vancouver, Canada, he attended the United Nations Habitat Conference. He hosted the annual RIBA conferences, as well as the large gathering in York of the Commonwealth Association of Architects in September 1976.

A high point, as it so often is for RIBA Presidents, was the awarding of the Royal Gold Medal for Architecture. In 1977, Lyons presented the honour to Sir Denys Lasdun, who had just completed the National Theatre. The previous year, for the first and only time in the Institute's history, the sovereign made the presentation. On 11 December 1975, HM The Queen visited RIBA headquarters at 66 Portland Place in a ceremony for Michael Scott. However, although bestowed by royal prerogative, the selection of Scott would have lain with an RIBA committee, in which Lyons had a major influence. Scott came from Dublin in the Republic of Ireland, and was therefore an outsider in the eyes of many English people.

From the Presidential podium, Eric Lyons was able to gather up all his values and not only repeatedly articulate them to his fellow architects, but also present them to a wider audience. In the *RIBA Journal*, he published 'The President's column' every month during his two-year term of office; magazines, such as *Vogue*, ran articles on him; the national newspapers covered his assertive opinions; and on BBC radio he sparred over questions and answers with listeners. As one critic said of him, he was 'somebody whose hobby might be described as conversation'.[69]

Lyons's principal passions kept surfacing. Always near the top of his agenda was his lifelong professional concern over 'censorship' in planning and aesthetic control, which he considered part of the general lack in public perception of 'an organic overview of the whole building process'.[70] On a related issue, and also close to his heart, was the ideals of community and, especially, as he had helped create with Span, the self-managing community. The illness suffered by state-run housing was not the fault of the architecture, Lyons insisted, but the lack of social responsibility. It was the architect's responsibility to work with the community to create a shared spirit.

It was about keeping 'small,' a catchword that had all but become Lyons's mantra by the time of his Presidency: 'I have kept a small office going, I believe in small buildings. I think good architecture comes from small groups working closely together. I married a small wife. Even if I don't totally believe that you can nourish life in such simple terms it is still a check against megalomania'.[71] What Lyons had been preaching for decades about the practicalities of keeping

Fig 1.17 Eric with Richard Lyons (left) and Ivor Cunningham (right) in his office, Mill House Studio, 1979.

small had become, by the 1970s, the new buzzword of the age, as exemplified by the economist E. F. Schumacher.[72]

'The great danger is that directly you go in for big scale production', asserted Lyons on the theme of smallness and referring back to the evils of controls, 'you're in the hands of fewer people. You're in the hands of bigger scale organisations, and bigger scale organisations suffer from their own bureaucratic cramps'.[73] This might have seemed an ironic position for Lyons, considering that he was in the midst of building one of the biggest council estates in the country at World's End, and a substantial new marina village in Portugal. Wasn't condemnation of the large public authorities, one critic asked him, like biting the hand that fed you? Lyons's quick response was 'You can bite with love'.[74]

Lyons's insistence on the small office as the 'life-blood of the profession' and his criticism that architects in large offices often did not have the breadth of experience found in smaller practices, sometimes antagonised the bigger firms and the architects who

ran them. But in the cold climate of the recession, when small practitioners were suffering most, he suggested that the bigger firms take on the smaller ones to help with the workload.[75] To give a greater voice to those in non-official architectural practices, Lyons had been instrumental in creating the Association of Consultant Architects (ACA) in 1973 when President-Elect of the RIBA. Aimed at the single or small architectural office, the ACA was not to be a rival to the RIBA, although Lyons no doubt enjoyed the adversarial challenge to authority. He was the ACA's first chairman.

With the building industry in its worst plight since the Second World War, one of Lyons's last tasks as RIBA President was to take part in a delegation to make sure that the Prime Minister was in no doubt about the state of crisis. Accompanied by Patrick Harrison from the RIBA and six other members of the building industry, Lyons spent an hour with the Labour PM, James Callaghan. Lyons felt dejected by the meeting and, as he walked away from No. 10 Downing Street, muttered 'There is no light in the sky, it's a grey scene' (Fig. 1.16).[76]

Fig 1.18 Ivor Cunningham at his drawing table in Mill House Studio, 1979.

Reflecting upon Lyons's two-year term as President, some critics believed that he had been naïve to think that he could make extensive changes, especially to the running of the Institute, bringing his 'small is beautiful' management skills to a bureaucracy that continued to bureaucratise and appear to represent large practices at the expense of smaller ones. As for his loud denouncements against planning controls, this is an issue with which architects today still continue to feel plagued.

Lyons had been an inspiration. As the architect, journalist and photographer John Donat said, he was 'one of the most candid, articulate and sharp-witted representatives of our guilt-ridden profession'.[77]

Back to Span

After his term of office as RIBA President ended in the middle of 1977, Lyons returned to a quieter, but still busy life. In 1979 he was appointed a Commander of the British Empire. But the best news was that Span was back, having reconstituted in 1976 after a six-year absence. The Gostling brothers, Frank and Jack, had been able to arrange the finances, returning as directors with Geoff Townsend and Leslie Bilsby. Lyons's two sons were both now architects: Antony had qualified after attending Thames Polytechnic and had practiced in his year out in the office on Vilamoura before forming his own private practice, and Richard had finished at the Architectural Association in 1968, worked on-and-off in the office, and become a partner in 1972 (Fig. 1.17).

However, it was not long after finishing his presidential term of office that Lyons began to have small, muscular twinges and bouts of paralysis. His left arm, especially, was giving him problems. He was diagnosed with motor neurone disease. Although this wasting illness progressed over two years, Lyons did not grow despondent, deriving equanimity from his fighting nature and the support of family and friends. His intellect never diminished and he kept designing, writing and conversing, and was as entertaining as always. Eric Lyons died on 22 February 1980 at Mill House.

Geoff Townsend had more or less retired by the time of Lyons's death; he moved to Angmering-on-Sea, Sussex, passing away in 2002. With the collapse of New Ash Green and the death of his wife Shura in 1969, Leslie Bilsby began developing properties in France, living for a time in Paris with his new wife, Annette Rigal. When Span revived in 1976, he was instrumental in land purchases. He died in 1990.

Span's builders, the Gostling brothers retired: Frank lives in Oxshott, Surrey, and Jack in Twickenham. Of Eric Lyons's architectural partners, Warner Baxter stayed on until 1982, finishing jobs, such as

Telford. He carried on in private practice and, now retired, lives in a Span house in Castle Green, Weybridge. John Metcalfe, too, set up in practice on his own, with an office in the Thames Wharf complex around Richard Rogers's office in Hammersmith. He retired to Hexham, Northumberland, where he later passed away.

Ivor Cunningham and Richard Lyons worked alongside one another at Mill House Studio for a few years after Lyons's death, completing the major projects of Vilamoura and Mallard Place, until Richard set up independently in 1985. For a time, between 1991 and 1994, John Metcalfe returned as a partner with Cunningham, completing a series of projects.[78]

Ivor Cunningham and his wife Annabel live just a five-minute stroll from Mill House, in a large Victorian house with many additions by Cunningham, where they've been since 1974.[79] Although the practice name of Eric Lyons Cunningham Metcalfe endures, Cunningham is the sole architect, now semi-retired (Fig. 1.18). He is the keeper of the flame, holding most of the surviving office archive and his own extraordinarily detailed memories.

Kate Lyons still lives at Mill House.

The architect in society

Just after his presidency at the Royal Institute of British Architects ended in mid-1977, Eric Lyons had his portrait painted. When it was completed, he decided not to present it as intended to the RIBA, as he did not care for it. Instead, the RIBA now displays two portraits of him. One is a bronze bust, a tousled-haired Eric by Keith Godwin. The other is an oil painting, by Walter Woodington, a calm almost muted portrait of Lyons in casual dress and pose. The work Lyons kept back was an intense, almost shocking canvas, an exceptionally fine work by Feliks Topolski, the artist today best known for his *Memoir*, a painted journey within the labyrinth of railway arches beside the Royal Festival Hall, a 14-year project featuring major figures of the 20th century with many portraits from Mao to Gandhi.

Lyons's portrait is painted with Topolski's hurried intensity in the strokes (Fig. 1.19). Half of his face gleams in brilliant white, the other half lies in shadow. A focal point is a favourite hand gesture that Eric often made when speaking – his right hand, painted in shades of jagged purple, is raised, thumb and fingers spread apart. He appears to be holding a mysterious, abstract volume, like a house seen in multi-dimensions. Then, again, perhaps there is nothing there, the abstract lines within the gestured space just the background representing his patterned shirt. Nevertheless, it is an enclosed space, held within his grasp, like the one in which *The Architect in Society* resides.

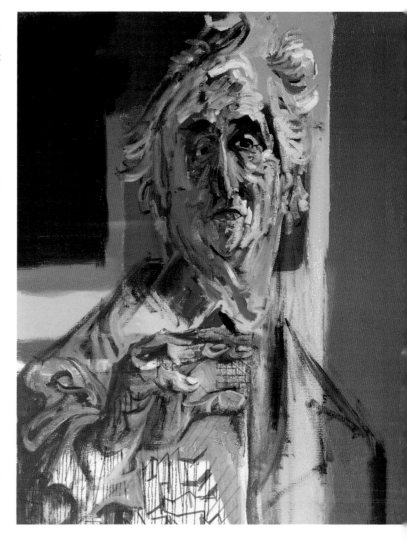

Fig 1.19 Eric Lyons, by Feliks Topolski, 1978.

Endnotes

1. Eric Lyons, 'Back to Blackheath', *Architect,* July 1971, pp. 37–42. *The Architect in Society* marked a victory by Eric Lyons and Span against the London County Council who had wanted the right not only to approve the colour that Hallgate was painted at the outset, which was a legal obligation, but to exercise that right in the future, which was not.

2. *The Times*, 21 July 1975, p. 5.

3. Interviews with Rita Kay, Eric Lyons's sister, by Ivor Cunningham, 7 March 1995, and by the author, 23 April 1999. Rita was two years younger than Eric. Rita asserted that Eric's middle name was Aaron, after his paternal grandfather, but that he changed it to Alfred. Lyons was to design the façade and interior for her clothing shop Kay Fashions, 151 Jamaica Road, London SE16, in 1959.

4. 47 Elmfield Road, London SW12.

5. Article of clerkship to John Stanley Beard FRIBA, dated 12 May 1930.

6. Alan Powers, obituary for Geoffrey Townsend, *The Independent*, 14 August 2002.

7. Information courtesy Elaine Penn, University Archivist, University of Westminster (formerly Regent Street Polytechnic), London W1.

8. Letter of recommendation from J. Stanley Beard, 11 January 1934; letter of recommendation from W. E. Trent, 9 April 1935.

9. Letter from W. Sydney Trent, 12 February 1936.

10. Letter from E. Maxwell Fry, 12 February 1936.

11. His initials 'EAL' appear in the 'drawn by' title box on drawings for the Impington Village College by Gropius and Fry in the RIBA Drawings Collection, PA357/1 (1–24).

12. Maxwell Fry, *Autobiographical Sketches* (London: Elek, 1975), p.149.

13. As remembered by Geoffrey Townsend in an interview with Ivor Cunningham, 4 October 1994.

14. Interview with Graham Morrison by the author, 20 March 2006.

15. Interview with Jack Howe by Ivor Cunningham, May 1995.

16. Transcript by Geoffrey Scoble, December 1999.

17. Correspondence with Ivor Cunningham by the author, 14 April 2006. Eric Lyons shared his birthday with Groucho Marx (as does the author).

18. Letter of recommendation from Andrew Mather, 7 November 1938. See Allen Eyles, *Odeon cinemas 1: Oscar Deutsch entertains our nation* (London: Cinema Theatre Association, 2002), p. 134.

19. Geoffrey Townsend was born and lived at 14 Trafalgar Road, London TW2 until 1945 when, at the age of 34, he married Winifred Warbanck. The following year, upon the death of Winifred's father, the couple purchased 86 Hampton Road, Twickenham, London TW2, the Warbanck family home, which Lyons altered into five flats, whilst also converting the adjoining stable block into a residence for the Townsends's own use. In 1956, they moved into a new home that Lyons designed for them: Linden House, Walpole Gardens, Strawberry Hill, Twickenham, London TW2. Letter from G. Townsend to Ivor Cunningham, 15 November 1994; interview with Louise Coleman (daughter of G. Townsend) by the author, 12 May 2006.

20. Peter left the company in 1952. Jack's first name is John.

21. Letter of recommendation from Harry W. Weedon, 9 March 1944.

22. Eric Lyons kept copies of his air raid shelter drawings that he did under Weedon. The title box, with the name of the project and architect's name has been clipped out of the sheet, for security purposes. Information concerning the shadow factories from Kate and Richard Lyons.

23. *Surrey Comet*, 27 August 1955, p. 5.

24. Interview with John Sheldon by Ivor Cunningham, April 1995.

25. Catherine Joyce Townsend, born 1922 in Gainsborough, Lincolnshire. Moved at the age of eight to Bawtry, South Yorkshire, when her mother remarried. She was no relation to Lyons's business partner, Geoffrey Townsend.

26. Mill House, 74 Bridge Road, East Moseley, London KT8.

27. Congress House, 23–28 Great Russell Street, London WC1. The competition was won by David du R. Aberdeen.

28. *Design 46: a survey of British industrial design as displayed in the Britain Can Make It* exhibition (1946), illustrated p. 98.

29. Tecta furniture and a McMurdo exhibition stand illustrated in *Designers in Britain*, 1949, published by the Society of Industrial Artists, of which Lyons was a member.

30. *Architects' Journal*, 30 July 1975, p. 250.

31. Interview with John Sheldon by Eric Cunningham, April 1995.

32. Bilsby insisted upon the replacement of Haynes for Henry Cushman, who had acted as Townsend's previous financial agent.

33. Leslie Bilsby claimed that the name Span was adopted on the intense lobbying of Eric Lyons, instead of other suggestions like Domus and Nubuild. *RIBA Journal,* November 1981, p. 52. The name gave the company the opportunity to play upon its meaning, as in the promotional literature: 'Span is a bridgehead… It spans the gap between the suburban monotony of the typical spec' development and the architecturally designed, individually built residence that has become, for all but a few… financially unattainable'.

34. Dunn was asked by Span to set up a similar store in Richmond, but declined because of the distance from Bromley. Pat Street, secretary to Geoffrey Townsend, thereupon opened Trend Interiors, on Richmond Hill, in 1960, financed by Townsend, moving across the street into a Georgian house converted by the architect Leslie Gooday. The furniture shop ran into the

1980s, furnishing many Span show houses and flats. Notes by Patricia Street, 18 April 2005.

35. Neil Bingham, 'The houses of Patrick Gwynne', *The Journal of the Twentieth Century Society: Post-War Houses* (London, 2000), pp. 30–44.

36. Leslie Bilsby was born in 1910 and came from Spalding, Lincolnshire. He worked for a year with his father, who ran a local building business, then found a job with a firm of builders working in Hampstead Garden Suburb, London. Bilsby attended evening classes, like Lyons and Townsend, at Regent Street Polytechnic, studying art. He married Shura Naumtchuk (died 1969) in 1934. They had three daughters: Tania, Caroline and Rosemary.

37. *Architecture and Building*, June 1956, pp. 218–19.

38. When Span Developments was formed in 1957, Townsend moved to the offices in one of the recently completed shops on the Richmond Road, part of Parkleys, which had domestic accommodation above. The Span sales office was on the ground floor.

39. 'The best of both wings', *House & Garden*, October 1957, pp. 74–77; July 1958, p. 19. The *House & Garden* front covers of both the June and July 1957 issues illustrated the Eric Lyons's Span show house in Blackheath, used that year by the journal as their 'House of Ideas'.

40. Interview with Michael and José Manser by the author, 16 March 2006.

41. Interview with Richard Lyons by the author, 17 April 2006.

42. Interview with Ivor Cunningham by the author, 2 May 2006.

43. *RIBA Journal*, May 1968, p. 215.

44. Interview with Kenneth Wood by the author, 17 April 2006.

45. *Architects' Journal*, 30 July 1975, p. 250. Lyons said that he tried, unsuccessfully, to patent a graphic method for producing formal perspectives easily.

46. Eric Lyons, 'Architects' pattern books', *RIBA Journal*, September 1976, p. 370.

47. R. Furneaux Jordan, 'Span: the spec builder as patron of modern architecture', *Architectural Review*, February 1959, pp. 108–20; Richard Findlater, 'Eric Lyons: the man about the house', *Punch*, 17 January 1962, pp. 142–44.

48. Eric Lyons, 'Too often we justify our ineptitudes by moral postures', *RIBA Journal*, May 1968, p. 216, an address given to the RIBA, 6 February 1968.

49. *Punch*, 17 January 1962, p. 142.

50. *Ideal Home*, October 1967, p. 52.

51. *RIBA Journal*, May 1968, p. 216.

52. *Building Design*, 17 August 1979, p. 2.

53. *RIBA Journal*, June 1963, pp. 219–42.

54. *RIBA Journal*, February 1961, p. 128.

55. The Act was the outcome of the 1965 report of the Planning Advisory Group to the Ministry of Housing and Local Government, dealing with suggested policies for controls on town and country environments. Ministry of Housing and Local Government Report. Planning Advisory Group, *The future of development plans* (London: HMSO, 1965).

56. *RIBA Journal*, May 1968, p. 216.

57. *Building*, 16 July 1976, p. 82.

58. *RIBA Journal*, March 1967, p. 101.

59. Eric Lyons, 'Managing without design?', *RIBA Journal*, October 1966, pp. 457–9.

60. *The Times*, 21 July 1975, p. 5.

61. Interview with J. T. Cadbury–Brown by the author, 5 March 2006.

62. *RIBA Journal*, December 1969, pp. 509–10.

63. 'The RIBA annual report', *RIBA Journal*, May 1976, pp. 195–210.

64. *Architects' Journal*, 16 July 1975, p. 5.

65. *RIBA Journal*, February 1975, p. 1.

66. *The Times*, 21 July 1975, p. 5.

67. *RIBA Journal*, January 1975, p. 5.

68. Interview with Owen Luder by the author, 4 April 2006.

69. *Building*, 8 July 1977, p. 47.

70. *RIBA Journal*, July 1976, p. 266.

71. *The Times*, 21 July 1975, p. 5.

72. E. F. Schumacher, *Small is beautiful: economics as if people mattered* (London: Blond and Briggs, 1973).

73. *Building*, 16 July 1976, p. 85.

74. *Building Design*, 17 August 1979, p. 2.

75. *Architects' Journal*, 5 November 1975, p. 932; *RIBA Journal*, March 1976, p. 86.

76. *Architects' Journal*, 22 June 1977, pp. 1162–3.

77. *Building*, 16 July 1976, p. 79.

78. Major projects were Millmead Hostel, Esher, Surrey; the refurbishment of offices in Great Peter Street, London, and an international conference centre at Warren House, Kingston Hill, Surrey, the last two for Imperial Chemical Industries.

79. Ivor and Annabel married in 1959 and have four children: Amanda, Jenny, Angus and Daniel. Between 1961 and 1974, the Cunninghams lived in a studio house Ivor converted at 18 Feltham Avenue, a ten-minute walk to Mill House. Their present home is 37 Wolsey Road, London (KT8).

"I don't believe that I emulate
Gropius architecturally but his rational
discipline was something that I needed.
I'm basically irrational."

Eric Lyons

The vast majority of the houses built in Britain, other than those erected by local and national government during the middle six decades of the 20th century, have never been the work of architects. The process of speculative building by which they were developed was not wholly ignorant of architecture, but generally managed quite well at the bottom of a food chain in which real, trained architects remained several steps removed. Despite this handicap, many of them are now listed buildings, and many others are exchanged for high prices and are highly valued. As a development company specialising in housing and using professional architects as a matter of course, Span was exceptional in breaking this pattern – its architects did not just design individual houses, but also the layout and landscaping of their setting. This chapter looks back before the time of Span to examine attitudes to speculative development in England, and the problem of its low quality that Span set out to solve. It will also look at the trends within English modern architecture during Eric Lyons's early years that show his designs to be part of a wider movement of ideas.

The speculative builder in history

To the historian, speculative building is a process that only partially reveals its inner mechanisms.[1] Statements of intent are almost entirely lacking and we seldom have more than legal documents, bankruptcy notices and the bricks and mortar evidence. How, we would like to know, did the terraces, squares, crescents and villas get their form, which in many cases delights us still? How did design, consumer taste and finance interact? Who was responsible for balancing supply and demand, and introducing design innovation?

There seems not to have been a great deal of conscious invention in British urban planning, and it was easier to see the bad results than the good. This was the result of a wave of urban planning agitation around 1900, by which time the terraced house lost its charm at all social levels and alternatives were increasingly sought. The middle-class flight to the suburbs (a long-standing phenomenon) accelerated, with opportunities opening up for lower social classes to do the same owing to improved transport and increased concerns for health. Improved mobility extended the practical boundaries for commuting and allowed versions of the reformed suburban villa (no basement, level access to back garden, coal delivery round the side) to replace the older terrace format with its rear extension and back alley. Span came after this phase, rearranging the existing types and beliefs in the light of experience and reflection, with a kind of passionate reasonableness.

Prejudice against suburbs

There had always been prejudice about suburbs, but speculative, suburban building was seen first as comic rather than tragic: the world of Mr Pooter in Brickfield Terrace, Holloway.[2] An interwar equivalent to Mr Pooter would undoubtedly have lived in a semi, built at a much lower density, not just as a result of customer choice, but also because of planning law (Fig. 2.1). According to Thomas Sharp, he would, therefore, become 'a hermaphrodite, sterile, imbecile, a monster, abhorrent, loathsome to the Nature which he worships'.[3] Interwar suburbs were the worst of two alternatives, using a lot of land whilst failing to produce visual coherence in the landscape. Sharp also wrote that:

Fig 2.1 'Motorville': The interwar suburban semi, as depicted by Thomas Sharp in *English Panorama* (London: J. M. Dent, 1938).

Fig 2.2 *The Small House Exhibition* at the RIBA in 1939 was a belated attempt to involve architects in improving poor suburban planning.

For a hundred years we have behaved like film-struck servant girls blinded to the filth accumulating around us by romantic dreams of worlds as yet and ever unlikely to be realised. More than anything else it is this pitiful attitude of escape which has brought the English town from its beauty and hopefulness of a hundred and fifty years ago to its shapeless and shameful meanness of to-day.[4]

His condemnation of the suburbs was shared by other young writers of the 1930s. It seems harsh to us today, but it must have reflected their own sense of frustration about lost opportunities to do something better in the face of what Clough Williams–Ellis in 1928 called 'the Octopus' – the force of the uncontrolled free market.[5] What had begun so promisingly in the planning and construction of the first garden suburbs and the Town Planning Act of 1909, the first of its kind, had gone terribly wrong by the 1930s, but governments seemed unable to correct it through further legislation. The historian Alan Jackson attributed the dismal result to lack of central government time and willpower, lack of properly qualified planning advisers at a local level, and lack of coordination between local authorities.[6]

For the Left, private enterprise in a free market was bound to lower cultural standards, and only the collaboration of intellectuals with the state could be trusted to deliver efficiency and fair shares to all. The romantic Right (along with a section of the Left) deplored the urbanisation of England that was so visible in the march of ribbon development, and which was disrupting the social hierarchy.

In the 1920s, freehold generally replaced leasehold because of the availability of mortgages and instalment plans. Compared to architects' one-off houses, the semis were produced efficiently, so that, before 1939, anyone with a steady job could buy a house with a mortgage and pay it off within 10 or 20 years, regardless of their class or background. If jerry-building[7] was sometimes a problem, it never reached the disastrous levels predicted by critics of the semi at the time, such as John Betjeman who wrote 'when … we realise that the luckless occupants will find themselves in a few years saddled with a slum … let us begin to think that there is something wrong with architecture today'.[8] The suburban semi effected an extraordinary transformation in British social class and went further towards solving the slum problem than any direct government intervention, whatever the cost in amenity and aesthetics. Cheap land was the necessary condition; loss of countryside and substandard urbanism the penalty, hence the pressure behind the Town and Country Planning Act 1947 to put power to refuse development into the hands of town halls and Whitehall corridors, rather than leaving the market to find its own levels.

The new freeholders enjoyed their limited opportunities to make their homes an expression of personal taste, which made the matter worse in the eyes of critics. The idea that suburbs epitomised 'the little man'[9] was read back from the way that the outdoor space was demarcated with hedges and dwarf walls, protecting each trivial attempt to establish identity through ornamental gardening. It was the problem of 'my pink half of the drainpipe' as the Bonzo Dog (Doo Dah) Band put it in 1968.[10] This response was undoubtedly snobbish, but at a time when there was widespread, intellectual doubt about the benign operation of the free market, its outward manifestation was unattractive. Because the 'spec' world managed to make money without the help of architects, they sided with benign control through public ownership, serviced by benevolent and modern-minded designers.

Outside the architectural discourse, the GPO film *Pett and Pott, a Fairy Story of the Suburbs* (1934), directed by Alberto Cavalcanti, shows how anti-suburban prejudice was projected from an elevated cultural position. Ostensibly a morality tale about the advantages of installing a telephone, the film represents, with expressionist exaggeration, the dreary repetitiveness of the commuter train journey suffered by all the suburban dwellers. Owing to the poor planning of the suburb, Mrs Pott has to walk to get to the shops and, as a result of her unhappiness, her marriage breaks down, whilst Mrs Pett, who has installed a telephone, saves her legs by ordering her groceries to be delivered. The general message of the film is less about telephones than about the awfulness of the suburbs in general.[11]

The modernist alternative

In the opening minutes of their political drama of 1936, *The Ascent of F6*, W. H. Auden and Christopher Isherwood have their 'Everyman', Mr A, describe '…the journey home again/ In the hot suburban train/ To the tawdry new estate,/ Crumpled, grubby, dazed and late'.[12] These words were included in the captioning of the Royal Institute of British Architects' exhibition, *The Small House*, in 1939, which was a belated attempt to involve architects in improving the situation (Fig. 2.2). A broadcast commentary on the exhibition stressed the importance of road planning and the creation of shared open spaces, instanced by a Swiss estate where houses had their own gardens, but a third of the total space was formed into a central green accessible from any of the 72 houses without crossing a roadway.[13]

The exhibition showed mainly European examples. In Britain between the wars, an architect-designed, cheap house was nearly always a council house in a Georgian or vernacular style, and so the work of architects carried the stigma of low status, however good it might be; a problem that persisted after the war. Modern architecture on the open market in the 1930s was, at the beginning,

Fig 2.3   Welch & Lander 1934 in The Ridings, Ealing (Hanger Hill Estate), designed flat-roofed modern houses with white walls interspersed with brick houses with pitched roofs, all to similar plans.

Fig 2.4   99-101 Park Avenue, Ruislip by Connell, Ward & Lucas 1935.

a glamorous new style, but it was a risky business proposition, as the infrequent occurrence of flat roofs in the suburbs attests. Architects, modern or otherwise, were not entirely excluded from the suburban development process, but the exceptions are rare enough to attract attention in themselves. In some places, such as Hampstead Garden Suburb and Welwyn Garden City, the land was held in trust and there was a commitment to special design quality. In some suburban developments where this did not apply, the developer decided to work with one architect to ensure consistency of quality, as was the case with the Hanger Hill Estate in Ealing where, around 1934, the builders Haymills employed architects Welch and Lander for nearly all the houses, flats, and for a hotel on Western Avenue (Fig. 2.3). Some of the houses were flat-roofed modern, with white walls, although these were interspersed with brick and pitched roofs, all to similar plans.

In 1934, the builders John Laing held a competition for designs for the Sunnyfields Estate, Barnet, for students of the Architectural Association, choosing respectable but relatively conservative models, but nothing changed. In some senses, Span was a continuation of these lonely pioneers, but with all kinds of differences. At Hanger Hill or Sunnyfields, all that was offered was a supposedly better form of house, but no rethinking of the

subdivision of land or the relationship between individual dwellings. Connell, Ward & Lucas's group of three houses in Park Avenue, Ruislip, (1934–5) was more radical to look at (Fig. 2.4), even after a compromise was reached with the local authority over their design, but they were still only a semi and a half, with plans that were symmetrical with each other, producing the same problem of overall composition that nearly all semis suffered, because the centre line of the party wall was marked by a piece of blank wall or a drainpipe, although the mirror symmetry of the elevations created the expectation of some sort of central focus.

For the design of private flats, as opposed to villas, architects of all kinds were more in demand. Flats between the wars ranged in style from neo-Tudor to modern, and examples of each kind oppose each other across Highgate North Hill, the modern example being Lubetkin and Tecton's Highpoint (1935). Many flats were built in the gardens of demolished Victorian villas – the scale of property that would originally have run to an orchard, kitchen garden, stable and coach house. Even today, at projects such as Fairacres, Roehampton, by Minoprio & Spenceley, or Frederick Gibberd's pre-war developments at Pullman Court, Streatham (1935), and elsewhere in the outer suburbs, we can see the fine trees that were preserved, with the building footprint fitted around them. These are much more like prototypes for Span, with the difference that Span flats seldom went above three storeys, altering the relationship between the interior, the trees and the sky to a more equal partnership. A closer equivalent to Span from 1930s British modernism is the forgotten and altered three-storey block Highfield Court, Highfield Road, Golders Green, by A. V. Pilichowski (Fig. 2.5).

Return to the terrace

Projects such as Highpoint, Lawn Road, Pullman Court and Highfield Court in the private sector, and Kensal House (1936) in the public, were reproduced in F. R. S. Yorke and Frederick Gibberd's influential book, *The Modern Flat* (1938), and were, at the time, the last word in modern movement thinking on the dwelling.[14] In European modernism, by contrast, as Yorke's earlier book, *The Modern House* showed, houses in terraces were considered a perfectly acceptable modern form.[15] Yorke compared contemporary suburban development in Ealing with terrace houses in Lloyd Square, Islington (1818), and a terrace of workers' housing in Amsterdam by J. J. P. Oud, who had completed several examples, including one at the Weissenhofsiedlung in Stuttgart in 1927. Foreign architects visiting London were rapturous about the 'modern' quality of Georgian Bloomsbury and similar places, finding there the sort of impersonal standardisation of buildings, set amongst mature trees and adequately spaced out, that they identified as essentially modern.[16] The terrace was favoured because it removed the pretence of individualism from housing, and Yorke argued that 'only

Fig 2.5   A closer equivalent to Span from 1930s British modernism is the three-storey Highfield Court, Highfield Road, Golders Green, by A. V. Pilichowski.

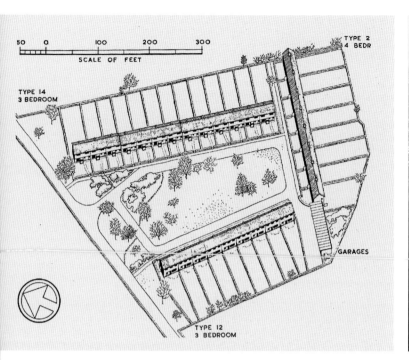

Fig 2.6a   Tayler and Green placed their housing in terraces whenever possible, as at Ditchingham, Norfolk, to avoid the broken-up look of semi-detached houses in the broad landscape.

Fig 2.6b   Terraced housing around a green at Ditchingham, Norfolk.

by the acceptance of a modern standard can there be any escape from the monotony that variety brings to the road in which every house, though obviously similar in plan, strives to look different from its neighbour'.[17]

This paradox was repeated through much of the literature aimed at the general public from before the Second World War to the early years of peace. Span developments showed how the paradox could be resolved. In place of the minor but meaningless variations of the suburban semi, Eric Lyons used a range of standard house and flat types, but found the *genius loci* of the site and enhanced it through the design and planting of the public spaces, so that you need never feel lost in a Span development. Similar claims can be made for the rural housing constructed between 1947 and 1970 by Herbert Tayler and David Green in Norfolk, which aimed to bring a new standard of sensitivity to the public sector, partly through carefully developed, standard house types, but also through adaptation to particular sites and forethought about planting and maintenance.[18] Tayler and Green placed their housing in terraces whenever possible to avoid the broken-up look of semi-detached houses in the broad landscape (Figs. 2.6a and 2.6b).

The terrace was not the only housing form used by Span, but it is important enough to deserve further discussion, and it is interesting to explore how English architects and commentators responded to it before the 1950s. Between the wars, state housing subsidies were only available for cottage estates with a density of 12 houses to the acre, the norm established by the garden cities. At these densities, there was no reason to build terraces, which consequently only occurred in a few private developments, given that the terrace still carried a stigma of the slums. In 1935, Berthold Lubetkin made a significant contribution with a terrace of houses in Genesta Road, Plumstead, in collaboration with Pilichowski, showing how concrete construction with a flat roof allowed a rethinking of the terrace form, with a compact, top-lit, spiral staircase in the centre of the plan, and an open plan, single room filling the first floor, but he did not get the chance to work in this manner again. In the final years before the war, Ernö Goldfinger and Denys Lasdun both presented houses they had built in London as they might look if extended by repetition into longer terraces. Goldfinger's three houses in terrace form at 1–3 Willow Road, Hampstead, completed in 1939 (and for which Leslie Bilsby, later to work with Geoffrey Townsend and Eric Lyons, was the contractor), were a deliberate attempt to recreate

Fig 2.7   1–3 Willow Road by Erno Goldfinger imagined as an urban square.

Fig 2.8   Speculative flats in mature existing landscapes at St Leonard's Hill, Windsor, by Gropius & Fry, presented an alternative to conventional suburban development.

the typical London urban form. He also prepared and published drawings showing the design extended as a terrace forming one side of a square (Fig. 2.7). Lasdun's single house at 32 Newton Road, Paddington, was published with photomontages, also showing it extended as a terrace and in other alternative forms.[19] Tayler and Green prepared a similar drawing based on The Studio, Duke's Head Yard, Highgate (1940), a design inspired in part by Ernst May's Romerstadt housing in Frankfurt (1926), although their drawing was not published at the time.

The alternative chiefly favoured amongst modernists was high-rise housing in a *zeilenbau* formation (parallel slab blocks equidistant from each other), which gained adherents owing to the demonstration of extra open space that it could give back, in comparison with conventional development.[20] Whilst Eric Lyons was in the office of Walter Gropius and Maxwell Fry in the 1930s, two schemes for speculative flats were prepared, one in Birmingham and one at St Leonard's Hill, Windsor (Fig. 2.8), both commissioned by Jack Pritchard's Isokon Company. Presented as a preferable alternative to conventional suburban development, these were notable for their mature existing landscapes, and the sort of lifestyle they promised for professional people could be seen as another precursor of Span, despite differences in height and layout. Such luxuries were expensive in land costs, however, and it was still legal

to build tenements (but not houses) at unhealthily high densities of 100 or 200 to the acre.

A project by the architectural writer Arthur Trystan Edwards, which hoped to secure massive state funding to grasp the slum clearance and resettlement problem, comes much closer, however, to proposing a Span-type planning solution than either cottages or tenement flats.[21] Edwards's two-storey terraces, each with at least 150 square feet of private outdoor space, were to be 'charming streets and quadrangles which represent a happy mean between garden suburbia on the one hand and the tall standardised block on the other', built at densities of 30 to 38 houses per acre (Figs. 2.9a, 2.9b and 2.9c).[22] The backs of his houses would be well-designed, unlike normal council houses, and many of them would face onto communal gardens enclosed by four connected terraces. Nothing was built to these designs, although they were widely published and discussed in magazines, which we may assume were seen by Lyons and Townsend.

However, Trystan Edwards's project opened up a debate about acceptable housing densities, which was carried forward by the housing consultant Elizabeth Denby, who became a strong advocate for the return of the terrace as a 'choice between two impractical and unnecessary extremes' represented by garden cities and flats. 'The rows of terrace cottages built in Regency days, with a small garden in front and a long one behind', Denby explained, 'were built at a density of 50 or 60 dwellings to the acre. That is the density at which we are now building flats'.[23] On this occasion, she suffered a patronising put down by Lewis Silkin, a future Minister of Health and Housing, who quoted back the ministerial norms as if nothing else were possible. However, in 1939, she was able to promote a full-size version of her ideas at the Ideal Home Exhibition in the All-Europe House, a terrace of houses laid out in a saw-tooth formation modelled on a development in Bromma, Stockholm, designed by Paul Hedqvist in 1932 (Fig. 2.10). The Swedish Prime Minister, Albin Hansson, who introduced the 'Folkhemmet' or 'People's Home'

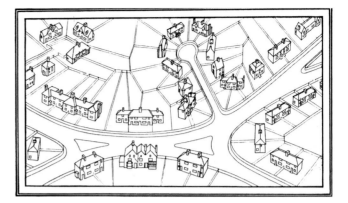

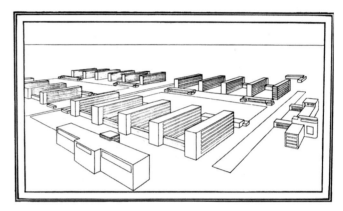

Fig 2.9a   A project by Arthur Trystan Edwards, described in *One Hundred New Towns for Britain* (1934), hoped to secure state funding to deal with slum clearance and resettlement problems. 'Villadom in "Open Developments"'.

Fig 2.9b   'Repetitive Blocks of Developments'.

Fig 2.9c   'Quadrangular Formations exemplify a happy mean'.

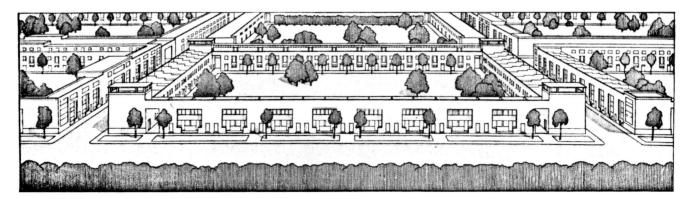

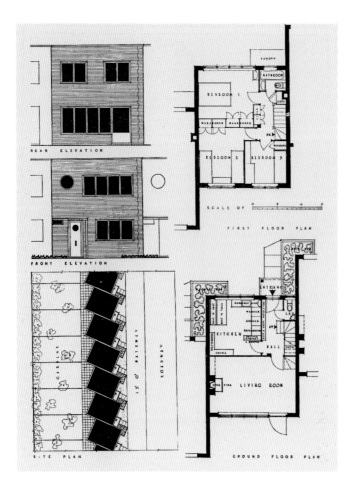

Fig 2.10 At the Ideal Home Exhibition 1939 Elizabeth Denby promoted the All-Europe House, a terrace of houses laid out in a saw-tooth formation modelled on a development in Stockholm, designed by Paul Hedqvist in 1932.

concept as the background to Swedish modern architecture and social democracy, lived here. Denby provided enticing images of Swedish life in her book, *Europe Re-Housed*, including compactly planned, timber, terraced houses built by one of the co-operative housing societies, looking very much like Span prototypes.[24] These co-operatives fulfilled the same investment function as building societies in Britain, but also built their own developments, housing one tenth of the population of Stockholm by 1934, although municipalities were also involved in housing finance. By these means, as Denby explained, Sweden avoided the absolute distinction between private and public sectors seen in Britain, both before and after the war. Bye-laws, she noted, also contributed to a feeling of collective pride in the look of the buildings after completion, 'giving an air of general gaiety to the streets by the gleaming paint and colourwash'.[25] The Swedish planning system was even able to reconcile conflicts between preservation and new building.

The courtyard as a housing form

Not only was the architectural form of the terrace open to new ideas, but also the layout of the houses in relation to grouping and access. Communal space in the form of courtyards was another completely traditional idea, found in the Inns of Court, Oxford and Cambridge colleges, almshouses, and in projects such as Waterlow Court, Hampstead Garden Suburb, by M. H. Baillie-Scott, and Guessens Court, Welwyn Garden City, but one which was waiting to be married to the right form of house and tenure. Furthermore, Walter Gropius's project for Christ's College, Cambridge (1936), although not a courtyard form in itself, acted to complete a court, with rooms organised traditionally off staircases, a system similar to later Span flats. The seclusion of college quadrangles and courts, with their carefully-detailed footpaths around central grass plots and restrained garden planting, contrasts with the urban squares, which in other respects they resemble, because cars and other vehicles are excluded. Additionally, the college will usually have a single main point of entry, with one court leading out of another, as often found in Span layouts. At Impington Village College, Gropius organised the plan so that after entering the famous 'promenade' that acts as entrance hall and principal circulation route, you are tempted out into a three-sided courtyard, which was built around a mature horse chestnut tree.

For more immediate examples of the creative arrangement of outdoor space in housing design, however, we should turn to the USA, where two of the famous schemes by Clarence Stein and Henry Wright, acting jointly as planners with Stein as architect, explored some of the issues current in post-war British housing layouts, and Span in particular. At Sunnyside Gardens in Queens (1924–7) Stein and Wright claimed to be continuing Raymond Unwin's theme, 'Nothing gained by Overcrowding', when they allowed the central area within each of the already delineated urban blocks to be reserved for communal use (Fig. 2.11).[26] This was an idea pioneered even earlier in London, especially in the Kensington Park area, where the backs of the houses enclose pleasantly-landscaped, shared gardens, entered through the individual gardens of the houses and maintained jointly by the householders. 'These common greens were intended for restful gatherings or for quiet play. They were not to be used as playground for any but the very young', wrote Stein.[27] Lewis Mumford, an early resident closely associated with the project, wrote: 'though our means were modest, we contrived to live in an environment where space, sunlight, order, colour – these essential ingredients for either life or art – were constantly present, silently moulding all of us'.[28]

At Radburn, New Jersey (1929), Stein and Wright's next scheme, they were in control of the layouts, and carried forward the now famous arrangement of restricting access to the front of the house to pedestrians, with vehicles entering back courts only, with garages for residents and pathways to back doors (Fig. 2.12).[29] This was the final reversal of the conventional distinction between front and back, which the other schemes mentioned had begun to dissolve. It was a completely logical separation, focused on child safety at a time of growing car ownership. It caught the imagination of post-war British planners, who tried to reproduce Radburn layouts in post-war new towns, but found that children and adults alike tended to congregate in the hard-surfaced traffic areas, whilst the ambiguity about entrance was a social hazard rather than an advantage. Span layouts similarly kept vehicles away from the front entrances, but were less diagrammatic in their separation, and therefore avoided the problems. The architectural style of Sunnyside and Radburn was not modern movement because the houses were designed in a simple Georgian or colonial style, well-adapted to the changing building lines and composed picturesquely from functional requirements. Nothing comparable to this existed in Britain, where the relationship between building modes and other cultural factors has been the subject of complex and often meaningless prejudice.

The romantic side of modernism

Thus far noted are some of the attitudes to private sector housing between the wars and some of the models that were being considered; some inside the relatively small sector of the modern movement, as defined internationally and some, like Sunnyside and Radburn, more concerned with planning form than building form. Is this enough to explain where Span 'comes from'? One further significant influence to be considered is the idea of romanticism in modern architecture, an aspect of modernism often excluded or denigrated and from which Span's critical reputation has suffered. Romanticism should not be understood as a retreat from modernism but as part of its maturing process. It may be

Fig 2.11   At Sunnyside Gardens in Queens, New York (1924–7), Stein and Wright allowed the central area within each of the urban blocks to be reserved for communal use.

Fig 2.12   At Radburn, New Jersey (1929), Stein carried forward the now famous arrangement of restricting access to the front of the house to pedestrians, with vehicles entering back courts only, with garages for residents and pathways to back doors.

identified in stylistic terms, with its preference for natural materials, associational forms and regional references. These, arguably, are secondary manifestations of what is, primarily, a metaphysical enquiry into the nature of life. As Gropius wrote: 'Catch phrases like "functionalism" (*die neue Sachlichkeit*) and "fitness for purpose = beauty" have the effect of deflecting appreciation of the New Architecture into external channels or making it purely one sided'.[30] In fact, he argued, 'the New Architecture is a bridge uniting opposite poles of thought'.

Between the wars, as is now widely accepted, there was a focus on the technical and mechanical in the 1920s, followed in the 1930s by a very different concern with nature. The 'second generation' of modernists, born between 1898 and 1918, included Alvar Aalto, Marcel Breuer, Charles Eames, Serge Chermayeff and Eric Lyons.[31] The move towards nature was shared by the first generation, amongst them the American architect Frank Lloyd Wright, for whom it was a constant theme, but the second generation made it their own. It carried over into the third generation, represented in Britain by figures such as Edward Cullinan and Peter Aldington, whose work is often more identifiably romantic in architectural form. Each of these generations explored the interaction between architecture and nature. Laszlo Moholy Nagy, for example, imagines that 'a white house with great glass windows surrounded by trees becomes almost transparent when the sun shines. The white walls act as projection screens on which shadows multiply the trees, and the glass plates become mirrors in which the trees are repeated. A perfect transparency is the result; the house becomes part of nature'.[32]

It is not so much the glass that is significant here in relation to Span, but the vision, similar severe neo-classical buildings placed in lusciously-planted surroundings in the late Georgian and Regency periods, with their elevations softened by climbing plants and trellises. What this passage suggests so powerfully is that the house acts as a projection screen for nature, and the art of designing is to deflect attention away from the building as an object and into the play of light and space to which it contributes, and which can be enjoyed from indoors. In these ways, some of the most moving architectural effects can be created apparently out of almost nothing. The medium is relationships, not objects. We could hardly be further removed from the attention-seeking but banal world of the standard semi.

One can say that a great deal of first generation modernism, which we associate with pure forms and machine-made surfaces, is romantic in its emotional effect, and more sensitive to landscape and site than was once imagined. Especially in respect of form, Eric Lyons was part of this tendency. In his typical Span work, he avoided the more demonstrative form-making of Aalto or Breuer. Chermayeff and Eames probably provide a better analogy, each of them through the houses they built for themselves. Chermayeff's house, Bentley Wood, East Sussex (1938) is a pure form, composed of rectangles created by a partially exposed, timber frame on a regular bay system that could have been multiplied as an urban form. In its landscape setting, however, as well as its timber structure and cladding, it qualifies as a romantic concept, very close to Moholy Nagy's vision of an exact balance of nature and

Fig 2.13 At Bentley Wood, Halland, East Sussex, Serge Chermayeff designed a house composed of rectangles created by a partially exposed, timber frame on a regular bay system in a romantic landscape setting.

Fig 2.14 Walter Gropius, Wood House, at Shipbourne, Kent (1936), one of several timber, modern houses in Britain of this period.

culture (Fig. 2.13). The Eames House at Santa Monica (1946) is rather similar in its effect, although built of industrial materials. It also responds to its setting and was perched on an expensively-excavated platform in order to preserve and benefit from an existing row of trees. When looking for the roots of Span, Gropius's Wood House at Shipbourne, Kent (1936), also deserves mention (Fig. 2.14). It is called that because it is built of timber, with timber window frames, and was one of several timber, modern houses in Britain of this period, more remarkable perhaps for its authorship than for what it was. The lesson for Lyons could have been that modern architecture could come in a range of materials, both 'traditional' and 'modern', without dilution of the concepts. It was this sort of steadfast adaptability that Lyons carried forward from the 1930s into the 1950s, when it became more common to look back to the 'pioneers', such as Gropius, in search of their more extreme moments, rather than their moderate ones.

Endnotes

1. Perhaps the best attempt to investigate suburban development in depth remains H. J. Dyos, *Victorian Suburb: a study of the growth of Camberwell*, (Leicester: Leicester University Press, 1961).
2. George and Weedon Grossmith, *The Diary of a Nobody* (Bristol: J. W. Arrowsmith, 1892).
3. Quoted in Robert Cowan, *Dictionary of Urbanism*, (Tisbury: Streetwise Press, 2005), p. 348.
4. Thomas Sharp, *English Panorama*, (London: J. M. Dent, 1938), p. 98. 1st edn 1936.
5. Clough Williams-Ellis, *England and the Octopus* (London: Geoffrey Bless, 1928).
6. Alan A. Jackson, *Semi-Detached London* (London: George Allen & Unwin, 1973), p. 321.
7. Jerry-builder: a speculating builder who 'runs up' unsubstantially built houses of inferior materials (Oxford English Dictionary, first use 1869).
8. John Betjeman, 'Antiquarian Prejudice' (1937), in *First and Last Loves* (London: John Murray, 1952), p. 49.
9. 'Mean and perky little houses that surely none but mean and perky little souls should inhabit with satisfaction', *op. cit.*, Clough Williams-Ellis, p. 15.
10. Title of song included on *Doughnut in Granny's Greenhouse* by the Bonzo Dog (Doo Dah) Band, November 1968, Liberty LBL/LBS 83158.
11. 'If you can imagine *Un Chien Andalou* reworked by Gilbert and Sullivan, you'll have the flavour of this unlikely product of the Grierson-supervised GPO Film Unit.... it's a satirical-ironical-irrational reverie, which contrasts the virtuous Pett family (who have a phone) with the disgraceful Potts (who don't). The latter are gleefully portrayed as the embodiment of everything un-suburban, with their libidinous continental ways and laxity with the hired help. Made for a pittance, it's radical, fun and probably left its sponsors aghast'. http://www.timeout.com/film/71030.html.
12. W. H. Auden and Christopher Isherwood, *The Ascent of F6* (London: Faber & Faber, 1936), p. 18.
13. M. Howlett, 'The "Small House" Exhibition', *RIBA Journal*, 7 November 1938, p. 26.
14. F. R. S. Yorke and Frederick Gibberd, *The Modern Flat* (London: Architectural Press, 1937).
15. F. R. S. Yorke, *The Modern House* (London: Architectural Press, 1934).
16. The best known instance was the Danish architect, S. E. Rasmussen's book, *London, the Unique City* (London: Cape, 1937). The German housing architect Bruno Taut's book, *Modern Architecture* (London: The Studio, 1929), included a section about the antecedents to modernism in late Georgian urban architecture in England.
17. *op. cit.*, F. R. S. Yorke, 1934, p. 18.
18. See Elain Harwood and Alan Powers, *Tayler and Green, Architects 1938–1973: the spirit of place in modern housing* (London: Prince of Wales's Institute of Architecture, 1998).
19. Goldfinger house: *Architectural Review*, April 1940, pp. 126–30; Lasdun house: *Architectural Review*, March 1939, pp. 119–32.
20. Walter Gropius, *The New Architecture and the Bauhaus* (London: Faber & Faber, 1935). Translated from the German by P. Morton Shand.
21. Arthur Trystan Edwards, *A Hundred New Towns for Britain*, (London: Simpkin Marshall, 1934).
22. Review by W. M. W. in *Building*, vol.10, 1935, p. 119.
23. Elizabeth Denby, 'Rehousing', *Architect & Building News*, vol.148, 20 November 1936, pp. 23–4. Abstract of paper on 'Rehousing from the Slum-Dweller's Point of View' read before the RIBA 16 November 1936.
24. Elizabeth Denby, *Europe Rehoused* (London: Allen & Unwin, 1938).
25. *ibid.*, p. 61.
26. Raymond Unwin, *Nothing Gained by Overcrowding!* (London: Garden Cities and Town Planning Association, 1912).
27. Clarence Stein, *Toward New Towns for America* (Liverpool: University of Liverpool Press, 1951), p. 27.
28. *ibid.*, p. 30.
29. See also Chapter 3.
30. *op. cit.*, Gropius, p. 19
31. The dates are taken from Philip Drew, *The Third Generation* (London: Pall Mall, 1972).
32. László Moholy Nagy, *The New Vision*, 3rd edn, (New York: Wittenborn and Company, 1946) p. 64.

"To me the dominating factor in layout design is the creation of space... visual space and funtional space."

Eric Lyons

Span arose from a dissatisfaction with the domestic building process, its restrictions, and its inability to provide an appropriate contemporary solution; it therefore aimed 'to span the gap between the suburban monotony of the typical speculative development and the architecturally designed, individually built residence that has become (for all but a few) financially unattainable'.[1] Its mission was 'to provide an environment – at the right price – that will give people a "lift"'.[2] 'Environment' is perhaps the most apt description for what slightly later was interpreted as a 'way of life',[3] or would nowadays be quoted as 'lifestyle'. Landscape was the primary basis for the success of Span; it was the essence of the schemes, as observed by the architectural critic R. Furneaux Jordan in 1959 who noted it was:

> ...something almost universally absent from normal spec'
> building and almost always present in good 18th-century
> building – landscape. This does not mean that Lyons can plan
> a pretty garden and has somehow persuaded Span to pay for
> it. The whole approach is through landscape. The landscape,
> the design of houses within an environment, is the starting
> point of the design from Lyons's point of view; the top selling
> point... from Townsend's.[4]

This quote mirrors the perception of architect and landscape architect Geoffrey Jellicoe in 1980, who acknowledged that Span's domestic housing was 'conceived more as landscape architecture than as architecture itself' and observed that 'The elegant Span housing... have [sic] been a success speculatively as well as aesthetically. "Good landscape is good business" was proved right'.[5] This chapter analyses the contribution made by landscape to the housing schemes; what the designers tried to achieve and how that was accomplished.

Historic context

By the end of the 19th century British housing was dominated by developers who paid little or no particular attention to landscape issues. At the turn of the century Ebenezer Howard promoted the concept of the garden city as an answer to the ills of the overcrowded industrial city.[6] Whilst he had only provided a diagrammatic model of what this entailed, showing 32,000-inhabitant-large garden cities as satellites to the big city, he later joined with the architect Raymond Unwin to develop Letchworth and Welwyn Garden City. Unwin's layouts were considerably freer in plan than any previous urban development, with low-density, abundant green spaces and large private gardens; he introduced cul-de-sacs, closes and roundabouts (Fig. 3.1). Few garden cities were actually developed, but many of the interwar developments showed the influences in design features that had been promoted by Unwin.[7] Yet the influence of the garden city travelled widely and it was far-reaching; it provided an international reputation in town planning, but also has been blamed for the extensive interwar suburban sprawl outside all major British cities.[8]

Housing policy was reviewed during the Second World War, with the Dudley Report (1944) providing the main official statement for post-war England.[9] It noted the many serious mistakes that had

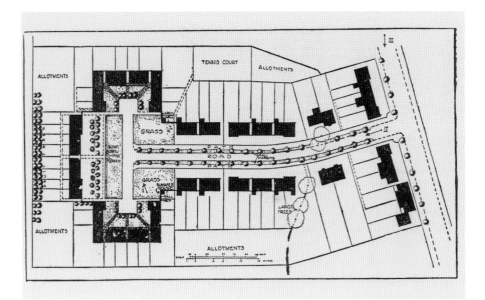

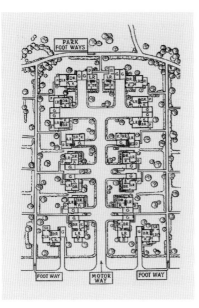

Fig 3.1 Raymond Unwin introduced a new vocabulary in housing design, placing low-density housing around cul-de-sacs and closes.

Fig 3.2a The Radburn principle segregated pedestrians and the motorcars by creating a cul-de-sac network of roads accessible by car.

been made, including the conspicuous separation between private and 'municipal' housing, insufficient community facilities (churches, schools, club buildings, shops, open spaces), poorly located housing in relationship to work, insufficient variety in housing types, the lack of smaller open spaces and playgrounds, and poor design quality of houses and their setting.[10] Following these shortcomings on site planning and layout in relation to housing, detailed suggestions were made on appropriate design and treatment. The importance of welding new residents in a community was widely acknowledged, and in order to create a satisfactory social life, smaller and more intimate neighbourhoods were required. New neighbourhoods were normally named after some local source or tradition, which helped to give immediate separate identity and local pride – yet they were not to be seen as self-contained communities of which inhabitants were more conscious than the town.[11]

These recommendations followed the neighbourhood theory that became so dominantly influential after the Second World War. It was a concept that had been appropriated earlier by the planner C. A. Perry,[12] yet it has recently been revealed that it was widely in circulation previously in the writings by William E. Drummond,[13] and in fact was the basis of the planning of Radburn, New Jersey

Fig 3.2b Plan of northwest and southwest residential districts, Radburn, New Jersey 1929.

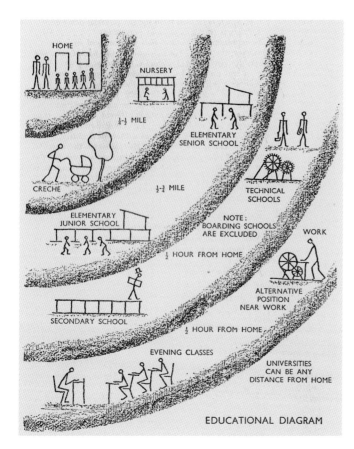

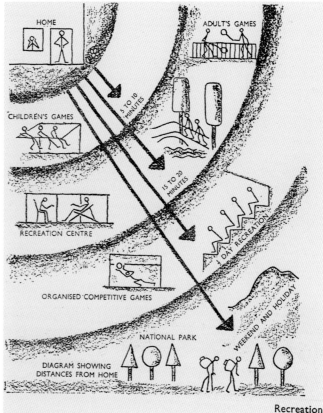

Fig 3.3a Neighbourhood theories formed the basis for much post-war town planning, with conceptual diagrams such as those by Gutkind. One of the main criteria for town planning was accessibility from the home: Educational diagram.

Fig 3.3b Recreational diagram.

(1929), where Clarence Stein segregated pedestrians and motor cars by creating a cul-de-sac network of roads accessible by car, whereas the front of the house faced onto the pedestrian network that linked in with a park system (Figs. 3.2a and 3.2b). The Radburn principle is now generally and loosely used in any housing layout where cars and pedestrians are separated and was extremely influential in post-war Britain.

In England the neighbourhood theory was partly overtaken by the National Council of Social Service that had initially promoted village halls as social centres in the countryside and, during the war, community centres in urban areas. They argued that 'One of the tasks of the community centre will be to create out of the neighbourhood which it serves, a community'.[14] It implied that the focus was on the building rather than the landscape, a view corrected by the landscape architect Brenda Colvin who argued

that 'Community gardens, even more than community hall and buildings, may, if suitably designed, foster the social unity of a group' (Figs. 3.3a and 3.3b).[15] Colvin asserted that vast areas of suburb had been visually ruined by the 'semi-detached repetitive pattern' and she promoted the type of mixed texture of old towns and villages, which 'lies largely in the mixture of sizes resulting from mixed-income groups, with all the variety of their different gardens, side by side, creating a sense of community and friendly relationship which can never arise where all is monotonous repetition'. (The later editions of Colvin's book illustrated these principles with modern schemes by Tayler and Green in Gillingham, Norfolk, and the third phase of Span's Highsett development in Cambridge.[16])

Whilst community and neighbourhood theories were discussed prior to the war,[17] the main application in Britain was found in the development of the new towns concept during and after the war.

The new town of Ongar, projected by Patrick Abercrombie in 1944 as an example of one of London's satellite towns, was to contain six neighbourhoods of 10,000 inhabitants each (Fig. 3.4). This was considered sufficient to require a community centre, two junior and infant schools and four nursery schools, as well as 70–100 shops. A density from 30 persons per acre up to a maximum of 50 per acre was incorporated in various dwelling types from detached houses to flats. (See also Chapter 4.) The neighbourhoods were surrounded by a strip of parkland, with narrower strips dividing the various housing groups within the neighbourhood.[18] The New Towns Act 1946 set out government procedure for a national policy of town design, with Stevenage announced as the first one that year; Crawley, Hemel Hempstead, Harlow, Hatfield, Basildon and Bracknell followed shortly after. Whilst these Mark I new towns differed in design, they all retained the neighbourhood structure with generous open space, green wedges and well-spaced-out houses. They provided a welcome range of issues for discussion, ranging from masterplan down to detail design, with the architectural press covering numerous examples of housing. The impact of this work was that when the much-trumpeted housing exhibition at Lansbury, East London, was opened (as part of the 1951 Festival of Britain) its design revealed little new, neither in architectural, nor in landscape planning, nor design terms, because the best architects were busily making their contributions in the various new towns.[19]

Building a community

Lyons had little time for the architecture generated in the new towns, which he found too widely spaced, and not sufficiently

Fig 3.4 Patrick Abercrombie's 1944 project for a new town at Ongar was based on the neighbourhood theory, with community centres and schools located in generous greenspace.

urban, referring to their layout as being conceived on a 'suburban prairie pattern'. He had found it a tragedy that they had had to wait so long for Cumbernauld to emerge.[20] Mark II new towns, such as Cumbernauld, Skelmersdale and Runcorn, had higher densities and were more compact, integrating urban motorways or public transport systems. In 1955 Cumbernauld was the first to breach the neighbourhood idea[21] creating 'a small town with a strong sense of place'.[22] The concept by Hugh Wilson featured a town centre on the central hill, within easy walking distance from the housing areas, and a complete segregation of pedestrians and vehicles. The masterplan, developed with landscape architects Bill Gillespie and Peter Youngman, exploited the topography and the distant views and proposed extensive forest areas on steep slopes, where development was technically impossible.

Lyons had included examples of housing layouts in Cumbernauld in an issue of *Architectural Design*, which he selected, edited and entitled 'Building a community'.[23] This confirmed his belief that grouped housing not only imparts the sense of community, but also makes economic and sensible use of land, is good town planning and enables modern building techniques by repetitive design.[24] Other examples confirm some of the sources of inspiration and influences which also affected the Span developments; a scheme of flats at Ponente del Mare on the Italian Riviera was included as an example of what might be appropriate along the coast in Devon and Cornwall. Siedlung Halen, Berne, Switzerland, a dense urban scheme in woodland by Atelier 5 – an example Lyons used in his slide shows[25] – showed that high- rather than low-density might be appropriate even when more space might have been available, as its density encouraged interaction and thus imparted this sense of community.

Also included was Jørn Utzon's (the designer of the Sydney Opera building) housing scheme at Elsinore, Denmark, an example of the spatial economy provided by a different building typology. Sixty court (or courtyard) houses were arranged according to the contours, providing an interesting, yet rhythmically controlled skyline. The essence here, however, is that a conventional layout would have only enabled 48 houses to be built and would not have provided any common land (Fig. 3.5). Paradise Row, Henley-on-Thames, a mix of courtyard, terraced houses and flats by Tom Hancock of Morton and Lupton, was also included as it incorporated an interesting innovation on the traditional Radburn principle, that Lyons considered a threat to the urban landscape. The Prestonpans development, a single-storey, high-density development by Edinburgh University Housing Research Unit, was included for the interest created with its complex of private and public courts, not for the design of the individual units. Lafayette Park, Detroit, a new neighbourhood of high-rise apartment

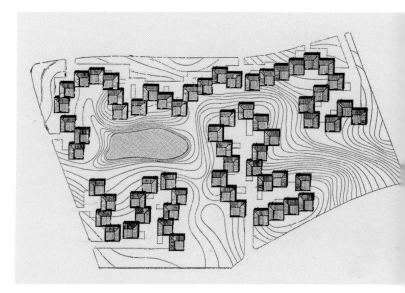

Fig 3.5   Jørn Utzon's housing scheme at Elsinore, Denmark (1958), was one of the sources of inspiration for Span housing in that it reduced private space for each dwelling and provided extensive communal space instead.

blocks and two-storey terraces by Mies van der Rohe and Ludwig Hilbersheimer, built around a park (which appears as an innovation on the Radburn principle, but without provision of private garden space) is within walking distance of the city centre. As a contrast to this modernist scheme a traditional settlement of Lindos on Rhodes provides an example of a courtyard development and organisation as an alternative to semi-detached housing or short terraces. Besides these real-life cases one futuristic example was included – 'mobile architecture' by Yona Friedman and R. Aujame, in which towns are given over to the pedestrian. They proposed that halls, markets and houses should be changeable and replaceable: 'Planning becomes bearable, because it is not definitive, and the possibility of correction or experimentation is still there'.[26]

The examples selected by Eric Lyons reveal the aspirations of Span in that they include a whole range of typologies, with the presumption that innovation in grouping might encourage a sense of community. In the selection it is clear, therefore, that he is unhindered by the style of the buildings, whether they be traditional, vernacular, modernist or futuristic. Lyons later appears to confirm this by quoting the planners' dictum that 'the external design of the individual house units is relatively unimportant', but then argues that layout is vital and that the design of individual units greatly affects the environment, prior to stating the general methodology for establishing a new development, with its priorities:

> To me the dominating factor in layout design is the creation of space, not just the road pattern, or just the segregation of traffic, or the convenient arrangement of sewers and services and so on; all this must be subservient to the spatial concept, that is to say, space where it is wanted and for what it is wanted: visual space and functional space. Buildings define space, and the space about buildings and the buildings should be integrated. This integration can only result from a creative design process to produce what I call the 'building landscape'. The landscape must be designed not only to adorn but to define the functions of space; particularly in urban scale it is the placing of buildings that matters, so that spaces are significant and the accesses convenient and so on. The soft furnishings of nature should not be used to obscure spatial relationships but to enhance them, and this means that the organisation of space must be right to start with. In other words, landscape should be the functional design of the space, not just a matter of bringing in a landscape-decorator to sprinkle some trees and cobbles around the place.[27]

With these principles established, Lyons continued to stress the importance of 'architectural *scale* and the sense of community that is imparted by compact groupings of buildings and the use of common space'. In this, the significance of the user was recognised in that having housing that expresses a community that does not in fact exist is not good enough, and that a community is needed: 'we need people to be involved in the creation and preservation of the environment'. The creation of communal spaces and the setting up of a framework so that residents can be involved with their environment can be an effective way to create a community.[28] It is probably one of the most important keys to the lasting success of the Span developments and explains why, whereas Lyons was asked to talk about the 'appearance of housing', he entitled his paper 'setting' and emphasised that we should 'design our whole environment'.[29]

Shaping the landscape

Whilst the designs of the various projects were considered holistically, many of the spatial decisions were taken at the planning stages, to which Lyons always contributed. After the initial project at Parkleys (1956), which was organised by Geoffrey Townsend (a fervent gardener with an interest in rhododendrons), Ivor Cunningham was employed with special responsibility for landscape.[30] He first designed housing schemes in Blackheath, but very soon progressed to designing the Span housing layouts and then onto actual dwellings. As, in time, Cunningham became increasingly involved with the buildings, additional help was required. Initially, Michael Brown filled the gap, contributing primarily to the planting of Fieldend (1961), where he later lived.[31] After a relatively short time, however, he left, to be replaced by the Dane Preben Jakobsen, who answered an advert in the *Architects' Journal*. Jakobsen had worked for a number of nurseries in Denmark, France and Great Britain before completing a Diploma in Horticulture at the Royal Botanic Gardens, Kew, and studying landscape architecture at the Royal Academy of Fine Arts in Copenhagen, under Professor C. Th. Sørensen, who was a significant influence on him. He worked for Span from 1961–9, where he was noted as a superb plantsman with a strong design sense, contributing to work at Southrow, Blackheath (1963), Highsett, Cambridge (1963–5), The Lane, Blackheath (1964), Templemere, Weybridge (1965), Holme Chase, Weybridge (1966), and New Ash Green (1969).[32]

Design philosophy

Despite the different backgrounds of the landscape designers, there are similarities between the various housing schemes, due principally to the strong concept developed by Lyons and Cunningham. Jellicoe wrote that Lyons was a rare exception amongst architects in that he had 'consistently held the balance between architecture and nature without which the average human subconsciously feels disoriented'.[33] He noted how the practice approached housing as landscape architecture, describing how, in contrast to 'the usual configuration of buildings encircling a space into which gardens have been inserted', it 'evolved a form of terrace houses enclosing common gardens in a single total landscape concept', the unity of which was 'partly achieved by ground modelling, so that, in contrast to the standard London square, vertical and horizontal have an agreeable plastic relationship'. He registered that there are small patio gardens, 'but that the collective gardens are so beautifully and intricately planted that they have maintained some mystique of nature without being disordered'. He concluded that in 'this age of concrete jungles and mass production of architecture, the preservation of human values is vital' and that a 'Lyons house is only for the sensitive and the appreciative, where the sight, touch and smell of a plant has as much meaning as a work of art'.

The Eric Lyons Cunningham Partnership (ELCP) effectively summarised the philosophy of its approach in an undated promotional booklet entitled *Landscape*:

> *The design of landscape is not confined to creating gardens or parks: it can help to create all kinds of different environments. ELCP believe that an important aspect of landscape design is to satisfy the functions of space; to express or underline certain aspects and even on occasion to obscure some of these functions. The introduction of Nature into the man-oriented urban environments can be decorative and soften the impact of hard building masses. ELCP use their landscape design skill in combination with their basic architectural skill with the specific objective of integrating the design of the whole. The two design disciplines join to provide a unique approach to the problems of creating places with individual identities. The spaces in between the buildings are not left to chance, and this integrated design process leads to a cohesive outcome where buildings help to create the settings and the settings enhance the buildings.*
>
> *ELCP have produced a great variety of different kinds of places by their positive approach and when they talk about 'identity' of place it is no academic matter. It means that places can be purposefully created so that each is readily recognised by its individual characteristics. The user can identify it and develop a relationship with the place itself.*
>
> *We all have affection for certain places in our lives; the great squares and avenues; the gardens and parks; the village green and the intimate lanes and byways. Most of these much-loved places have been formed by the pressures of long historical changes. In our work we endeavour to create places with comparable qualities either for 'instant' effect or to provide the basis for further growth and change in the course of time. Our aspiration is to create places that people will enjoy.[34]*

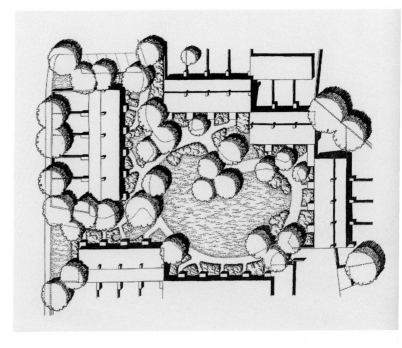

Fig 3.6   The traditional arrangement of front and rear garden as standard provision for new housing was first questioned in a 1957 project at St Nicholas Street, Coventry, where front gardens were omitted and a communal garden was provided instead.

Fig 3.7 In Span schemes the dominance of the car was challenged by not dictating the layout in favour of the car. By being forced to proceed through the communal gardens these became informal meeting places, thus enhancing the community spirit.

Whilst the fashion for British post-war housing dictated a number of distinct typologies – for example, flats in an open landscape with a sprinkling of trees with flowing line-type paths approximately along desire lines and two-storey housing with front and back gardens – an early Span scheme, such as Parkleys, provides a clearly different character. Here, there is a clear articulation of spaces; quadrangles connected with the flats that encourage communal activities or informal meetings, whilst the planting provides a clearly garden-type character with shrub belts and tree planting. The nature of the layout was determined by rectangular areas that were reminiscent of Scandinavian functionalism, be it with a more adventurous range of plants, courtesy of the British climate. Private gardens were later excluded from developments of houses as for schemes of flats, and the resulting approach is what Cunningham liked to refer to as 'wall-to-wall landscape carpeting'[35] or as 'with the landscape washing up to the buildings'.[36] Whilst these terms are suggestive, they are perhaps slightly disparaging of the difficult process that appears to have taken place to create purposeful places with building blocks and planting. The fact that the maintenance became the responsibility of the residents' association instead of a local authority enabled the aftercare of the complicated landscape structure to be guaranteed.

Front and back

For most of the 1950s the front and rear garden remained standard in Span housing. This traditional arrangement was first questioned in a 1957 project for a housing scheme in St Nicholas Street, Coventry (Fig. 3.6). Not having front gardens opened up substantial possibilities, as it was not now necessary to adhere to a strictly geometrical layout determined by footpaths, and enabled more flowing designs. These provided an easier way to create informally, interlinking spaces and, therefore, more flexible use of the place. Rear gardens were seen as 'private places for individual foibles, where people can pursue outdoor creative skills, can keep their toddlers in safety and hang out washing',[37] and were thus considered a necessity. Front gardens, however, were considered as the best symbols of the lifestyle of the inhabitants and as a means of separating their dwellings from the outside world. These factors were considered to be redundant in private developments where residents' associations existed. Whilst the Coventry scheme did not come to fruition, the idea of communal space at the front of housing was incorporated in the design for Corner Green Phase 1, Blackheath, (1959) and this became the model for subsequent developments.[38]

The layout of Span developments used a number of standard house types, rather than specific ones designed for each site, which had distinct marketing advantages. The standard types were mostly designed so that they enabled some flexibility with regard to the orientation, or with a number of types arranged so that they could

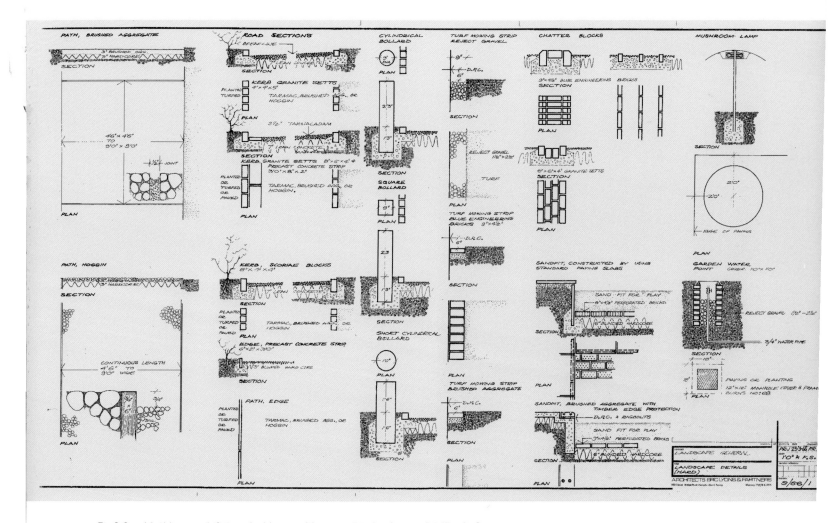

Fig 3.8   Nothing was left to coincidence with respect to landscape detailing in Span
housing schemes, as this sheet with standard details signifies.

all face a central communal space. The lack of front gardens in the later schemes enabled the central lawn to be extended up to the building blocks, whilst in other places shrub and tree planting was used to break up the monotony of repetitive housing. Planting provided its own rhythm and created places in conjunction with the buildings. It was also used to create an illusion of more extensive space that is not only attractive visually, but also provides a magnificent informal playground for children.

Cars and parking

The car and car parking greatly affect the domestic landscape in design terms; in Span schemes the dominance of the car was challenged by not dictating the layout in favour of the car. Cunningham noted how he liked people to approach the Span developments 'with some style' and not dominated by the car.[39]

Instead of parking alongside the road in front of each house, Span produced separate car parks, or 'car squares' that were screened off and 'served as a connection between the walker in the gardens and the driver on the road' (Fig. 3.7). Drivers would turn into pedestrians and move through the communal gardens, which would thus serve as informal meeting places, an important advantage over examples by other developers, where proximity to the car becomes the main design criterion. Similarly, the preferred manner of grouping garages in separate courts provided visual and practical advantages that were exploited in most of the Span developments.[40] This arrangement, which was common to continental housing of the 1950s and 60s, certainly serves its purpose of shaping a community, as most residents tend to know each other, which furthers a sense of security and belonging,[41] and it is only regrettable that this approach is so rarely shared with new developments today.

Nothing was left to coincidence with respect to the detailing of the landscape; all features from signs, number plates, lamp posts, garden lamps and bollards were specifically selected or purposely designed (Fig. 3.8). The Scandinavian style mushroom-shaped outdoor lamps became a signature of Span housing developments (Fig. 3.9). First used at Parkleys, they were designed by Lyons and produced by Frederick Thomas.[42] Each consisted of a '30 in. diameter shallow dome on a stalk of 1½ in. diameter steel tube, both units are stove enamelled green. The fittings stand just over 3 ft high'.[43] Contrasting strongly with other types of municipal lighting, these lamps provided an immediate sense of a garden environment. In 1960, at the time when Elizabeth Beazley noted that British 'standards of outdoor design have dropped to a very low ebb', she was able to commend the garden of a Span house for the type and quality of detailing it maintained.[44]

Planting

The early Span planting schemes by Cunningham, like their site planning, are primarily concerned with functional issues. An example such as The Keep, Blackheath (1957), which still features small front gardens, had them divided from communal space with low and medium-sized shrubs such as: *Lavendula* 'Hidcote', *Berberis verruculosa, Cotoneaster simonsii, Tamarix gallica, Erica x veitchii,* and *Spiraea thunbergii.* Additional strips of shrub planting serve as buffer zones to soften the lines of buildings and direct cars into allocated car parking, with strategically planted trees reinforcing this. Shrubbery planting includes a whole range of popular nursery material from the 1950s, including: *Rhus typhina, Cortaderia selloana* (pampas grass) and *Fatsia japonica* at corner positions; whilst *Rosa rugosa* 'Blanc Double de Coubert', *Rosa chinensis, Rosa omeiensis pteracantha, Rosa rugosa, Spiraea x vanhouttei, Olearia x haastii, Juniperus x media* 'Pfitzeriana', *Philadelphus* 'Manteau d'Hermine', *Cornus alternifolia* 'Argentea', *Cornus mas, Sambucus nigra* 'Aurea', *Berberis stenophylla, Cotoneaster conspicuous, Kalmia latifolia* and *Arundinaria japonica* are generally used in small groups and tend to be repeated in places (Fig. 3.10). Trees planted in this scheme include *Betula pendula* in pairs or threesomes in strategic corner positions; the majority of further trees are used singly, either intended to mature freely in their location, including *Sorbus x thuringiaca, Ulmus parviflora, Prunus* 'Tai Haku', *Gleditsia triacanthos*; or to achieve a considerable size relatively quickly, such as *Acer saccharinum.* Since Corner Green Phase 1 forms the first communal green without divisions for front gardens, strategic planting becomes more informal, but it is structurally no less important. There is now a subtle distinction between the communal space privacy required, resolved with strategic projections in places, with smaller plant groupings, that give a sense of the domestic, rather than the larger communal or public scale. It is interesting to note that the overall plant selection at Corner Green Phase 1 retained a similar palette to The Keep.

Fig 3.9 The Scandinavian-style mushroom-shaped outdoor lamps provided an immediate sense of a garden environment; they were first used at Parkleys in 1956 and became a signature of Span housing schemes.

Fig 3.10   Planting schemes by Ivor Cunningham in early Span projects such as The Keep, Blackheath (1957), were primarily concerned with functional issues, and still incorporated front gardens.

At Fieldend, the planting prepared by Michael Brown and Cunningham develops the Corner Green Phase 1 approach; here the palette is more restricted and with more consistent use of a number of selected plants to provide cohesion (Fig. 3.11). Whilst a row of large plane trees (*Platanus x acerifolia*) is used to emphasise enclosure – something Cunningham considered a mistake as the terraces already provided this – other planting is informal. The centre is dominated by birch (*Betula pendula*) planted in a large drift; there are some *Larix europaea*, *Robinia pseudoacacia*, *Koelreuteria paniculata* and *Sophora japonica* planted at irregular spacings. Unlike at The Keep, the planting provides a more naturalistic appearance. Low planting in the centre is used to contain the informal path system and separate it from the grass areas. *Hypericum calycinum* predominates here in large groupings, with *Erica carnea*, and *Vinca*

minor. Smaller and larger odd corners to the sides have been planted with a slightly wider range, in much smaller numbers than plants used in the centre, with some low groundcover sub-shrubs such as *Hebe buxifolia*, *Hebe lycopodioides*, *Pachysandra terminalis* and *Hedera helix*; or with some ferns in a more shady position, including *Adiantum pedatum*, *Scolopendrium vulgare*, *Polypodium* and *Dryopteris*. These are included within mixed shrub masses, incorporating *Juniperus x media* 'Pfitzeriana', *Amelanchier laevis*, *Cornus stolonifera*, *Cotoneaster dammeri*, *Cotoneaster horizontalis*, *Cytisus x kewensis* and *Pieris japonica*. To one side *Taxus baccata* 'Repandens' has been used to emphasise the rhythm of the entrances to the houses. *Hedera helix*, *Jasminum officinale* and *Clematis paniculata* are used to cover the bare end of walls of the terraces.

45

Fig 3.11 Planting design at Fieldend emphasised the creation of enclosure with an open space in the centre, surrounded by dappled light of birch trees and with more garden-type plants near the houses.

With Jakobsen, the practice gained someone with considerable ambition with respect to developing planting design, and he was later identified as one of the main plantsmen of his period. Indeed, he had led a new movement of corporate landscape planting that was pioneered at Span housing, such as Templemere, influencing a generation of landscape architects (Figs 3.12, 3.13a and 3.13b). The range of plants used by him increased substantially over earlier Span schemes and the way they were used changed also. Jakobsen's writings explain his theories, identifying 'juxtapositioning' 'as the essence of all planting design'.[45] Juxtapositioning saw planting design as an artistic expression that took its cues from related spatial theories that also involved a full understanding of scale, proportion and balance. For this purpose, planting was divided according to its habit and function within the scheme, such as multi-stemmed sculptural dominants, backdrop, background, anchor domes, bold spiky accent, intermediate, carpet, vertical linear facer and bold broadleaved facer. At Templemere, for example, he provided a lavender groundcover that was 'used in a manner that an artist applies paint to a canvas, mauve highlighted by accents of *Cortaderia*'.[46] The range of plants in this scheme includes a large selection of shrubs including *Rhododendron* 'Bengal Fire', *Buddleia fallowiana* 'Lochinch', *Caryopteris clandonensis*, *Cornus asperifolia*, *Cornus mas* 'Macrocarpa', *Cornus stolonifera* 'Flaviramea', *Cytisus scoparius*, *Hypericum calycinum* and *H.moserianum* and *Lavendula spica* 'Hidcote'. Several trees were already on site, but moved into new positions, and additional ones added, including *Betula alba*, *Larix principis-rupprechtii*, *Gleditsia triacanthos* and *Robinia pseudoacacia*. Plants with a spike-like structure within the planting include *Arundo donax* 'Macrophylla', *Phormium tenax*, and *Arundinaria japonica*.

Jakobsen continued to apply his artistic approach to structural planting at New Ash Green. Unlike Warrington New Town a few years later, where planting was dictated by ecological principles, at New Ash Green there was little attempt to link up with the natural vegetation of the region. Whilst alder (*Alnus glutinosa*) and hornbeam (*Carpinus betulus*) were used predominantly in certain areas, the dominant tree planting in others was beech (*Fagus sylvatica*), which were consciously applied as natives and used primarily on the edges of the development. It was noted that trees were not to be planted in lines but should be 'informal in content & outlook the planting to be similar to the beech hangers normally found on chalkland'.[47] These informal woodland plantations had incidental underplantings of field maples. Other trees used were exotics from different parts of the world, including *Acer saccharinum* 'Wieri' (a pendulous form), *Alnus cordata, Betula albosinensis septentrionalis* and conifers *Picea omorika* and *Pinus peuce*. Except for the alder, these trees were primarily used within the housing areas, thus emphasising directional, visual and aesthetic criteria, rather than concerns over nativeness, which continues to be such a prominent issue today.

Fig 3.12   Preben Jakobsen's planting schemes, such as those pioneered at Span housing at Templemere, influenced a generation of landscape architects and set new standards for corporate landscape planting.

Span's urbanism

When Lyons promoted 'urbanity' and admitted that 'urban building is the only kind that really interests me', he did not mean an emphasis on inner city building, but intended this to be understood as a contrast to low-density development that 'is strangling every town in the country and contaminating the country around every town'.[48] In fact, most of the Span housing developments are located in traditional suburban areas around London, as in Blackheath, Weybridge, Ham and Twickenham, but they maintain densities that are appropriate in urban areas without losing a sense of space. Lyons referred to these houses with small rear gardens that achieved the same densities as apartments (60 persons per acre) as 'town houses', as used at the Cedars, Teddington, in 1958.[49] The sites for Span developments were carefully selected and generally had well-established vegetation of mature trees. Several in Blackheath were in the grounds of large Victorian houses, whilst a few of those in Weybridge are located within the curtilage of

Oatlands Park, an important landscape park famous for its early 18th-century refashioning by the artist and landscape gardener, William Kent. Others were former nurseries or gravel pits, sometimes with extensive planting, sometimes with very limited vegetation, as at Fieldend. Sites like these provided additional opportunities for land re-shaping instead, in order to provide interest, but lacked the instant maturity.

Whilst recognising the need for preservation of 'the finest of our past' and 'the not so fine if it cannot be replaced by better',[50] Lyons had few qualms about being accused of 'cannibalising the Victorian gardens of demolished mansions'.[51] In fact, he seems to have relished the fights with planners and other officials to achieve the kind of developments that enabled an instant new landscape to be created, that provided 'the cosy embrace of his landscaping'. He questioned the need for zoning, which had been useful considered in the light of polluting factories, but was less so with modern, clean and noiseless

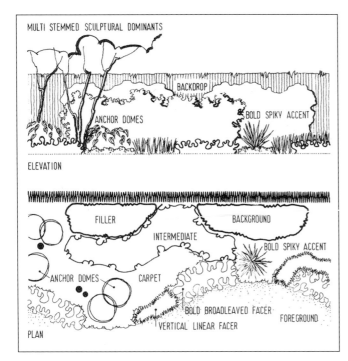

Fig 3.13a Jakobsen's theories identified 'juxtapositioning' as the essence of all planting design, dividing plants on the grounds of habit and function within the scheme.

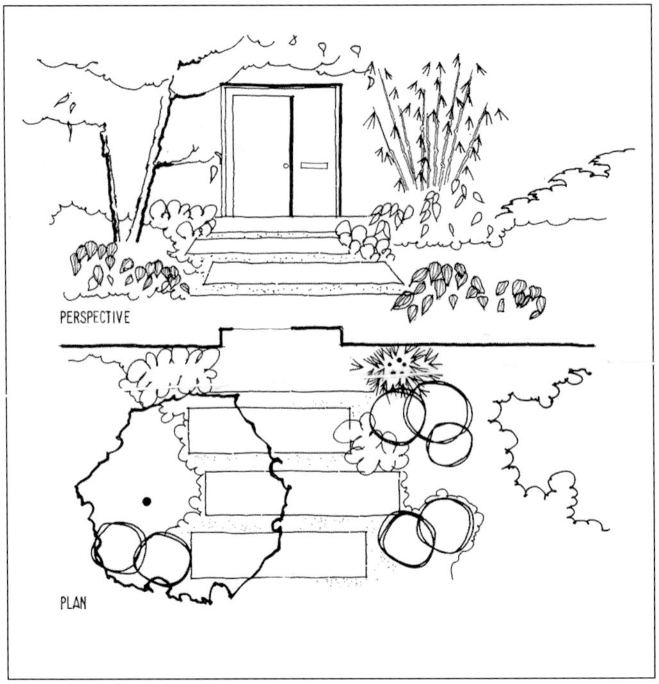

Fig 3.13b Enframement of an entrance using plants of different heights.

industries. This increased travel to work and removed 'essentially communal activities in special areas remote from housing'. In this context he liked to quote Lewis Mumford, who suggested that 'we have to "re-assemble the parts of the city… uniting them in a new pattern that shall offer much richer resources for living than either the congested and disordered central metropolis or the outlying areas reached by its expressways"'.[52] Span's small-scale, new housing in places where this is most needed, on previously developed sites within an existing suburban framework, was seen as providing a welcome alternative to large-scale, greenfield developments on the edge of town without appropriate infrastructure.

Lyons's commitment to high densities, whilst not sacrificing his idea of community and his landscape ideals, becomes clear from the 1963 redevelopment proposals for World's End, Chelsea. Conceived as a deck scheme over two storeys of car parking, with a number of 19-storey tower blocks integrated within an overall six-storey terrace system, the emphasis was on landscape with a series of 'newel posts' filled with earth enabling trees to mature, with lawned areas completing 'the illusion of natural parkland'.[53] The scheme, that can be interpreted as incorporating various ideas in some of his favourite prototypes (Ponente del Mare, Siedlung

Halen and Lafayette Park), was being promoted as representing a village atmosphere 'but a village in a modern setting', incorporating a church, a school, a pub, shops, a community centre, a club, gym, playing fields and open spaces, with community facilities paid for by the 765 dwellings for 2,500 people.[54] The scheme has been criticised because there was little money left for the communal facilities due to the higher-than-expected structural costs.[55] yet it has long been acknowledged as one of the best high-density, high-rise schemes in Britain that also created an interesting environment.[56]

Simultaneously with extending the community and landscape ideals to developments with high density, Lyons was involved in exploring whether these could be translated into a proposed village for 6,000 people at New Ash Green, Kent. The new village was separated into four compact neighbourhoods, divided by green wedges that led to the centre, reminiscent of other post-war British new towns. A ring road encloses the neighbourhoods with cul-de-sac feeder roads leading to tightly-grouped, terrace housing responding to the contouring. From here a separate walkway system leads to the village centre. The housing areas were planted with woody vegetation, meaning that the two- and three-storey housing was soon integrated within the landscape and the village became invisible. The overall wooded character of the village is rare within the post-war new towns, but is also found in Milton Keynes (1967; landscape architect Peter Youngman) and Warrington New Town (1968; landscape architect masterplan Sylvia Crowe; later Rob Tregay and others); the latter is strongly inspired by Dutch and Scandinavian examples, which might have also influenced the wooded treatment at New Ash Green, since Cunningham had lived in both the Netherlands and in Sweden and Jakobsen, who prepared the planting plans, was particularly familiar with the latest developments in Denmark.[57]

By the late 1970s approaches to modernism were seen as rather a cliché and were derided for their austerity and, as a result, Lyons and Cunningham continued to be innovative and to explore new approaches. Mallard Place, Twickenham, (1984) was one of these late developments that provided a high-density estate of two- and three-storey buildings with two courtyard blocks. Situated on a former industrial works, the location is what would currently be called a brownfield site on an exquisite location at the edge of the Thames. The development takes good advantage of its riverside setting, where mature trees have been retained and where the slope down to the river and private moorings has been designed with quality hard landscape detailing and planting. The development forms a cul-de-sac, with family houses with small rear gardens, mainly to the quiet edges of the site, whilst one of the courtyard blocks fronts the busy Strawberry Vale. Car parking is located around the buildings in the centre of the site, where the relationship between the buildings is tight, but with well-resolved spaces. Yet, unlike the earlier schemes the cul-de-sac does not provide a focus for community life, which is here provided by the communal swimming pool and a long lawn, which lie between the house blocks alongside the Thames. In contrast to earlier Span schemes, Mallard Place is exuberant in its architectural detailing, which relishes in a rich use of materials, colours and textures.[58] This is a considerable step away from the earlier schemes yet it continues to provide a model for its integration of buildings in a landscape.

Time, place and architecture

This chapter has shown that the designers of the Span developments followed a total landscape concept, in which the houses formed some of the building blocks, albeit the most important, in order to create a place where community life may be enacted. The emphasis on communal gardens that were well-designed functionally as well as aesthetically, without or with little traffic, created civilised environments that were safe playgrounds. By delegating cars outside the communal gardens, the latter became informal meeting places as well as places for communal activities. These housing environments provided a 'way of life' that was an attractive alternative to the bland open spaces left in other contemporary developments. Although the designers had intended their schemes to be populated by a broad range of people, the uptake due to the very nature of the housing as speculative developments, was rather middle class and they have sometimes been referred to as 'middle class ghettos'.[59] It seems that this, however, is an unfair criticism, since it was only possible to achieve environments like these outside the social housing realm, which is bound up in bureaucracy of planning systems and guidelines, even more so than speculative housing. Eric Lyons showed that with well-argued rationales and persistence it was possible to realise schemes that were innovative and set new standards.

Whilst other developers observed Span's successes in marketing their houses and copied the style, they were rarely as successful, since the significance and importance of the quality of the landscape were frequently not properly understood: indeed, Nicholas Taylor spoke of a 'sub-Span style'[60] when discussing the external appearance. Probably the most important factor in Span's success was the framework that it put in place to ensure a community, the setting up of the residents' associations. These not only guarantee a consistent external appearance of the buildings, but are primarily responsible for the maintenance of the communal landscape over time. Yet in the post-modern era, many of these modernist values are being questioned, particularly in a world dominated by issues of security, personal choice and sustainability. The example of the Span schemes shows that some of our presumptions may require re-evaluation in the light of their continued success. For example, the absence of shrub layers in housing environments to maintain security creates boring environments and reduces their use as potential playgrounds, therefore removing an important feature that, in fact, encourages community life. Increasing choice is considered to be a democratic right and, in the currently popular responsive environments theory, this includes aspects such as permeability and personalisation.[61] Many Span developments are within a cul-de-sac arrangement and have, therefore, a limited permeability, yet, within the smallish size of the developments on infill sites, other solutions would frequently have been difficult. The residents' associations seek to restrict personalisation of places by individuals, but then everyone must have known what they were buying into! Whilst many of the building materials used within the Span developments may not be considered sustainable today, there are a number of very important lessons to be drawn.[62] Additionally, the Span schemes continue to provide a model for social sustainability, which at the beginning of one of the largest house building programmes in British history, is perhaps the most significant lesson, particularly if the message that its landscape is the primary basis for this, can be communicated.

Endnotes

1. Span Promotional Literature (c.1960s), RIBA Span Archive Box 3/1.
2. 'Eric Lyons and G. P. Townsend', *Architects' Journal*, vol. 121, 1955, pp. 72–73.
3. Caroline Moorhead, 'Eric Lyons: Building gardens with houses in them', *The Times*, 21 July 1975.
4. R. Furneaux Jordan, 'Span: the spec builder as patron of modern architecture' *Architectural Review*, February 1959, pp. 108–220.
5. Muriel Emanuel, *Contemporary Architects* (London: Macmillan, 1980), p. 496.
6. Ebenezer Howard, *Garden Cities of To-morrow* (London: Swan Sonnenschein & Co, 1902).
7. See Raymond Unwin, *Town Planning in Practice* (London: T. Fisher Unwin, 1909).
8. J. M. Richards, *The Castles on the Ground: The Anatomy of Suburbia* (London: John Murray, 1946); Brenda Colvin, *Land and Landscape* (London: John Murray, 1947), p. 195.
9. See Ministry of Health, *Design of Dwellings* (London: HMSO, 1944); Leo Kuper, 'Social science research and the planning of urban neighbourhoods', *Social Forces* vol. 29/ 3, 1951, pp. 237–43.
10. *op. cit.*, *Design of Dwellings*, p. 11; taken from Association for Planning and Regional Reconstruction, *Housing Digest: An analysis of housing reports 1941–1945* (London and Glasgow: Art and Educational Publishers, 1946), p. 42.
11. Frank Schaffer, *The New Town Story* (London: Paladin, 1972), p. 71.
12. C. A. Perry, *The Neighbourhood Unit: A Scheme of Arrangement for the Family Life Community* (London: 1929); *Housing for the Machine Age* (New York: Russell Sage Foundation, 1939).
13. Donald Leslie Johnson, 'Origin of the neighbourhood unit', *Planning Perspectives*, 17, 2002, pp. 227–45; in 1898 Ebenezer Howard had written about 'wards' instead of neighbourhoods.
14. National Council of Social Service, *Our Neighbourhood: A Handbook of Information for Community Centres and Associations* (London: National Council of Social Service, 1950), p. 18.
15. *op. cit.*, Brenda Colvin, p. 211.
16. Brenda Colvin, *Land and Landscape* (London: John Murray, 1973), pp. 317–19.
17. See, for example, Catherine Bauer, *Modern Housing* (London: George Allen and Unwin, 1935), pp. 153–67.
18. Patrick Abercrombie, *Greater London Plan 1944* (London: HMSO, 1945), pp. 168–71.
19. See Annabel Downs, *Peter Shepheard* (Reigate: Landscape Design Trust, 2004), pp. 67–8.
20. Eric Lyons, 'The housing project: setting', *Housing Review* Vol.11/12, 1962/63, p. 168.
21. *op. cit.*, Schaffer, p. 73.
22. Sheila Harvey, *Reflections of Landscape: The Lives and Work of Six British Landscape Architects* (Aldershot: Gower, 1987), pp. 120–1.
23. Eric Lyons, 'Building a community', *Architectural Design*, 30, 1960, pp. 344–55.
24. Eric Lyons, 'Urban housing', *The Estates Gazette,* Vol. 179, 1961, p. 883; *op. cit.*, Eric Lyons, 1962/63, p. 169.
25. *op. cit.*, Eric Lyons, 1962/63, p. 171.
26. *op. cit.*, Eric Lyons, 1960, pp. 344–55.
27. *op. cit.*, Eric Lyons, 1962/63, p. 168.
28. *ibid.*, pp. 170–71.
29. *ibid.*, p. 167.
30. Ivor Cunningham (b.1928) commenced his studies with an architectural course at the Medway School of Art. Following completion of his architectural studies at the Architectural Association and landscape planning under Brian Hackett at the University of Durham, a British Council grant enabled him to continue with a further year's landscape studies at the Agricultural University in Wageningen under Professor J. T. P. Bijhouwer. On his return he was elected an Associate of the Institute of Landscape Architects. Working for an eighteen-month period for Brenda Colvin and Sylvia Crowe, dealing primarily with their architectural needs, he helped to re-design a pleasure garden on the Lincolnshire coast destroyed after the 1953 flooding, and a caravan site in the same area. He was then employed in the office of Eric Anjou, Stockholm, for six months designing a variety of projects. He returned to England to work for Eric Lyons in November 1955. See also Chapter 1 for further biographical details.
31. Michael Brown (1923–96) studied architecture at the Edinburgh College of Art, qualifying in 1951. He first worked for the London County Council school division, and then in private practice in London. In 1955 he was awarded a scholarship to the Department of Landscape Architecture at the University of Pennsylvania, under Ian McHarg, who was a significant influence on him. He then worked for Dan Kiley in Vermont, with projects including the Saarinen House, Ohio, and the Rockefeller Institute, New York. He taught at Pennsylvania before returning to work with Eric Lyons in 1960, then set up in private practice in London in 1962. See also Obituary 'Michael Brown', *The Times*, 18 March 1996.
32. Preben Jakobsen (b.1934) set up his own practice in 1969, for a short time living in Hove and then Cheltenham, where he co-operated much with his wife Maggie, an architect. See also Geoffrey and Susan Jellicoe, Patrick Goode, Michael Lancaster, *The Oxford Companion to Gardens* (Oxford: Oxford University Press, 1986), pp. 290–91.
33. Geoffrey Jellicoe, 'Lyons, Eric (Alfred)' in Muriel Emanuel (ed), *Contemporary Architects* (London: Macmillan, 1980), p. 496.

34. Eric Lyons Cunningham Partnership, 'Landscape', undated promotional brochure.
35. Ivor Cunningham, 'Spick and Span', seminar at Royal Botanic Gardens, Kew, 7 March 1980.
36. Ivor Cunningham, 'A Span site revisited – Corner Green, Blackheath, London', *Landscape Design* no. 137, 1982, pp. 29–30.
37. *op. cit.,* Cunningham, 1980.
38. This innovation was one of the approaches that was criticised in Lyons's schemes, for having 'in front of his houses systematically eliminated all the more natural systems of protection by fences or hedges. There is something slightly absurd about a great expanse of grass, "freely landscaped" as the handouts put it, which then has immediately to compromise its freedom by being peppered with little notices'. See Nicholas Taylor, *The Village in the City* (London: Temple Smith, 1973), p. 98; Taylor quotes Ian Nairn's television programme on Span. This emphasises issues concerning the use of these communal spaces, and raises particular issues with respect to play and dogs. Semi-private front gardens are an issue that continues to be topical in urban design theories today, but the success of this feature in the middle-class Span environments can be measured by the fact that they have not been changed by the residents.
39 *op. cit.,* Cunningham, 1980.
40. *ibid.*
41. See James Strike, *The Spirit of Span Housing* (Strikeprint, 2005).
42. *ibid.,* p. 56.
43. *Architectural Review* 141, 1967, p. 164.
44. Elizabeth Beazley, *Design and Detail of the Spaces between Buildings* (London: Architectural Press, 1960), pp. 12, 123.
45. Preben Jakobsen, 'Shrubs and groundcover' in Brian Clouston (ed), *Landscape Design with Plants* (Oxford: Heinemann Newness, 1977), p. 48.
46. *ibid.,* p. 41.
47. Drawing number 1037-130, Span Kent New Ash Green, Planting and contour layout, Landscape Zone 2 – perimeter, signed PRJ, 29/11/1967.
48. Eric Lyons, 'Working for a spec. builder', *Architects' Journal*, 27 March 1958, pp. 457–8.
49. David Pearce, 'Spanning the years', *Building Design*, 24 August 1979, pp. 11–12.
50. Eric Lyons, 'Urban housing', published lecture at Town and Country Planning School, Reading, 1961, p. 8.
51. *op. cit.,* Taylor, 1973, p. 139.
52. Eric Lyons, *op. cit.,* 1962/63, p. 170. The quote is probably from Mumford's influential *The Culture of Cities* (New York: Harcourt Brace, 1938).
53. *Architectural Review* 142, 1967, p. 379.
54. 'Under way, the big village', *Chelsea News*, 11 October 1963.
55. *op. cit.,* Taylor, 1973, pp. 159–60.
56. David Pearce, 'Success one step ahead', *Building Design*, 29 February 1980, p. 2; Frederick Gibberd, *Town Design* (London: Architectural Press, 1967), p. 329, Gibberd (the designer of Harlow New Town) notably does not include any Span schemes.
57. See also 'Green belt problems: Nibblings in Kent', *Architects' Journal*, 1 January 1964, pp. 9–11; and Chapter 5.
58. The scheme appears to adhere to some of the principles and solutions expressed in *The Essex Design Guide*, but it takes it well beyond this in the exploration of its architectural language. *The Essex Design Guide for Residential and Mixed Use Areas* (Essex: Essex Planning Officers Association, 1973).
59. Astragal, 'Notes & topics', *Architects' Journal*, 21 May 1969, p. 1351.
60. *op. cit.,* Taylor, 1973, p. 95.
61. Ian Bentley, Alan Alcock, Paul Murrain, Sue McGlynn and Graham Smith, *Responsive Environments: A Manual for Designers* (London: Architectural Press, 1985).
62. For example, the structure of communal spaces means that sustainability features, such as rills and water tanks to collect rainwater for re-use (in toilets for example), could easily be incorporated rather better than within schemes where all the land has been subdivided to individuals.

"It is a little piquant to get a housing
medal for building a design that
has previously been solemnly and
publicly declared 'detrimental to the
amenities' by your local council."

Eric Lyons

Designs for Span took about 60 per cent of the workload of Eric Lyons and Partners. Housing projects for local authorities accounted for most of the rest – and far exceeded Span in volume terms (3,012 dwellings compared with 2,134 for Span). Very different briefs ensured a wide variety between the public and private schemes. Lyons was adept in building to high densities, and whilst his work for Span anticipated the interest in low-rise, high-density schemes by a decade, in public housing (apart from a scheme at Longmead Road, Thames Ditton for Esher Urban District Council) he was constrained to design medium and high-rise flats until the late 1960s. From 1952 the Conservative governments sought to make it easier for private developers to secure building licences by allowing local authorities to transfer part of their own quota, and the abolition of controls in November 1954 opened a floodgate to volume building for sale. Ian Nairn made his reputation writing about the 'grisly parody of the English village street' that resulted, 'put together without any wish to make the whole greater than the parts'.[1] Whilst most private housing was repetitive and unimaginative, Nairn did, however, find a few developers taking heed of critical taste and, around London at least, a few schemes retaining mature trees, grouping their units carefully, and aiming for a clean, crisp appearance. In particular Nairn celebrated 'the pioneer efforts of one architect, Eric Lyons, and his clients, Span'.

The formation of Eric Lyons and Partners
Eric Lyons and Geoffrey Townsend first practiced together in 1938. Townsend's interests from the first were in speculative housing, producing basic designs for small terraced housing around his

native Whitton and Twickenham.[2] Following their respective war work, in 1945 Lyons and Townsend resumed their practice in the Twickenham area, where Townsend secured war-damage work and commenced a block of flats before more restrictive licensing and betterment controls in 1947 made private building even more difficult. These early flats, Oaklands, and a block on a war-damaged site in Jameson Road, Bexhill, were unexceptional in building design, although significant in that Lyons conceived the frontage space as integral with the blocks whilst Townsend arranged for their future maintenance through a residents' committee to which all occupants paid a small sum.[3]

From this the pair turned to terraced houses, Lyons evolving a simple cross-wall design of yellow brick and lightweight façades, used at a handful of small sites developed by Townsend trading as Hampton Cross Properties. However, as an architect could not then also trade as a developer, and realising the impossibility of finding a client willing to take on their ideas, Townsend resigned his membership of the Royal Institute of British Architects (RIBA) in 1953 to take on a much larger project, initially as Bargood Estates, at Ham Common. This was Parkleys, the scheme of 175 flats off Ham Common on the Richmond/Kingston boundary that made the reputation of what was to become Span (Fig. 1.1). Meanwhile, the builder Leslie Bilsby was building up sites around his home on the Cator Estate in Blackheath for the local architect C. Bernard Brown. When in 1954 Bilsby needed an architect for a four-acre site there, for which he had outline planning permission but no design, he turned to Lyons and Townsend, to whom he was introduced by

Fig 4.1 Parkleys, Marlowe Court, showing the vista through the building – a clever integration of dwelling and landscape.

Geoffrey Dunn of Dunn's Department Store, Bromley, furnishers of many show homes in the 1950s, including that at Parkleys.

At this time, Lyons formed his own independent practice. Townsend's connections with both architecture and building, as well as his close association with Lyons, made Span different from other firms, but it was Lyons who was most admired for bridging the gap between speculative work and the creative approach most architects of his generation found only in the public sector. The rare link between architect and developer permitted Lyons an unusually free hand, involved from the first site selection and with complete control of the whole scheme from briefing to site supervision and landscaping. Yet the blocks still had to be simple for 'the architect has to design and organise so that buildings can be produced at the same cost as a builder's scheme providing the same accommodation', as Townsend explained.[4] Lyons deliberately kept his office small. When Ivor Cunningham joined in November 1955 there were four architects and a junior, and by 1968, when the firm was at its busiest, there were twelve. Amongst the many assistants were several who went on to independent careers designing housing, amongst them Robert Bailie (1965–7), John Darbourne (1958–60), Geoffrey Darke (1958–61), John Malyan (1956–9), Graham Morrison (1975–8), Geoffrey Scoble (c.1954–7), Royston Summers (1971–2) and Kenneth Wood (c.1953–5), whilst Bill Pack (an assistant before 1955) went on to partner the commercial architect Cecil Elsom. Lyons's partners included Gilbert Powell, Warner Baxter and Ivor Cunningham.[5] Most important was Ivor

Cunningham: he was involved initially in the landscaping at Parkleys and The Priory, but subsequently had a hand in the overall layout of the developments. Landscaping help was provided first by Michael Brown and then by Preben Jakobsen.[6]

The first Span schemes

Span set out to show, in Townsend's words, that 'architect-designed houses and flats can be produced to sell at competitive prices, and to show the developer the necessary margin of profit'.[7] The choice of sites was critical. Around London they chose desirable, leafy areas already popular with commuters, beginning in Richmond and Twickenham, and later advancing to Weybridge and Byfleet; Bilsby brought in Blackheath. Outside London they built in Cambridge, Hove, Oxford and Taplow; schemes in Bristol and Cheltenham were only partly realised due to lack of demand. Lyons declared himself interested in 'group housing', combining privacy with the desire to create communities, and consciously adapting the Georgian terrace and garden square to modern materials. Roads were deliberately kept narrow and separated from pedestrian walks and communal areas, advertised as safe for children's play. Lyons sought to keep his roads private (unadopted) in order to circumvent bye-law requirements concerning their width and materials, facilitated at Blackheath by the presence of the private Cator Estate as ground landlord. Lyons also courted controversy with his developments' modern appearance and relatively high densities.

J. H. Forshaw and Patrick Abercrombie in the *County of London Plan* (1943) had divided the capital into three rings of population density, and this was one of their few recommendations to be immediately and firmly adopted.[8] To express their ideas of a fluid 'mixed development' of houses and flats they expressed these densities not in numbers of dwellings but as 'persons per acre' or 'ppa', as championed in the late 1930s by Elizabeth Denby. By 1951 the density for much of south London, including Blackheath, had been reduced, to 70 ppa.[9] Lyons's densities were often above this figure, with The Lane, Blackheath, reaching 75 and Parkleys 74 ppa. Such densities were very different from those realised by most architects working for local authorities or private developers, who averaged 30–40 ppa for low-rise schemes. So, although the locations were suburban, Lyons's aesthetic was as urban as those of his near contemporaries at the Regent Street Polytechnic, Gordon Cullen and Ralph Erskine. An advertising brochure from c.1962 explains that 'the work of the Span Group proceeds from the basic principle that all Span Projects should be designed integrally as a background to the contemporary social pattern. It is a work against Subtopia'.[10] Or, as Bilsby explained, 'I wouldn't say it was a "village" atmosphere we try to create, rather an urban community with some of the characteristics of the older single-ownership villages'.[11]

Parkleys (1956) was a development entirely of flats, mainly of two-storey linked blocks set around courtyards, with parts of the ground floor left open to give access. Like the earlier houses for Hampton Cross, they adopted a simple cross-wall construction that meant the main façades could have near-continuous bands of glazing. Lyons worked almost always with the Czech émigré engineer Zigmund Pick. More decorative three-storey blocks at Parkleys were built to an H-plan which was repeated only at Applecourt, Cambridge, (while Park Gate, Hove, has similar open panelwork), which have the effect of squat point blocks against the general mass of two-storey terraces and quadrangles. In early sales brochures, Span described its style as 'happily and unselfconsciously itself, aping no other age'.[12] The first schemes had tile hanging between the rows of windows, perhaps inspired by its vernacular use in the Sussex Weald; from the late 1950s weatherboarding gave a more elegant finish. The building firm for the early schemes was E. Gostling Ltd. of Hampton, whom Townsend had met in 1928 and who re-emerged in the 1960s to work in Weybridge, at New Ash Green and on the later developments at Blackheath.

Other schemes in the 1950s were mostly built by Wates Ltd – responsible for Parkleys – and a firm whose own low-rise schemes owed much to Span. Most of the flats repeated the basic type plans, A, B and C, of two or three bedrooms, B and C with a dining area or study off the main living room.[13] The more complex sequence of terraced house plans began with T1 in Twickenham and the popular T2 in Blackheath and Teddington; variants included a staggered T2Y, and the wider T7 and T8. A three-storey version at Foxes Dale, Blackheath, became T3, including No. 2, the *House and Garden* 'House of Ideas' (1957).[14] Larger units were also used in higher-income developments at Weybridge and in parts of New Ash Green, Kent. In some, extra accommodation was under a butterfly roof (the R range of houses), including the *Woman's Journal* 'House of the Year' (1965), No. 1 Foxes Dale, as well as houses at Oxford and Cambridge. Internally, however, the room sizes are small, although the construction encouraged some of the ground floors to be open plan and many fitments and cupboards were built-in. The first scheme (unrealised) to omit front gardens was designed with T2 houses at Coventry. It was later followed by Corner Green, Blackheath, but with T7 and T8 houses.

The landscaping was as important as the buildings themselves, softening and obscuring the densities and intended to appear mature from the first. Lyons himself claimed that 'as a designer, I have always been interested in place rather than one-off buildings on isolated sites. That's why I am interested in landscape'.[15] Cunningham indicates, however, that Lyons's interest was in creating spaces and a sense of place, leaving the rich detail of the actual planting to him. This was seen at Oaklands, which had a communal space but little planting,

Fig 4.2 Thurnby Court, Twickenham, a later development of the Parkleys-type flats that is particularly well-maintained.

and in his estate for Esher Urban District Council (UDC). At all Span projects a residents' society was formed: 'It takes the worries of window cleaning, garden upkeep, exterior repairs etc. off the shoulders of individual owners and generally helps to create and preserve an intelligently friendly atmosphere,' explained the sales brochure.[16] Townsend served as the first chair of the Parkleys Committee until the residents felt able to run it themselves.[17] At most estates Span held the freehold – those at Oxford and Cambridge being the main exceptions – but since the 1980s they have passed to the residents' societies. Townsend was also a pioneer of endowment mortgages, negotiated through Henry Cushman and the Alliance Building Society, and a Span package included all surveyor's and legal fees.[18] Other building societies were suspicious of Span's unconventional appearance and construction, until the first dwellings began to be resold at a substantial profit, some doubling their value in four years. In the late 1960s, however, building societies suffered a credit squeeze that coincided with Span's introduction of steel elements into their construction at New Ash Green; they were unwilling to offer mortgages on such designs, which they regarded as 'non-traditional'.

Span in Blackheath

Parkleys was followed by a smaller development of two-storey flats in quadrangles at Thurnby Court, Strawberry Hill (1958) (Fig. 4.2), and houses in The Cedars, Teddington (1958). But, meanwhile, Span's attention had turned to the Cator Estate in Blackheath, a charming preserve of late 18th-century and early 19th-century terraces and villas, most notably Michael Searles's The Paragon, a terrace of linked pairs dating from 1794–1805 which had been carefully restored after war damage by Bernard Brown (who won a Festival of Britain Merit Award for his pains) with Leslie Bilsby as his builder. The area's history was stoutly defended by the Blackheath Society, founded in 1937, and Blackheath Park – the core of the Cator Estate – was becoming admired for its 'Regency character'. But many of the houses had been damaged beyond repair, and the long gardens and backland nurseries of Blackheath Park and the roads immediately to its north and south, were ripe for speculative development. Lesley Bilsby was on hand to do just that.

In October 1953 the Ministry of Housing and Local Government (MHLG) granted permission on appeal for a development of houses and flats at The Hall (submitted by Leslie Bilsby Limited but later redesigned and the subject of further opposition from the local council). Another application, first made by Bilsby in June 1954, was for Priory Park, 61 flats and 49 garages, later known as The Priory, which in 1956 became the first development in Blackheath Park constructed by Span (Fig. 4.3). It was followed by three houses in Foxes Dale. The relatively large size of these houses, with their three storeys, two bathrooms and first floor sun terrace, proved hard to sell at the time and part of the site was passed on to the architect Peter Moro to build a house for himself.

Fig 4.3   The Priory, Blackheath, the first of Span's developments in the area, also follows the pattern of Parkleys.

Fig 4.4   The Plantation, the site of a former nursery, was one of Span's most controversial sites in Blackheath, and one of Lyons's most dense developments.

Another scheme for houses on nursery land, the Morden Plantation on Morden Road, was initially rejected on grounds of access, but by February 1956 Greenwich Council was summoning other arguments against modern building in Blackheath, claiming that they were 'completely out of harmony with the Georgian character of the area, which has been carefully preserved on the adjoining estate of this council'.[19] This was a reference to the Pond Estate, where Sir Albert Richardson had been brought in as consultant at the behest of Lewis Silkin, Minister of Town and Country Planning, after Lewisham Metropolitan Borough (MB) had tried to build alongside the heath on the site of Searles's Little Paragon. Lewisham and Greenwich Councils had gone on to develop four-storey flats and bungalows to which Richardson gave a neo-Georgian veneer. The Morden Plantation scheme was one public inquiry initially lost by Span, although the site was eventually redeveloped by them as The Plantation (Fig. 4.4), with Bilsby taking part of the site for a house for himself designed by Walter Greaves.

In the early 1960s Greenwich MB could still claim that the 'architectural treatment, although satisfactory in itself, is out of character with its setting in Blackheath Park'.[20] The London County Council (LCC), as overall planning authority, was initially more sympathetic, consenting in June 1956 to the building of The Keep and Corner Green on a former caravan site off Morden Road Mews. The Keep, the first realised scheme where Ivor Cunningham handled the overall layout, was altered to meet planners' requirements, but Corner Green was one of Lyons's personal favourites. It was opened in December 1959 by Henry Brooke, Minister of Housing and Local Government, to mark the completion of a million houses by private enterprise since 1945 (Fig. 4.5). Its layout owed much to Charles Reilly's vision of communities developed around village greens (see below) and to the bisection of the site by a railway tunnel. The houses are served by an access road to the rear, and the central green is amongst the most private and densely landscaped of all Span works:

> The best decisions we made about external materials was the
> choice of mild stocks … Corner Green look[s] much better
> for it – the soft golden colour in distant views and the crunchy
> texture and mixed colours seen close to. Corner Green has
> survived (or matured) as the best of all the Span schemes. The
> layout had the simple idea of a central green pedestrian area
> and the ground formation and the planting used strong shapes
> to underline the functional use of the space (which is what I
> think 'building landscape' should be used for) and it looks good
> even in winter.[21]

Span's greatest fight was over the Little Paragon, five linked houses by Michael Searles destroyed in 1942. The sensitive site overlooking

Fig 4.5 Corner Green, Blackheath, with terraces of houses around an enclosed green, firmly separates pedestrian areas from parking.

Fig 4.6   South Row, Blackheath, flats and a terrace of houses built after Span's most contentious public inquiry.

the Heath was deliberately excluded from Albert Richardson's housing scheme. Bernard Brown's company, Paragon Developments, sought to rebuild the terrace as it had The Paragon, but found it uneconomic. In February 1959 Lyons made an application for a three-storey block of 23 flats, incorporating an innovative corner plan, with ten maisonettes set over garages in a range to the rear designed to limit views of Richardson's work.[22] LCC officers were minded to approve the scheme for Nos. 3–30 South Row, provided that the roof profile was simplified and the materials used met their approval. It was, however, opposed by the Royal Fine Art Commission and members of the LCC's Historic Buildings Sub-Committee, and was eventually rejected by the Town Planning Committee. For the public inquiry that followed in 1960, W. A. Eden of the Historic Buildings Division produced sketches to show how flats could be inserted behind a façade that followed Searles's style and proportions. The artist Victor Pasmore, who

lived nearby, wrote in support of Lyons's scheme, extolling how the design had 'architectural vitality'.[23] It was approved, the inspector E. W. Berridge considering that Eden's 'fake' would 'cast doubt upon the authenticity of the adjacent buildings and assume an importance which it could not justify or sustain'.[24] Ironically, South Row won Eric Lyons a MHLG Housing Design Award when finally completed in 1963 (Fig. 4.6).

However, the LCC and Greenwich Council continued to oppose the building of more Span estates in Blackheath Park, suggesting that they would have a serious effect on the neighbourhood's character and offering to prepare a comprehensive plan for Blackheath to divert development towards 'its less attractive parts'.[25] In 1963 a general policy for Blackheath Park sought to keep new housing behind existing building lines, and secured the listing of fifteen buildings for their architectural interest, whilst allowing 'a good modern design on good open sites'.[26] Far from being 'open', the Span sites became tighter and denser, as at The Lane, and further dwellings were tucked into high-density schemes, such as The Keep and Corner Green. To celebrate a victory in November 1958 over the choice of materials and colour of paintwork at Hallgate (1958) – 26 flats added at the entrance to The Hall (Fig. 4.7) after an initial scheme for large houses was dismissed as uneconomic – Lyons commissioned a sculpture from Keith Godwin, a local resident, friend of Bilsby and collaborator on several Span projects. Depicting a man struggling under the weight of the concrete lintel he supports, and named *The Architect in Society*, for Lyons 'it depicts with rare and wry humour the architect's real position today under pressure on the one side by the needs of a society, on the other by the restrictions of planning authorities. If it is not a good likeness, it is roughly the way I feel at times'.[27]

By 1964 Span had built 600 units around Blackheath Park, and Greenwich MB commented that 'intrusion of this type of construction, with the approval of the LCC, has now become so widespread that it would be futile to resist it further'.[28] The schemes from the 1960s are often tightly packed into difficult backland sites, Lyons complaining that The Lane had 'the shape and proportion of a banana'.[29] Today, the area takes its distinctive character from the combination of Regency and Span developments, and the mature landscaping of both. That Span estates were not diluted in their execution was due to Lyons's sheer determination to defy the planners, termed by him 'aesthetic controllers', and restrictive building regulations – of which he was an outspoken critic – ironically, perhaps, given the stringency of Span's own covenants. He won around 20 housing medals from the MHLG, three in 1964 alone. As he confessed to *The Times*, 'it is a little piquant to get a housing medal for building a design that has previously been solemnly and publicly declared "detrimental to the amenities" by your local council'.[30] Above all, Lyons was his own man, declaring his standards and sticking to them. As he explained: 'Our output was fantastically high for a small unit because I was able to set the conditions out myself and provide the means of responding very quickly'.[31]

Span outside London

Outside the London area, Span's most ambitious venture was in Cambridge, on land owned by Jesus College, where Leslie Bilsby knew the bursar. Here, as also at The Paddox, Oxford, where the land was held by St Edward's School, the leaseholding arrangements differed from those estates where Span was the ground landlord. Highsett, in Cambridge, replaced a number of Victorian villas, including one formerly owned by the keeper of the Botanic Gardens. To preserve as much of this planting as possible, Lyons originally proposed a fifteen-storey tower for the second stage with the encouragement of Leslie Martin, a Fellow

Fig 4.7   Hallgate, the block of flats encloses the Hall development where it meets Blackheath Park.

Fig 4.8   Park Gate, Hove, Span's first major scheme completed outside London, comprises flats that provide a link between Parkleys and South Row in planning and scale.

Fig 4.9   Templemere, Weybridge, the most luxuriant of Span's developments in Weybridge. The houses are carefully grouped to reflect the scale of the 18th-century landscape.

of Jesus College and by then working on the first of the low-rise, high-density studies developed with Patrick Hodgkinson, West Kentish Town. After Lyons's tower was refused planning permission in both 1958 and 1960, a compact scheme of houses was agreed. The first stage of the original scheme is a quadrangle of flats and maisonettes, in collegiate fashion and with a similar fortress quality given to it by its high surrounding walls. On two sides the ground floor is partially open – the two upper storeys are supported on pilotis – with views through the street gates right through the block to the shrubberies beyond, laid out mostly by Ivor Cunningham. Whilst some flats repeated the small type plans found at Parkleys, new larger plans gave some living rooms a dual aspect. The fourth side has maisonettes set over garages, making the overall plan form far more complex than is usual with Span housing. The cross-wall construction was, for once, partly concealed to allow a greater horizontality, with continuous bands of glazing. The second phase was of T8 houses similar to those at Corner Green, but for the last part of the development, amidst Victorian trees and lush infill planting by Preben Jakobsen, the Eric Lyons Cunningham Partnership, as the firm had just become, developed a more luxurious plan-type to meet a growing demand. This was the 'R' series of three storeys with broader frontages and projecting bays, blond brick and concrete lintels contrasting with white weatherboarding, a type repeated at The Paddox (1965).

Henry Cushman, the Alliance Building Society agent working with Span, lived in Hove, where he brought in Park Gate for Span and another scheme near the cricket ground in Wilbury Road (which was not realised for lack of demand). Park Gate was a four-storey block of 47 flats built in 1957–60 around an internal courtyard, and with access by lifts as well as stairs, but with type plans similar to Parkleys and The Priory and that subsequently adopted at South Row (Fig. 4.8). At The Park, Cheltenham, a three-storey development of flats was designed by Dick Towning Hill, a Bristol architect whose work Lyons admired for the quality and economy of his designs. Some other schemes for Span outside London were less successful commercially, including the charmingly named Pitch & Pay at Sneyd Park, Bristol, also by Towning Hill. Here, a series of linked houses was built in 1963, but they did not sell well and the remainder of the site was taken over by local developers Chivers. At The Verneys, Cheltenham (1963), Lyons designed a scheme of 'patio' houses, less than half of which was built. More successful, both critically and commercially, was Cedar Chase, Rectory Road, Taplow (1966), 24 houses built using a strong black and white palette and with planting by Preben Jakobsen. It won an award in the MHLG's 'Good Design for Housing' scheme in 1967, when it was described by the judges as 'an outstanding example of how to use the minimum amount of materials to greatest effect, producing simple but very effective domestic architecture'.[32] The idiom was repeated at Marsham Lodge, Gerrards Cross, one of Jakobsen's final schemes with Span and completed in 1969.

Span also built extensively around Weybridge in Surrey, in the 1960s dubbed 'the Beverly Hills of England' for the exclusive estates springing up around it, and where some of the firm's most imaginative fusions of housing and landscape were realised.[33] Sandy soils and landscaping from earlier large villas, made for a mature, wooded landscape in which Span set five developments in the 1960s – including Lakeside, built in 1969 by Calderhead and Scoble, the practice formed by two of Lyons's early assistants. The first and best known of Lyons's Weybridge developments is Templemere (1965). In a lecture to the RIBA he explained that:

> it was not until we moved on to a beautiful site at Weybridge that we started having enough confidence to move away from the kind of external spaces we have been creating. Because of the enormous scale of some splendid cedar trees on the site I attempted to approach the problems of spatial organisation quite differently, to try and create less defined space. The space flows on like a water course and loses itself in all directions, bubbling around the trees and clusters, going down into the wood and disappearing.[34]

Cunningham remembers that on their first walk round the site together, he and Lyons realised that courtyards would not work and that the houses had to match the scale of the mature 18th-century landscape, part of the Oatlands Estate. A new house type,

LI, was given a bold octagonal shape and arranged in outward-facing groups, an expressive form that could hold its own against the vast Cedars of Lebanon. The first scheme included flats to the same shape, but the site values were very high and houses made better commercial sense (Fig. 4.9). It was followed by Castle Green (1965) almost opposite, a series of smaller T2A houses set within mature trees; Brackley, with much larger T16 and T17 three- and four-bedroomed houses; and finally Holme Chase, a one-off design with butterfly roofs for the entrance porches. There followed two simpler schemes for sites nearby at Byfleet acquired by Townsend; Weymede (1966) and Grasmere (1967), the latter with a prototype of the K2 houses subsequently used at New Ash Green.

Public housing by Eric Lyons

Eric Lyons claimed that he:

> never had anything to do with public versus private. With Span it was a kind of soft option for an architect, because I hadn't got any clients and therefore the best way was to try and manufacture some, and so people got together around my ideas. I was interested in creating what is now called community housing: a community in the sense of self-management and co-ownership, but also an expression of a community.[35]

However, he did take on many public projects (not all of which were built), although he became increasingly vocal in his criticism of housing management in the public sector – his responsibilities as President of the RIBA giving him the opportunity to speak out.[36] He also built a block of 36 flats with an assembly hall and nursery on a secluded site overlooking Hampstead Heath for the Soviet Trade Delegation (1957), an unlikely client brought in through Leslie Bilsby, whose wife was a Russian émigré.

What is remarkable is how different Lyons's public housing schemes are from his Span work, although much of it was meticulously detailed despite the difficulty of working as a consultant to a large authority. The low-rise components of the Haddo Estate (Wheatley House and Ravenswood) by his assistant Robert Bailie, commissioned in 1958 by St Pancras MB and built in 1963–5, are more reminiscent of Span housing than anything by Lyons himself.[37] Lyons's first public commission in 1948 from Esher UDC comprised a mix of two-storey houses, three-storey flats and old peoples' bungalows. This reflected the requirement of the time for mixed development that made most effective use of land and available government grants, and provided a range of housing that suited a clientele for public housing. This included more single people and couples without families than became the case with public housing later in the 20th century. The layout of long terraces

Fig 4.10 Pitcairn House, Hackney, for the London County Council, since altered by the addition of a pitched roof.

Fig 4.11 Castle House, Southampton, flats for the city council on the site of the medieval keep and, perhaps, Lyons's most popular public housing.

Fig 4.12 'Streets in the Sky' at Castle House. Each 'street' or access deck serves three floors of flats.

set behind kidney-shaped village greens suggests the influence of Sir Charles Reilly's scheme for Woodchurch, Birkenhead, a controversial proposal of 1944 subsequently widely promoted as 'Reilly greens'.[38] As Reilly would have wished, the land immediately in front of the Esher houses was also to have been maintained as a communal space by the local authority, but proved too expensive. Nevertheless, the rows of terraces around a shared green, with clear separation between pedestrian pathways and access drives to groups of garages, anticipate the more compact Corner Green. The houses themselves are much larger than most popular Span types, with double frontages.[39]

Esher was followed by work for the LCC, for whom Lyons prepared two schemes for the western extension of its Frampton Park Estate, Hackney. The main east part of the estate was built 1952–4 to conventional designs by W. A. Cessford Ball, leaving a small area on Mare Street, which was cleared only in 1956. Lyons first prepared a three-storey scheme with shops fronting Mare Street, but when the LCC valuer reported that nearby shops on Wells Street had proved impossible to let, in early 1958 he produced a new, more radical design.[40] This was a single ten-storey block of flats, Pitcairn House,

with broad access balconies on every third floor; internal stairs gave access to the flats on the floors above and below (Fig. 4.10).[41] This seems to have been the first built example of such a plan in Britain, Ernö Goldfinger's proposal for Watford Rural District Council at Abbotts Langley (1955) having been rejected by the planners.[42] The concept made for efficient planning and a faster lift service in very tall blocks, although at the time Pitcairn House was judged an expensive building as there was no compensating low-rise in the building contract.[43] The use of upper walkways was to become a feature of Lyons's later public housing schemes, uniting a series of superficially very different looking buildings.

Southampton was one of the most progressive housing authorities in the post-war years. In the 1920s the city had seen a great expansion with the building of cottage estates, both public and private. The 1950s saw a greater mix, with low-rise housing and high-rise flats on suburban sites combined with high-density, medium-rise development where land was available in the centre. In November 1953 the Corporation's Housing Committee resolved to look at slum clearance, following the presentation of the government White Paper, *Houses: the Next Step*.[44] By May 1954 it had identified seven areas for clearance and, although the MHLG offered subsidies for only one, the city decided to take on the rest anyway. Southampton had no shortage of land – it had had no difficulty in extending its boundaries in 1954 – so there was no pressure to redevelop its centre at a high density, save from a real commitment to clearance. But Southampton's city centre has moved northwards over the past 150 years, leaving the medieval core on its historic peninsular very run down. One site in the old city centre was of particular interest, and was next to that where the council had erected its first housing in Bugle Street in 1904.

This curious site was not strictly slum clearance, for it had formerly been occupied by the medieval castle keep. Ruined by the 17th century, the remains were incorporated into a fantastic mock medieval castle, built by the Marquis of Lansdowne in 1804 and which only lasted until 1818. Then the motte was lowered and a Zion chapel built on it, which survived until July 1959. On 4 January 1957 the chair of the Housing Committee and the chief architect, Leon Berger, were asked to suggest architects for the redevelopment of the site. In March, Eric Lyons was invited to meet the sub-committee, as were the firm of Powell and Moya; when the latter declined, YRM were interviewed instead. Lyons was commissioned, although it was only in September 1958 that he was formally asked to prepare plans. Then he was asked to submit designs for a meeting in December, a deadline he could not or would not meet. Instead he presented his scheme at the February meeting. The delay seems to have been because he was originally offered a larger area at Castle Hill, for which he designed three and four-storey flats but, as the site conditions were so poor, he was forced to revise his scheme in favour of a single, twelve-storey block on piles, approved in June 1959. The plan with three floors served from one corridor was repeated from Pitcairn House (Figs. 4.11 and 4.12).

A tender from J. Hunt Ltd. was approved in January 1960, but the plans were then refused government loan sanction as being too expensive. Lyons was reluctant to make reductions without compromising his design, and in April a revised tender for £234,796 11s 0d from Hawkins Bros Ltd was approved. Work began later in 1960 but dragged on – in January 1963 Lyons was hauled before the committee to explain the delay, and in March it was still unfinished. But his care was justified by the block's success as a new landmark for the old motte. Much is made of the steep contour, with two entrances and lines of garages set one above the other facing in opposite directions. Above the smooth, brick finishes of these entrance levels and their surrounding walls, the block has a rough texture formed of exposed aggregate pre-cast panels. Its form is slim, but the profile has a serrated edge – for every one of the 72 flats has a south-facing balcony flush with the façade and is reached

Fig 4.13   Shawbridge, Harlow, a relatively high-density scheme for the Great Parndon area of the new town, executed in dark brick.

Fig 4.14 Mayford, Oakley Square, Camden, medium-rise, high density housing commissioned by St Pancras Metropolitan Borough and including a children's home, anticipates many of the ideas found at World's End.

via partially open access decks set within the body of the block and facing north, with an irregular pattern of struts to its balustrades.[45] The placing of three sets of doors on a single floor not only saved space, but also proved convivial and popular. 'The front doors with their own porches, mats and even house names open on to little streets. The Council calls them deck access. The residents know them as streets. It is called the "most successful block in the South of England", claimed the local paper.[46] Bill Meering, interviewed in 1981 and by 1996 the chair of the Tenants' Association, said: 'We do have a true community spirit here. The open corridors allow people to meet. I think more should have been built like that'.

The growth in Britain's population in the 1940s and 1950s led to increases in housing targets for the new towns established after the war. At Harlow, designated in 1948 with a planned population of 60,000, the target was raised in 1963 to 90,000. Already proposals had been made for the development of the south-western area, Great Parndon, at a density of 70 ppa rather than the 40 ppa of the earlier neighbourhoods such as Mark Hall, and an open competition was held in 1960 for the first phase. This was assessed by Lyons's friend H. T. (Jim) Cadbury-Brown and won by Michael Neylan, with an innovative scheme subsequently built as Bishopsfield. Later sites were developed in Harlow's traditional way, with the Development Corporation and private architects taking on some 200–250 houses and their attendant road layout. Lyons and Cunningham designed a scheme, Shawbridge, for a twelve-acre site near the area's main shopping centre, to a modified Radburn plan, which was built in 1962 (Fig. 4.13).[47] Garaging is set on cul-de-sacs to the rear, whilst the housing is concentrated on pedestrian courts away from the through road, with a mix of old peoples' flats and houses, and with flats bounding the main road. Particularly striking are the materials: Keymer black brick and white-painted boarding, anticipating that at Taplow and which have led to its being called 'the coal hole' locally.[48]

The Southampton and Harlow projects, and an unrealised private scheme for Rise Park, Nottingham, were followed by a series of developments for London boroughs and the Greater London Council (GLC), which helped to sustain his practice after Span's fall. Lyons was invited to design an estate for St Pancras MB at the invitation of Frederick MacManus, who was appointed town planning consultant to the Council in September 1962. St Pancras was unusual for a London borough in having no architects department in the post-war period, passing all its extensive housing programme to private practices selected on the basis of simple sketches and an interview (to avoid a formal RIBA competition using an outside assessor). Lyons was commissioned in early 1963 in preference to Stirling and Gowan, the other suggestion by MacManus. He was asked to produce a design for a sensitive site south of Oakley Square, where the Council had decided to redevelop the frontage houses – as well as the run-down area behind – against

Fig 4.15   World's End, a sketch of an early version of the scheme.

the wishes of local residents; the north side of the square was one of the first three rehabilitation projects run by the Borough.

Lyons's scheme of 183 units, designed in late 1963 at the moderately high density of 136 ppa, imposed by Forshaw and Abercrombie across inner London, placed family dwellings in low-rise maisonettes set around courtyards, and smaller flats in ten-storey towers, subsequently reduced to eight. A system of broad walkways on the second floor served all the flats, linking the upper maisonettes to the lifts in the towers and giving what Lyons described as 'a sociable means of access' away from cars.[49] A revised design presented to what had become the London Borough of Camden in September 1966, further reduced the total height down to seven storeys, limited the number of plan-types to five, and ensured that almost all the largest (three-bedroom) units were at ground level with patio gardens. Half the car parking was hidden under the two eastern garden courts and adjoining buildings.

The scheme also now included a small children's home, for eight youngsters and two carers. Work finally began on site in early 1968, and the development was completed in 1971, when it was named Mayford.[50] The result is a complex and introverted development, relieved by its use of planting and warm brown brick (Fig. 4.14).

Lyons's one very large scheme was at World's End, for Chelsea MB. Chelsea's gentrification left little room for public housing to relieve a long-standing waiting list of 1,300 families, although the Borough had been imaginative in the 1940s in taking on very large houses and converting them to flats. The one area open to the Council for redevelopment was at the western, 'wrong' end of Cheyne Walk, near London Transport's Lots Road Power Station, where in 1955 the Council had built its Cremorne Estate to the designs of Armstrong and MacManus. The area beyond Beaufort Street, filled with small streets of low-rise housing, was not developed because of rising

Fig 4.16 World's End, Chelsea, Eric Lyons's largest commission, executed with H. T. Cadbury–Brown and John Metcalfe. A detail of the corner of this massive development by the Thames.

costs and the difficulty of rehousing over 2,000 people. Only in 1961 did the Council turn again to the site, as the forced surrender of property requisitioned in the war aggravated its housing shortage still further. But to make a worthwhile addition to the Council's stock, the rebuilding had to be to a much higher density than the 136 ppa for which the area was zoned. The Cremorne Estate had been built to this density, and Chelsea MB believed that the MHLG would accept a zoning of 250 ppa across the two estates, meaning that what it termed West Chelsea could be developed at 338 ppa. But the LCC, who were the planning authority, would not be persuaded. It did, however, ask for a sketch scheme showing how the accommodation might be arranged.

Chelsea MB found itself in a dilemma, unwilling to produce serious plans without knowing if a high density would be permitted, but needing to produce a detailed scheme if it was to have a

chance of realising its redevelopment. A sketch proposal by the Borough surveyor containing two 26-storey towers was refused in November 1962 by the LCC, who conceded only a density of 150 ppa, as it felt that tall buildings would 'mar traditional views from the river'.[51] The Council recorded that had the permission been granted there was 'every possibility' of it holding a competition for the design; instead, on the advice of its counsel, whilst making an appeal to the MHLG, it interviewed a number of 'eminent Architect Planners', and in early 1963 appointed Lyons to prepare a preliminary scheme.

With his experience of planning inquiries Lyons was a perfect choice. His scheme for what he later described as 'a complete metropolitan village' was welcomed enthusiastically by all sides of the council.[52] By October 1963 Lyons had produced a revised scheme and a model, and two versions were taken to public inquiry. A Councillor Brooks appealed to residents opposing the scheme to take a philanthropic, long-term view and sell up, and the local press portrayed a battle between locals on the waiting list and incomers, who were just beginning to show that working class Victorian housing could be restored and sold for high prices.[53] By 1965 a house in Chelsea was selling for £15,000 compared with £5,500 in Battersea. As the *Chelsea News* remarked of the scheme: 'It is cheering news that hundreds of real old Chelsea people are not likely after all to be pushed out of their home town just because people better able to afford to live there have moved in'.[54]

The public inquiry was held in January 1965 and its result announced in August. The inspector, W. H. Loney, recognised that there was an urgent need for additional housing in the Borough and that, in principle, any redevelopment should have more units than previously existed on the site to alleviate, rather than add to, the waiting list. He preferred the taller of Lyons's two schemes, which allowed more open space, but, in the lower version, he liked the way the shops were set at ground level in their traditional location along the King's Road. But there were small details of daylighting infringements and vehicle exits that needed revision, so Loney rejected the scheme. However, the principle of high density was won and a third scheme, submitted in March 1966, duly incorporated the 'best features' of the previous two, and was granted permission in August 1966. Another inquiry in February 1967 saw the incomers, amongst them the actress Susannah York, lose their campaign against the Compulsory Purchase Orders on their homes.

Lyons's plan comprised a figure-of-eight necklace of flats on five and six storeys, set around two orthogonal courtyards and served by a walkway at second floor level that also connected the seven, originally eight, 18 to 21-storey towers. In addition, there was to be a school, children's home, community centre, old peoples' flats, a church, shops and underground car parking; the ornate World's End public house on the King's Road was reprieved in the early 1970s. The construction was a reinforced concrete frame made of load-bearing walls and flat slab floors, remodelled for maximum wind resistance after the disaster of Ronan Point.[55] The larger flats were in the lower ranges, originally also with some artists' studios that were eliminated in the final version. Each flat had its own private balcony, which caught the sun for some part of the day, and the windows were carefully framed to give reassurance to those alarmed by heights. At a time when tall buildings were beginning to be questioned, the orthogonal shapes and brick cladding – the latter suggested by Cadbury-Brown – were an attempt to invest the scheme with a greater humanity than found in many high-rise developments elsewhere, and a clear progression from Mayford (Fig. 4.15).

Fig 4.17   Westbourne Road, Islington, flats and houses for the local council.

Fig 4.18   Fieldend, Aqueduct, Telford, housing for Telford new town.

Fig 4.19   St Michael's, additions to the Delhi Street Estate for the London Borough of Islington.

Fig 4.20   The Friars, Southwark, one of two schools built by the London County Council to Lyons's designs.

The detailed design of World's End coincided with the development of New Ash Green and, moreover, Lyons had never designed such a big building. Jim Cadbury-Brown, however, had just completed his Gravesend Civic Centre and buildings at Essex University, and had space in his office. The two formed a new partnership, the Eric Lyons Cadbury-Brown Group Partnership, with Cunningham and Metcalfe as the other partners, to share the responsibilities of larger projects whilst continuing their individual practices. Cadbury-Brown and Metcalfe produced the working drawings from Lyons's basic design, and the school, offices and church are essentially their work.[56] The contract was let in 1969 to Holland, Hannen and Cubitts, and building began in early 1970 to a revised yardstick on the western half of the necklace. However, faced with a brick shortage and labourers' strike in 1972, the firm asked for two ex gratia payments, which the Royal Borough of Kensington and Chelsea refused. Work virtually ceased and Cubitts removed some of their equipment from the site while conducting secret negotiations with the Council's staff.[57] A year later the contract was re-let, ironically given the experience of New Ash Green, to Bovis. Greaves Tower was completed in April 1975 and the last part of the estate, its office component reduced, was let in early 1977 (Fig. 4.16).[58] It was the last of the great comprehensive developments; a very different culture existed in the late 1970s to that of a decade before, with vandalism a problem in the second phase and complaints that the

estate was difficult to police. The *Architectural Review* reported that 'an architect walking through the scheme would find himself entranced', but asked 'how does the layman view it?', reflecting the divergence of culture seen between middle class architects and their clients – something that Lyons was taking up as President of the RIBA from 1975 to 1977.[59]

Eric Lyons also built low-rise public housing in two developments for the London Borough of Islington. The enterprising and charismatic chief architect Alf Head solicited a number of schemes from specialists in low-rise, high-density development, amongst them Darbourne and Darke; Andrews, Sherlock and Partners (who designed three schemes for Span); and Pring, White and Partners, mainly for backland, infill sites. Lyons was commissioned in 1969 to design a large scheme on an open site at Westbourne Road (behind Pentonville Prison) comprising 268 houses, 132 flats, sheltered housing, a community hall and a medical centre, along with seven shops. The layout is almost a classic Radburn plan, with parking in cul-de-sacs around the perimeter, save that the site is bisected by a street containing garages underneath the flats, which breaks up the pattern of small pedestrian courtyards defined by low brick walls (Fig. 4.17). It was followed in 1972–9 by a slightly smaller scheme, but to a higher density, of two-storey houses and flats at Delhi Street, near York Way, laid out in rows rather like traditional northern back-to-backs.

Late works

That Lyons claimed a faith in competitions as 'an avenue to discover what resources he has within himself' when in 1974 he became President of the RIBA, may owe much to the impact on his own career of winning one.[60] In 1972 he won an open competition organised by the Portuguese developers Lusutor to design a holiday village on the Algarve near Faro. Only the first phase of Vilamoura was realised by the time of his death in 1980 and subsequent phases were continued by Ivor Cunningham and Richard Lyons to Eric Lyons's masterplan. The experience of the Mediterranean led Lyons to re-appraise his ideas of modern architecture. This first phase again includes orthogonal towers of flats, which give Vilamoura the look of a walled town approaching from the landward side. Behind are lower houses, shops and apartments leading towards the large marina. His approach became less puritan, Lyons explaining that 'I started to wonder how one does build places people will have affection for', which led him to a greater inclusiveness: 'References to the past in a context of indigenous scale and character suddenly means that architects are no longer talking to themselves'.[61]

This new idiom, with pitched roofs and elaborate decoration in brick and tile, informed both his last public housing projects, for the London Borough of Islington and Telford Development Corporation, and one unusual scheme for Span, at Mallard Place by the Thames at Twickenham. Fieldend, at Dawley, the oldest part of the new town of Telford, was a large and varied scheme on reclaimed industrial wasteland, its neo-vernacular, terraced houses contrasting with eye-catcher blocks of flats termed 'lodges', 'towers', and 'barns', the latter with steeply pitched roofs tall enough to contain two floors of accommodation. As at Vilamoura there was an emphasis on tiled roofs, varied brickwork and contrasting paint colours (Fig. 4.18). Mallard Place, laid out by Cunningham and completed by him in 1984 after Lyons's death, is a close-knit, inward-facing community of flats and houses, but it differs from earlier schemes in placing houses and garages together and the higher proportion of private gardens. The style is quirky, a mix of Vilamoura and the *Essex Design Guide* for modern housing in village settings.[62] Even the development at Telford he called 'slightly eclectic, slightly nostalgic', confessing that it represented the architecture of the times, when reaction against modernism was at its height.[63] The use of decoration was still more pronounced in an addition made by Cunningham to Delhi Street, on the site of a derelict Victorian church, with tile hanging and timber framing (Fig. 4.19). It makes a strange place to end the story of such champions of simple, modern design.[64]

Eric Lyons was essentially a specialist in designing the best possible housing to the tightest of budgets on the most awkward of sites. He did, however, design three schools, one at New Ash Green and

two for the LCC in Southwark, commissioned in 1960 and built on a single contract in 1962–4. Both Albion and Friars Primary Schools had been damaged in the war and the LCC was concerned that the government was restricting funding for rebuilding its substandard primaries, a policy that continued through most of the 1960s. The two schools were built to a similar plan, one the mirror image of the other, with a two-storey classroom block linked by a long corridor to an assembly hall which can be partly subdivided as a dining room, kitchen, and a library and staff accommodation set around an internal courtyard. At Albion School there was also a schoolkeeper's bungalow, whereas at the Friars School the old schoolhouse was retained. Margaret Trehearne designed glass for the internal courtyard at the Friars (Fig. 4.20). For a design of its date there is a considerable amount of corridor space, indicating, perhaps, that Lyons was not a specialist here, but providing useful experience for his subsequent primary school at New Ash Green.[65] Lyons's claims as a clever designer of social housing have always been overshadowed by his success with Span. As he admitted to John Donat in 1976, 'Working for a local authority client, I look back over the work and I can see now that you wouldn't think it had come out of the same office'.[66] In the same interview he explained that all his work came out of a series of common denominators, with a high degree of standardisation and repetition. What comes out of a study of his public work, as well as that for Span, is that he worked with two sets of denominators, one for his low-rise housing that is becoming rightly celebrated, and one for high-density flats that remains little known.

Endnotes

1. Ian Nairn, 'Spec-Built', *Architectural Review*, vol. 129, no. 769, March 1961, pp. 162–81.
2. Conversation with Ivor Cunningham, 15 February 2006. See Chapter 1 for further biographical details.
3. 'Oaklands, Constance Road, Whitton', *Architects' Journal*, vol. 108, no. 2796, 9 September 1948, pp. 244–6; 'Jameson Road, Bexhill', *Architect and Building News*, vol. 199, no. 4297, 27 April 1951, pp. 485–7.
4. 'Men of the Year', *Architects' Journal*, vol. 121, no. 3125, 20 January 1955, pp. 72–3.
5. Eric Lyons, 'Architects' Approach to Architecture', *RIBA Journal*, Third Series, vol. 75, no. 5, May 1968, p. 215, based on a lecture given on 6 February 1968.
6. See Chapter 3 for further biographical details.
7. Richard Findlater, 'The Man About the Houses', *Punch*, vol. 242, no. 6332, 17 January 1962, p. 143.
8. J. H. Forshaw and Patrick Abercrombie, *County of London Plan* (London: HMSO, 1943), p. 115.
9. *Administrative County of London Development Plan* (London County Council, 1951), pp. 44–6; Elizabeth Denby, *Europe Rehoused* (London: George Allen and Unwin, 1938, 1944), p. 263.
10. *Living with new ideas*, undated (c.1962) sales brochure held at Greenwich Heritage Centre.
11. *Woman's Journal*, April 1965, p. 54.
12. *op.cit., Living with new ideas.*
13. See the *Gazetteer* for a description of type plans.
14. *Architects' Journal*, vol. 125, no. 3248, 30 May 1957, pp. 809–11; *House and Garden*, vol. 12, no. 6 /102, June 1957, pp. 36–40.
15. Eric Lyons, 'Architecture and Place', *RIBA Journal*, Third Series, vol. 83, no. 10, October 1976, p. 407.
16. *op. cit., Living with new ideas.*
17. Information from H. H. Milnes, first resident of Gray Court, Parkleys, in 1955. See Chapter 6 for a discussion of the role of the residents' society.
18. George Mansell, 'The New Housing spells better Homes', in Frances Lake (ed) *Ideal Home Book* (London: Daily Mail, 1956), p. 55.
19. Greenwich MB Council Minutes, 2 February 1956
20. Greenwich MB Minutes of Proceedings, 4 June 1959, referring to building on the site of 97 Blackheath Park.
21. Eric Lyons, 'Back to Blackheath', *The Architect*, vol. 1, no. 6, July 1971, pp. 36–42.
22. Personal communication from Ivor Cunningham, 15 February 2006.
23. Letter from Victor Pasmore, 10 January 1960, in GLC/AR/ HB/02/0455, South Row, London Metropolitan Archives.
24. Kenneth J. Robinson, 'Period Flats Rejected', *The Observer*, no. 8810, 8 May 1960, p. 17.
25. *Blackheath Reporter*, vol. 2, no. 12, 24 February 1962, p. 3.
26. Greenwich MB, Minutes of Proceedings, 23 January 1963.
27. *Architects' Journal*, vol. 130, no. 3360, 10 September 1959, p. 149; no. 3364, 8 October 1959, p. 303.
28. Greenwich MB Minutes of Proceedings, 27 March 1960.
29. *op. cit.*, Eric Lyons, 1968, p. 217.
30. *The Times*, 21 May 1968, p. 6.
31. *Building*, vol. 227, no. 6854, 18 October 1974, p. 92.
32. *Architects' Journal*, vol. 146, no. 20, 15 November 1967, p. 1248.
33. James Fletcher Watson in conversation, July 2003.
34. *op.cit.*, Eric Lyons, 1968, p. 217.
35. John Donat, 'Mid-Span', in *Building*, vol. 231, no. 6943/ 29, 16 July 1976, pp. 81–2.
36. *The Architect*, vol. 121, no. 3, March 1975, pp. 21–3.
37. St Pancras MB Planning and Housing Development Committee Minutes, vol. 4, November 1958, p. 1760; information from Robert Bailie, 2001.
38. Lawrence Wolfe, *The Reilly Plan: A New Way of Life* (London: Nicholson and Watson, 1945); *Architects' Journal*, vol. 100, no. 2598, 9 November 1944, p. 346.
39. *Architects' Journal*, vol. 108, no. 2807, 25 November 1948, pp. 490–2; vol. 118, no. 3054, 10 September 1953, pp. 318–22.
40. Lyons was commissioned in 1955, and the first scheme was rejected early in 1957. London Metropolitan Archives, LCC/MIN/7693.
41. *Architectural Review*, vol. 12, no. 720, January 1957, pp. 42–3; vol. 125, no. 744, January 1959, p. 69.
42. James Dunnett and Gavin Stamp, *Ernö Goldfinger* (London: Architectural Association, 1983), p. 86.
43. Report, 18 February 1958. London Metropolitan Archives LCC/MIN/ 7702.
44. Ministry of Housing and Local Government, *Houses: the Next Step*, (London: HMSO, 1953).
45. *Architects' Journal*, vol. 130, no. 3360, 10 September 1959, p. 149; no. 3364, 8 October 1959, p. 303; *Architectural Review*, vol. 129, no. 755, January 1960, pp. 59–60.
46. *Southern Evening Echo*, 21 November 1981.
47. See Chapter 2 for discussion of the Radburn layout.
48. *Architectural Review*, vol. 129, no. 767, January 1961, pp. 34–5; vol. 140, no. 833, July 1966, pp. 42–3; Frederick Gibberd, Ben Hyde Harvey, Len White et al, *Harlow, the Story of a New Town* (Stevenage: Publications for Companies, 1980), p. 178.
49. There seemed to be concern that the south side of Oakley Square would lose its economic worth if council housing was built behind it. Eric Lyons, Report to St Pancras Planning and Housing Development Committee Minutes 16 January 1964 (Plans Sub-Committee December 1963); *Architectural Review*, vol. 137, no. 815, January 1965, p. 43.
50. LB Camden Planning Development Committee Minutes,

26 September 1966, 29 January 1968; information from
Ivor Cunningham.

51. Reported in Chelsea MB Minutes of Proceedings, November 1962.

52. *Building Design*, no. 274, 14 November 1975, p. 17.

53. Chelsea MB Minutes of Proceedings, January 1965.

54. *Chelsea News*, 20 August 1965. House prices from *Chelsea Post*, 22 November 1964.

55. This was a 23-storey block of flats in Cleaver Road, Newham, built using a prefabricated system (Larsen Neilsen), which collapsed on the morning of 16 May 1968 with the loss of five lives.

56. H. T. Cadbury-Brown, *Architects' Lives*, National Sound Archive, 9 July 1997.

57. A single militant crane operator had infiltrated the site and interrupted the work schedule in one of a number of attempts to radicalise the building industry in the early 1970s.

58. Chelsea MB Minutes of Proceedings 1961–5; Royal Borough of Kensington and Chelsea Minutes 1964–75.

59. *Building Design*, no. 274, 14 November 1975, p. 17; no. 339, 18 March 1977, pp. 12–13; *Architectural Review*, vol. 162, no. 967, September 1977, pp. 172–6. Jim Cadbury-Brown in conversation, February 2005.

60. 'A New Lease for Lyons', *Building*, vol. 227, no. 6854/ 42, 18 October 1974, p. 93.

61. 'Lyons Untamed', *Building Design*, no. 459, 17 August 1979, p. 2.

62. *The Essex Design Guide for Residential and Mixed Use Areas* (Essex: Essex Planning Officers Association, 1973).

63. 'Mid-Span', *Building*, vol. 231, no. 6943/ 29, 16 July 1976, p. 86.

64. *Architects' Journal*, 21 December 1981, pp. 1063–4. In 2005, Mallard Place received the Historic Housing Award, celebrating 60 years of housing.

65. Report DE7/403 (SO 124) 6 February 1961. LCC/MIN/3816, London Metropolitan Archives; LCC Council Minutes 1959–65; *Architectural Review*, vol. 133, no. 791, January 1963, p. 14.

66. *Building*, vol. 231, no. 6943/ 29, 16 July 1976, p. 83.

CHAPTER FIVE

New Ash Green: Span's
'latter 20th century
village in Kent'

Patrick Ellard

"This is the most exciting scheme
I have ever undertaken."

Eric Lyons

As consultant architect to Span, Eric Lyons shared Leslie Bilsby's ambition to expand operations into a wider field. As a team they had grown restless with the restrictions of the limited and, in certain instances, the poor quality of the sites they had acquired. Bilsby, buoyed by the popular success of the earlier Span housing schemes, proposed designing and building an entire town! After consideration, however, it was felt that an undertaking of this scale might be beyond the means of Span, and Lyons thought a smaller self-contained village-sized project would form a more realistic proposition. Both Lyons and Span were excited by the possibility of conceiving a new type of 'comprehensive' development, one which would facilitate the creation of a new community. Lyons stated 'This is the most exciting scheme I have ever undertaken'.[1] Clearly, Span was not in a position to fund a 'comprehensive' development on their own, but Ernest Haynes, the chair of Royal London Mutual Insurance Society Limited, was in sympathy with Span's position as a progressive housing developer and in 1960 gave its financial backing: 'I liked what they had done and felt that this was an organisation which we could support and help to achieve something worthwhile in the housing field... Someone has to blaze a new trial in housing and Span are doing this'.

A new kind of village
In 1961 Span became aware of the impending sale of two adjacent farms, Newhouse and North Ash in Ash, Kent. Bilsby immediately saw potential in the 430 acres of gently undulating, Kentish countryside: a central plateau could become the community centre with shops and other amenities, while the residential areas would radiate outwards, with an open field, neighbouring woods and meadow being retained. One of Span's subsidiary companies, Span Royal London Investments Limited (SRL) bought the two farms for £35,000 when they came up for auction in November 1961. In 1962, as part of the process of seeking planning permission, a document entitled 'A new village near Hartley Kent, New Ash Green' was produced, the name New Ash Green being derived from the name of the two farms. The document explained the fundamental intentions of the new village:

> This is an outline proposal to design and build an entirely
> new kind of village in attractive surroundings with all
> appropriate services and communal facilities for between
> five to six thousand people... One of the inherent qualities
> of the traditional English village is a sense of compactness,
> or continuity of building yet within a sense of freedom in the
> surrounding countryside and the enclosed open greens, or
> spaces. In New Ash Green a compact and well defined village
> is proposed, embedded in the surrounding countryside... The
> architectural quality of the village will be achieved by a close
> relationship between buildings and landscape.[3]

It was intended that New Ash Green would provide a wide range of accommodation and cater for various sizes of family and age range. Reference was made to the type of amenities that would be provided (such as community buildings, shops, primary school and church), and the sloping open field first seen by Bilsby was to become a park with miniature lake and a glass-domed swimming pool! Provision would also be made for light industry to the north of the village. The residential areas were grouped in five zones which were to be divided into 10–12 neighbourhoods, each with its own residents' society. In addition, Geoffrey Townsend felt that a project of this scale necessitated the introduction of a new management body, the Central Society that would oversee the wider needs of the Village.

In general terms, there is an approximate similarity to later masterplans and the design that appeared in the 1962 document, in that the exploitation of the site's geographical features, positioning of the residential zones and central placement of amenities with certain modifications, would be retained. However, much of the architecture illustrated in the document has a rigid rectilinearity in terms of its appearance and layout, although a more informal arrangement of housing was evident in some of the residential zones. With regard to social ambition and potential audience for New Ash Green, the 1962 document did include the revealing statement that 'The architectural setting is intended to give the new society a background reflecting, and in sympathy with the lives and aspirations of an alert and forward looking community'.[4] The use of the term 'society' emphasises how ambitious Span was and, also, that it believed there was a receptive audience for a new and unique environment. Townsend recalled the optimism of this period: 'We thought the Village was exciting in a way that it was trying to create a society for people, it wasn't just doing a spec. built job of selling houses'.[5]

The battle for New Ash Green
On the 15th November 1963 SRL applied to the Kent County Planning Authority for permission to develop the site as a new village, with appropriate services and communal facilities for 5,000 to 6,000 people. On the 14th of January 1964 the Planning Authority refused to grant planning permission on the grounds that they believed provision for new housing in Kent was already being made, local transportation could not cope with increased demand, and that the land was of agricultural value. Another issue that mitigated against Span's proposal was that the land was part of a proposed extension of the green belt. There was also opposition from Dartford Rural District Council (RDC) and the Parish Councils representing Ash, Fawkham and Hartley. They were concerned about the installation of sewers and drainage and the consequent spoilation of the countryside.

Span appealed against this decision and an official enquiry was held in July 1964. In their defence, SRL stated that the siting of their new development was appropriate and that Kent County Council had not made adequate provision for London commuters looking to relocate. They also questioned whether the area was of such great landscape value, suggesting that it was 'no more than pleasant rural countryside'.[6] SRL also stressed that the site was situated within a 'proposed' extension of the green belt and that New Ash Green would generate some opportunities for local employment. It was also emphasised that the Span and Lyons collaboration had established a reputation for design excellence and had won many awards for its work. As a means of pre-empting objections to the cost and inconvenience of installing the Village's infrastructure, SRL said that Span would contribute to these costs at the early stages of the project.[7] However, at the end of the enquiry, the inspector's report again recommended the refusal of planning permission, largely reiterating the perceived difficulties expressed during the first application.[8]

This report was sent to the Minister of Housing and Local Government, Keith Joseph, in September 1964, but a decision was deferred due to the impending general election.[9] A Labour victory on the 14th October 1964 saw Joseph replaced by Richard Crossman, who recognised the importance of his first major planning decision. The favourable report produced by his Parliamentary Secretary led Crossman to overrule the inspector's decision and grant planning permission for New Ash Green. A letter received by the solicitors acting on behalf of SRL from the Ministry of Housing stated that 'a village of the kind proposed would make a useful and imaginative contribution to the problem of housing in the outer metropolitan region'.[10] The letter declared that local transport would not be overburdened as a proportion of the residents would work locally and not have to use the train service. It was also felt that the scheme could be tolerated from an aesthetic point of view even if it was situated within a proposed extension of the green belt.[11] Crossman understood that, as a finite development, New Ash Green represented an ideal solution to the problem of urban sprawl:

> I think you will find, when it is completed, the people are going to realise that this model village, and the contrast to Hartley itself, will show up what's wrong with the ghastly development in this part of Kent for the last ten years. It's been the worst kind of development – unplanned, spasmodic, what is now described as seepage, seepage into the area. I want to see planned concentrated building, preserving all the countryside intact, so as to stop this seepage. It is because I wanted to have a model in Kent of what ought to be done that I gave the sanction for this plan to go ahead.... this may well be a model of how to get civilised modern community living in an area of beautiful landscape.[12]

As a partner in the Lyons practise, Ivor Cunningham adds further detail to the reasons behind Crossman's decision:

*He'd seen villages being ruined and made suburban by
accretions of development around them. This was a wrong way
of dealing with the countryside as it ruins existing villages, it
swamps them and they lose their character. If you build a new
village then you don't need to extend all the smaller villages,
it is an alternative form of strategic planning. I think that was
probably the main reason, he knew from his own experience
of where he was living that villages were being swallowed and
becoming suburbs.*[13]

Span and Lyons were well-accustomed to opposition from local
planning authorities and representative bodies, and the lengthy
court proceedings that often accompanied each new housing
scheme proposal. Once planning permission had been approved,
local councils at county, district and parish level were required by
law to co-operate with Span. Despite this reassurance nothing
could have prepared them for the intense controversy that followed
Crossman's announcement at the end of November 1964. For a
period of almost three years New Ash Green became the subject
of fierce media scrutiny and national controversy. Local Labour MP
and chair of Dartford RDC, Leslie Reeves, became one of Span's
most vocal detractors and said in December 1964 that New Ash
Green would receive approval 'over my dead body... We will defy
the Minister. Make no mistake about it'.[14]

As a private development, New Ash Green was unusual in that it
aimed to provide housing for owner occupiers and local authority
tenants and was, thus, deemed a social experiment. It was envisaged
that the London County Council and the Dartford RDC would both
provide tenants, but Leslie Reeves refused to negotiate with Span
on the matter, which led to the full allocation of 450 houses being
accepted by the newly-named Greater London Council (GLC).
Reeves also expressed another criticism – of Span profiting from
land speculation. The land had been purchased at its agricultural
value of £80 per acre, totalling £35,000. After planning permission
had been approved, each acre at development price was then
valued at £6,000, making the entire 430-acre site for New Ash
Green worth £2,500,000. Leslie Bilsby was always quick to refute
these claims: 'Ridiculous, millions will have to be spent before we
can hope to make any profit'.[15] Span also argued that only 190 of the
430 acres would be built upon and that they were not only building
houses, but also providing shops, community centre, library, church
and schools. At the end of December 1964, New Ash Green had
even become a subject of heated discussion in the House of Lords.
Lord Esher was at pains to defend the project:

*My Lords, I should like to say straight away that the architect
of this development, Mr Eric Lyons, has in my opinion made
what is possibly the outstanding contribution of any private*

*architect to domestic architecture in this country since the
War. Some share of the credit must go to the developers,
Span, to whom he has acted as consultant for many years.*[16]

Opposition to New Ash Green was further consolidated with
the formation of the Hartley and Ash Rural Preservation Society
(HARPS) in March 1965. The first entry in the HARPS minute book
described its intended aims as 'forming an Action Committee and
to raise funds for legal advice to prevent the development of the
village of New Ash Green'.[17] HARPS's campaigning was extensive
and unrelenting. In early November 1965 Leslie Reeves met
with HARPS to plan its strategy, notes taken during the meeting
revealing that 'The Dartford RDC had agreed to adopt reasonable
delaying tactics... Mr Reeves did stress, however, that his delaying
tactics required the continuing support of his Council and this he
hopes to obtain'.[18] To coincide with the first anniversary of Richard
Crossman's decision, an illustrated fifteen-page Memorandum
was sent to the Prime Minister Harold Wilson.[19] In the House
of Commons on 9th December, Wilson's response to the
Memorandum formed an explicit endorsement of
Crossman's ruling:

*We all recognise that this part of Kent has seen a much bigger
population increase in the past few years than any other
and that siting of extra houses there has been unplanned,
uncoordinated and not in the best interests of planning. What
my right hon. friend is trying to do is to keep old villages
unspoilt and to encourage the concentration of new building
into model communities... but my right hon. friend, I believe,
has taken the right decision.*[20]

Design and concept

In early January 1966, Dartford RDC received the first masterplan
for New Ash Green and detailed plan of the first neighbourhood,
Zone 1 (37 houses, five maisonettes, eight shops and 50 garages).[21]
The masterplan only indicated the positioning of each of the
residential neighbourhoods and amenities and failed to satisfy the
Committee who wanted to view the entire development with the
similar degree of detail seen in the drawings for Zone 1.
A Committee member felt that the development would be
'piecemeal': 'Are we going to get the village in penny packets like
this?.... We have got to look at every brick and tile on this four acre
site'.[22] Lyons declared his frustration with the malevolence of the
Committee in a newspaper interview: 'The people who oppose the
scheme are obviously trying to do everything they can to delay or
hinder it'.[23]

Lyons contempt for planning authorities was well known and
previous exchanges had led him to form the opinion that many were

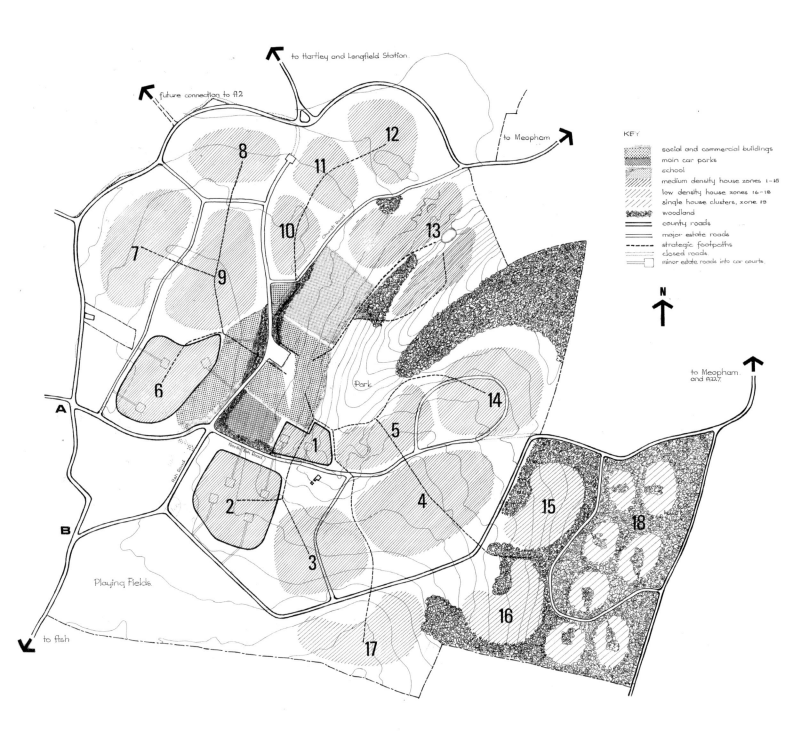

Fig 5.1 New Ash Green Masterplan, Eric Lyons and Partners for Span-Kent Limited, 1967, indicating 18 residential zones, which would be built in various densities.

simply inexperienced and unqualified to make informed decisions. The fact that the masterplan only indicated the general disposition of the residential neighbourhoods and amenities was quite intentional because, after establishing the range of house types and the overall characteristics of the development through the drawings for Zone 1, the design and planning of later neighbourhoods would be derived from Lyons's empirical approach of improvement and modification. This process relied on Lyons's aesthetic discernment and the feedback received from residents' societies. It was a policy that had been developed through Lyons's unique working relationship with Span: 'I was able to set the conditions out myself and provide the means of responding very quickly. That was great and that kind of peace is efficient and exhilarating and self-rewarding… I don't think design decisions are better because they take longer'.[24] With the exception of a few minor conditions, the New Ash Green masterplan and Zone 1 were given approval by Kent County Council Planning Committee in July 1966, followed by approval for Zone 2 in October 1966. During the summer of 1966 HARPS began to recognise that it was unlikely to prevent Span's model village of New Ash Green becoming a reality. The battle had been won, although Span and Lyons had to accept that valuable time had been lost.

Published in 1967, the promotional brochure for New Ash Green included a statement that neatly encapsulated Span's aspirations: 'The village is planned as a whole place, created for 20th-century living and providing for 20th-century people's needs'.[25] Despite the immense difficulties that Span and the Lyons practice had experienced in receiving planning permission and approval for their designs, the concept behind New Ash Green and the geographical positioning of the residential zones and amenities remained essentially the same. However, the new masterplan now indicated that the residential areas were to be divided into 18 zones (Fig. 5.1), built in varying densities (seven to 15 houses per acre), with Redhill Wood (Zone 18) being a 'low density' neighbourhood comprising 50 plots for individual, owner-built houses.[26] Lyons believed that neighbourhoods of between 100–150 houses were an appropriate size in terms of their management by individual residents' societies, with the 'Village Association' forming part of a unique two-tier management system 'responsible for maintaining the private roads, the playing fields and community buildings and The Minnis and all the Village grounds'.[27]

The chair of each neighbourhood residents' society would be known as the 'representative member', with one of these performing the dual role of chair of the central Village Association.[28] For those residents arriving in New Ash Green during the latter half of 1967, one of the key attractions was the possibility of becoming actively involved in the running of the Village itself. This was a point emphasised in the Span publicity brochure: 'Thus, the ownership

and management of the village is substantially in the hands of its residents, each of whom is able, through his representative member, to have a share in deciding how the village is to be run'.[29] It was intended that the residents' societies (and Village Association) would not only bestow a sense of control and contribution to the quality of the environment, but also encourage social integration. Through the provision of the planned amenities such as the shops, studios and proposed area set aside for light industry, some residents were hoping to find employment within the Village itself. Span also believed that residents would integrate with existing communities and make a positive contribution to the quality of life in the area.

The close working relationship that existed between Eric Lyons and Span allowed Lyons to follow his creative instincts unimpeded and for Span to facilitate the realisation of these ideas. Lyons spoke of 'The enormous benefit of a client who gave me an extraordinarily free hand, which I believe to be almost the most important factor'.[30] By giving Lyons 'total control', he was now in a position to create a 'total environment' on a scale never before undertaken by Span. Lyons found himself in the privileged position of directing every aesthetic facet of the housing schemes he designed for Span. It was this position that ultimately gave the designs a consistency and coordinated cohesion which contributed to their success. Lyons commented: 'I have responsibility for design, layout, contract supervision and landscape design, and I expect to be consulted on suitability of sites and type of development. In other words, therefore, a full service'.[31]

Initially, Lyons was unenthusiastic about the use of the word 'village' because of its historical connotations; he felt the design and concept behind New Ash Green were setting a precedent. However, for convenience and promotional purposes, the term was adopted, but as a means of appeasing Lyons, New Ash Green became the 'Latter 20th Century Village in Kent'.[32] However, New Ash Green, in some respects, would emulate the way in which settlements have developed through history – from the centre outwards. The issue of history and the traditional village was explored in one of the first major articles to be published on New Ash Green, based on interviews with Lyons and Leslie Bilsby. Lyons described the Village as:

Designed for today, for a multitude of different ways of individual living. We haven't discarded everything from the past, but where we have borrowed, it has not been sentimentally or nostalgically. I think it is uncompromisingly new, but not new for the sake of novelty… we might be near to a village situation in that the houses are grouped, terraced and clustered in a traditional village, but not in a 'semi-detached manner'.[33]

While Bilsby was keen to stress that New Ash Green would in no way form a pastiche of the traditional village, he did concede that 'People who really want to live in an old English cottage won't find any at New Ash Green. It's true that there's a cottage feeling about the smaller houses we're building there, especially inside, but what we are doing is providing homes that are sympathetic with the countryside'.[34] This article featured a series of drawings of New Ash Green by Gordon Cullen, including the 'Wents', the central walkway through New Ash Green's first neighbourhood, Over Minnis. The image was frequently reproduced in later publicity material (Fig. 5.2).

It is inevitable that New Ash Green embodied certain facets of the traditional village and, to a certain extent, Lyons and Span were conditioned by their own perception of the constituent elements that formed a village-type of development on the scale they envisaged. A building programme that worked from the centre outwards in pockets of development would cause the

minimum amount of disruption to residents in the completed neighbourhoods. The shopping centre was centrally placed for ease of access and was the first of the Village amenities to begin construction in February 1968. The informal clustering of the houses around common areas has obvious associations with the village green and Span also placed New Ash Green within the history of the local area by naming the residential neighbourhoods after the field names that appeared on an 18th-century tithe map of Ash Parish. Neighbourhood names were also taken from historic events and figures associated with the area. Kentish terms such as 'minnis' (meaning common land or open space) and 'went' (meaning path or way) were adopted.[35]

There are similarities that can be drawn between the ideology of the Garden City Movement and New Ash Green. Garden city pioneer Ebenezer Howard proposed the creation of a network of planned communities and Bilsby shared his ambitious nature,

Fig 5.2   The 'Wents', Over Minnis, by Gordon Cullen, showing the three shops that were built on the neighbourhood to provide basic amenities for early residents while the main shopping centre was under construction.

Fig 5.3   Grasmere, West Byfleet, Surrey, Eric Lyons and Partners. This development
allowed Lyons to prototype six houses from the K-range.

declaring that developments similar to New Ash Green could be
replicated across the country: 'Five hundred villages like New Ash
Green could be built in the next five years and 250,000 people
housed in exceptionally pleasant and functional environments'.[36]
Like the Garden City Movement, Span wished to combine the
advantages of both the city and the countryside and also bring
together residents from different backgrounds and income levels.
Despite these undeniable associations, when discussing New Ash
Green's origins, Lyons was reluctant to accept this connection,
stating that 'It is not to be a Garden City, but a lush, green
urbanism – the Verdant Village'.[37] Lyons, however, professed a great
admiration for contemporary, domestic, Scandinavian architecture.
Housing schemes designed by Alvar Aalto, Ralph Erskine and Arne
Jacobsen were set within wooded or landscaped areas, with their
houses relying on the use of brick, vertical wooden cladding, and
mono-pitch roofs. Furthermore, Tapiola, a housing project in Espoo,
Finland (designed during the early 1950s), placed houses amongst
the wooded hills and around open areas and parks. Tapiola has
even been referred to as a Finnish 'garden city'. Interviewed by the

BBC in 1968, Lyons gave his personal perspective on New Ash
Green and its relationship to historical precedents: 'We are going
to telescope history and we shall probably make some mistakes.
But history has made a lot of mistakes and on the whole we are
probably winning because we are trying to anticipate the mistakes
that history did make and try to prevent them from happening'.[38]

Building New Ash Green
Building Span and Landscape Span had been formed to handle
the increased workload generated by the development of New
Ash Green, whilst all other matters pertaining to the Village were
dealt with by Span-Kent Limited. Span proposed to build 2,000
homes and all the Village amenities between 1966 and 1971. Eric
Lyons and Partners designed a specific range of house types for
New Ash Green, the intention being to cater for a wide variety of
family size and also allow these families to then move around the
Village, in response to their changing needs. Lyons had understood
that the inability to do this on many of the early Span schemes
had proved problematic: 'For the first time we've got a big enough

Fig 5.4   Construction of first houses on Over Minnis, showing Lyons's combined use of both
modern and traditional building materials.

scheme, we've got a wide spectrum of income and size and range
of housing and it's been designed deliberately for this purpose'.[39]
Six house types were prototyped at Grasmere, Surrey, (1967) and
the distinctive style of New Ash Green's K range (K for Kent) was
established: wide frontage, mono-pitch roof, blue/black asbestos
tiles, vertical wooden cladding and angled front porch (Fig. 5.3).[40]

The K range of house types was advanced, not only in terms of
appearance, but also in their use of materials and methods of
construction. The houses were built of brick flank and party walls
with a central steel A-frame and horizontal purlins (Fig. 5.4). The
walls, front and back, first-storey floor and roof were constructed
of prefabricated panels, brought into position by crane and
attached to the A-frame and purlins. The houses were unique in
their construction, borrowing techniques that had previously been
applied to industrial buildings. Lyons described this approach:

*The structure is based on a simple principle of a centre
frame containing four metal columns that house the staircase
trimming, the heating, services etc. – all standardised. We
have produced from this basic core house a method of
construction consisting of large pre-formed timber floor panels,
wall panels and roof panels. The panels are made in the
factory on the site.*[41]

The K range of house types exemplified Lyons's understanding
of the use of standardisation, which at the same time permitted
a degree of variety. The houses were given the designation of
A to N and a number which indicated the number of floors the
property possessed, i.e. the K3N three-storey town house; the
standard K2A house; and the single-storey K1A bungalow. The
Lyons team also devised a standard floor plan which incorporated
a flexible arrangement of internal spaces and could accommodate

the addition of single or double-height projections. Lyons's quest to experiment and innovate was driven not only by his personal pragmatism, but also his desire to extend the skill of the builder. In effect, Lyons and Span rationalised traditional building techniques as opposed to adopting industrial system building, and they understood the commercial benefits of house production, which in theory would allow a faster and efficient method of construction.

However, in pushing Span's capabilities, Lyons did not want purely functional and technical issues to dictate decision-making: 'Directly an architect is thinking about use he automatically becomes sensitive to use. Directly he's in a machine that's producing he's got to think of the machine, not of the people. And therefore he stops thinking creatively in the terms I'm talking about'.[42] Span erected an assembly shop at New Ash Green which produced the wall, floor and roof panels, with the steel A-frames prefabricated at a factory in the nearby town of Dartford. The fact that many of the dimensions for the windows and doors were non-standard highlighted Lyons's belief that these proportions were correct for their use and that he was not prepared to simply accept what was commercially available. Tom McKenna worked for Span as a carpenter and foreman at New Ash Green during the late 1960s and shared many discussions with Lyons. He gives a compelling account of how Lyons, often accused of being an autocrat, collaborated on-site with his labour force:

> *Eric brought enthusiasm to the men, talked to the men. He*
> *could do a sketch on the back of an envelope and you got a*
> *picture of the buildability of what he was getting at. If you had*
> *a query with Eric, he would take the query on board. Then he'd*
> *draw on a piece of paper and it came back at you, he saw your*
> *problem and adapted it to suit. Then he'd sign the envelope*
> *and that was your instructions, you were covered to carry out*
> *that innovation. He was a great character.*[43]

The principle external materials of the Span-built houses at New Ash Green were brick, asbestos tile and wood.[44] The rough-sawn, vertical wooden cladding was treated with a rust-coloured stain on the early neighbourhoods, which allowed a greater visual integration between the houses and their surroundings. Dependent on house type, the chief internal features of the houses included built-in storage, kitchen with storage/divider unit, cupboards and preparation surfaces, large sliding door, exposed structural purlins, vinyl tiles laid as standard throughout ground floor and cathedral ceilings in first floor bedrooms (Fig. 5.5). The houses were decorated according to the paint and wallpaper offered by Span to residents.[45] Lyons applied an empirical approach to the design of the house interior:

> *I never design a room, or a set of rooms with the furniture*
> *arrangement in mind. It's a waste of time. But I do know the*

Fig 5.5   Interior of Over Minnis house showing how a fitted storage/divider was used as a means of providing enclosure for the kitchen.

Fig 5.6   Over Minnis from North Ash Road, showing the integration of architecture with hard and soft
landscaping, and the retention of mature trees found on the site.

optimum dimensions within which the users can arrange
things. I know which dimensions are flexible and which are not.
You can't predict how people will use rooms, so you have to
provide flexibility for them to make their arrangements.[46]

Early neighbourhoods

A 'topping-out' ceremony was held in May 1967 to celebrate the
completion of the first house – 34 Over Minnis – and the official
launch of New Ash Green 'At Home' was held on 21st September
1967, with Sir Keith Joseph as guest. Span and their consultant
architects would have enjoyed the irony of witnessing their project
being endorsed by the former Minister for Housing, who had
represented a government that had refused planning permission for
New Ash Green.

To ensure a speedy completion, Over Minnis only consisted of
33 houses, derived from the use of ten different house types. Four
of these designs were used as show houses to demonstrate the

diversity of accommodation that would ultimately be provided. The
most striking innovation in terms of planning can be seen in the
way the majority of the houses were positioned facing outwards.
Lyons gives an explanation for this change in approach: 'When you
are building small bundles of houses you tend to strive, perhaps
too hard, to establish some kind of introverted situation in order
to make it work in its own right. This Village project provides
the chance to extend the experience we have had'.[47] As a means
of maximising natural light penetrating into the houses, solar
orientation was taken into consideration at the planning stages of
a new neighbourhood. A unique feature was the inclusion of three
shops (bank, newsagent and the Span Shopping Service) positioned
along the 'The Wents'.[48]

In creating a modern vision of living in the countryside, the
development of New Ash Green presented a new and exciting
challenge to Lyons's team. They had never before had the
opportunity to incorporate open fields, large areas of woodland

and other dramatic geographical features into their designs on such a large scale. Ivor Cunningham and his assistant Preben Jakobsen formulated the planting policy and landscaping principles for the Village, a process that was always conducted simultaneously with planning and architectural decision-making as Lyons explained:

> *The architect designed the landscape hand in hand with the design of the dwelling, and it was the integration of all the elements – building, planting, pavings, roads, car parks, children's play spaces etc – that created an ambience and scale hitherto unknown in housing for ordinary people. It created an 'identity of place' and gave the residents a pride and interest in their place.*[49]

At New Ash Green, the size of the open spaces provided was maximised by the use of compact terraces of various configurations. The areas on the periphery of each neighbourhood were simply landscaped and formed shelter belts, whereas the neighbourhoods themselves relied on more exotic planting of a formal, architectural kind. Span also continued their policy of retaining existing mature trees found on site (Fig. 5.6). The aim was to establish an indigenous planting style, much in the same way there had been an effort to create an indigenous style of architecture for the Village. This is apparent on an enclosed green on the west side of the neighbourhood, where the physical enclosure is created by the use of angled brick walls and the single-storey projections of the two K2F house types at the each end of the space (Fig. 5.7). The K2E and K2F house types were deemed to be of the correct scale in relation to the size of the enclosed space they were creating. The space is dissected by a brushed aggregate path and steps, each step incorporating a line of 'plinth header' brindle engineering bricks, with the conventional brindle engineering brick used as a coping on the surrounding walls. By varying the lateral position of each step, it permitted the groundcover planted to seemingly encroach randomly onto the edge of the path. Part of the path then splits off, taking you to a secluded corner of this semi-private space. Hypericum was often used as groundcover, giving a subtle splash of colour, with phormium chosen for its sculptural qualities. Trees selected included ornamental horse chestnut, staghorn sumac and two catalpa trees positioned on a grassed area opposite the K2E and K2F houses.

As Over Minnis consisted of only 33 houses, the only full-size neighbourhood completed by Span was Punch Croft. For this reason it represents a fully-realised neighbourhood of the size envisaged by Lyons for the rest of the Village. Lyons described his approach to the design of Punch Croft:

> *In Zone Two the layout provides a system of four courts that are cul-de-sacs and the walkways are situated within that*

Fig 5.7   An enclosed green at the west side of Over Minnis, shows the high quality of landscaping later evident throughout New Ash Green. As previously seen on earlier Span housing schemes, the ubiquitous mushroom light was used to complement its landscape setting.

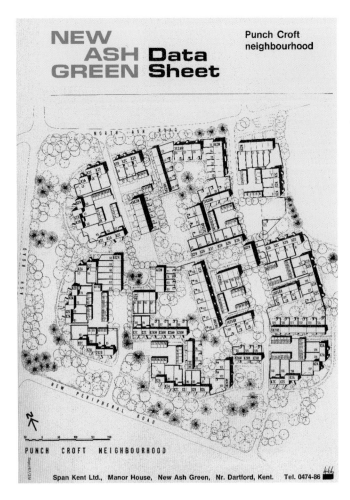

NEW ASH GREEN Data Sheet

Punch Croft neighbourhood

PUNCH CROFT NEIGHBOURHOOD

Span Kent Ltd., Manor House, New Ash Green, Nr. Dartford, Kent.   Tel. 0474-86

Fig 5.8 Data Sheet: Punch Croft neighbourhood. Other Data Sheets produced by Span illustrated the floor plans of the various house types available in New Ash Green.

pattern. The houses on the periphery tend to face outwards and those in the centre of the zone have their prospect at the back of the house, through relatively small semi-enclosed gardens. Every house has an open prospect at the back or the front.[50]

The concept of having access to a common green was a design policy maintained throughout the development, giving to each neighbourhood its individual identity and sense of place. By developing the themes explored earlier in the design of Over Minnis, the composition of Punch Croft displayed a greater spatial complexity (Fig. 5.8). Lyons believed that each neighbourhood should work at an 'intimate pedestrian level'.[51] The compact arrangement of the houses, pathways and common green spaces would encourage greater social interaction between the residents (Fig. 5.9). The width of the pathways would bring residents into closer proximity as they traversed the neighbourhood, and the conscious positioning of the kitchen sink at the front of certain house types would make those inside more likely to be seen by those walking past.[52]

Whilst valuing the social benefits of associational behaviour engendered by the physical form of each neighbourhood, Lyons strove to achieve a balance between 'art and science' and placed importance upon the role of aesthetics in the decision-making process.[53] The juxtapositioning of the houses was also influenced by their visual interrelationship. Lyons commented that 'the real things that create pleasant places are organic arrangements of buildings' and landscaping was a means of enhancing space, as opposed to merely filling it.[54] He believed that the intelligent use of space represented 'visible evidence of community'.[55] The positioning of the housing and the spaces they enclose also provides a sense of excitement when moving through Punch Croft as, from the periphery, views of the common greens are restricted to gaps between the terraces. On entering Punch Croft, by moving through the compressed space between the houses, the common greens open up and a glimpse of the next common can be seen through a similarly limited view between the houses in the distance, an experience described by Lyons as one of 'mystery, change, surprise'.[56] Yew and laurel hedges were used as another means of creating smaller enclosed cell-like spaces in front of houses or to enclose a common green.

As a means of attracting residents of various ages and financial means, the narrow-fronted, flat-roofed K2N was available at a 95 per cent mortgage rate with no down-payment.[57] Referred to as the 'newly wed houses', the common greens enclosed by terraces became known as 'newly wed squares'. Another house type to appear exclusively on Punch Croft was the K3N 'townhouse', with its living room situated on the first floor, providing impressive views of the surrounding common greens.

Community life

To promote New Ash Green, Span placed a series of advertisements in various newspapers, including *The Observer* and *The Guardian*, 'Emigrate to New Ash Green' and 'Your Span Plan for the Weekend' being two of the slogans used. Leslie Bilsby described the potential audience for New Ash Green and the intentions of Span's advertising campaign:

> *Whilst the houses may attract would be purchasers, people will not actually buy unless they are in sympathy with the ideals of New Ash Green. Such people are not easily classified under the broad heading usual in research, because they represent an attitude as much as an age or socio-economic group. There is a personality type to whom we tailor our selling message... New Ash Green is 'social pioneering' and represents a fairly unorthodox concept... it is necessary to define the advertised image very clearly so that we can sell the concept first, and the house afterwards... The promotional programme for New Ash Green is geared to challenging people's accepted norms in housing.*[58]

For the 1968 Ideal Home Exhibition at Earl's Court in London, the Span stand included a full-size house from the K range; this encouraged thousands of visitors to view Over Minnis and its showhouses. Span's house prices ranged from £6,500 for the three-bedroomed K2A to £8,000 for a four-bedroomed K2D. Whilst house prices at New Ash Green were marginally higher than other parts of Kent, Span said that this difference took into account the cost of the Village amenities they planned to build. Two weeks after the launch in September 1967 almost all of the houses on Over Minnis, and one hundred houses from the layout plan of Punch Croft, had been sold.[59] Those arriving in the late 1960s came from a diversity of backgrounds and different parts of the country, although many could be described as archetypal Span residents drawn heavily from the design, architectural and teaching professions. A key factor that united the early inhabitants was the wish to embrace the concept of 'a new way of life for you and your family'.[60]

Making the commitment to move out to the country at a point when the Village was still under construction, encouraged a sense of excitement amongst the early 'pioneering settlers'. The limited road access, poor bus service and copious amounts of mud were all deemed to be part of the 'fun'. Regardless of social class and profession, a noticeable proportion of the early residents were at the same point in their personal life cycle – under 30 years of age and married with young children. They shared a collective

Fig 5.9   The compact arrangement of houses on Punch Croft gave the neighbourhood greater spatial complexity and increased opportunities for associational behaviour.

enthusiasm and determination to make New Ash Green work and enjoy its benefits, and there was no difficulty in filling positions on the residents' societies. The 1960s has been seen as an era of great optimism and the concept of New Ash Green seemed to strike a chord with the prevailing attitude of young families looking for a suitable place to live. It was the wish to embrace something new, to experience a lifestyle that differed from the conventions of urban and suburban existence that underpinned the 'pioneering-spirit' that prevailed at the time. Architect Brian Hardcastle and his family moved into a house on Over Minnis in 1968. From day one he sensed an atmosphere of great optimism: 'In the early days people came because they wanted to be here. Generally speaking, they were young professionals, not necessarily wealthy but starting off their married lives, with young kids and enthusiastic about the place. There was so much enthusiasm about New Ash Green'.[61]

The inevitable consequence of like-minded residents sharing the same environment was a thriving social life, supported by the friendly and co-operative attitude of the Span management and sales teams based at their headquarters, the Manor House. Residents enjoyed the relaxed, informal atmosphere at the Manor House, where they found the staff more than willing to deal with any issues that might arise. Architect Jim Harbinson and his family were amongst the first to move into Punch Croft in 1968. He

recollects the feeling of conviviality that permeated the Village at the time:

> It was like a social experiment as much as an architectural experiment and that was what really attracted me to it… This was a totally new concept and was very exciting. We couldn't wait to get in! From day one there was a common endeavour to advance the social life. There was a party once-a-week in the Manor House which welcomed new residents. On the first day we moved in, two or three people called at the door to see if we needed anything or needed help. These were people who had arrived maybe a week before. So you had a tremendous community feeling about the whole place.[62]

As well as the parties held at the Manor House during 1968, Span planted 'Richard's Tree' to commemorate the birth of the first child in the Village (Fig. 5.10), followed by a champagne reception held at the Exhibition Hall next to the Manor House, hosted by Leslie Bilsby. The tennis courts built were intended to be the first stage of the conversion of the Manor House into a 'country club' for the residents, and tennis matches were held between sales staff and residents during the summer of 1968. Later in the year Span helped to organise a communal firework display. Those living in New Ash Green during this period describe it as an open, tolerant

Fig 5.10 Ceremonial Planting of Richard's Tree, Over Minnis, 1968, a Span-organised event to commemorate the birth of the first child in New Ash Green.

Fig 5.11 KL house type kitchen interior on Lambardes, where houses were larger in comparison to those built on other neighbourhoods.

Fig 5.12   View of Lambardes 'Triangle'. Subtle use of mounding ensured that paths were partially hidden when viewing across this triangular-shaped green.

and friendly place. Don Allbury, a manual worker from London and early Punch Croft resident, saw his neighbours who worked in the media professions as having a significant role in the development of the Village: 'There were some very influential people… Mike McNay who worked on *The Guardian* and Peter Sissons, so you had access to information'.[63] A proliferation of groups and societies was founded, including a Film Society, Wives Group, tennis and football clubs, Churches Association, and Scout and Brownie packs.[64] First published in May 1968, the Village journal *The New Ash Green Argus* gave the new community a 'voice'; early editions were produced using a photocopier and paper supplied by Span. With *Guardian* writer, Mike McNay as editor, *The Argus* provided a forum for residents to discuss important issues affecting their community.[65]

Regardless of the continual building work and landscaping at various stages of maturity, the environment that early residents entered was a very different one to anything they had experienced before. Even those who had previously lived in Span properties understood that New Ash Green represented Lyons's unique response to a rural setting. The design of New Ash Green also had an impact on the children living in the Village. Traversing the Village would mean crossing few, if any, main roads, and the generous provision of common greens to play on presented an endless variety of spaces to investigate. Margaret Burningham, who moved to Punch Croft in

1968, comments: 'I think it was a good place. Where we were our kitchen faced onto the green so your kids actually could play outside and you didn't have to worry about traffic. You had also got the nursery. I think it was absolutely brilliant for children, it was ideal'.[66]

Later neighbourhoods and the shopping centre

The Lambardes (Zone 5) and Knights Croft (Zone 3) neighbourhoods were put on sale in May 1968.[67] Lambardes, when complete, would consist of 57 houses taken from the KL (L for link) range. The KL range introduced six new house types to New Ash Green. Their design was derived from the L1 and T2Y house types built earlier at Templemere (1965). The most striking feature of these houses was the floor-to-ceiling windows at ground level. The continual evaluation and modification of house types had become an important part of Lyons's working method.[68] Lyons explained this approach: 'I am a rehasher, and I believe in rehashing, although I call it an evolutionary process…. I believe this evolutionary attitude towards one's work can sustain and discipline thinking'.[69] In contrast to the earlier neighbourhoods, the houses at Lambardes were larger in size, more spacious and built at a lower density (Fig. 5.11), and this was reflected in the prices (a three-bedroom KL1 cost £7,500 and a four/five-bedroom KL6 cost £11,000).[70] In terms of its planning, Lambardes emulated the staggered terraces and fan-shaped clusters first developed at Templemere, achieved by linking the houses using an angled entrance porch. Three arcing terraces to the west of the neighbourhood are used to create a triangular-shaped enclosure (Fig. 5.12). To give additional visual interest to this space, the displaced soil generated during the building of the houses was used to create a subtle mounding, which gradually slopes up around the edge before sweeping down to the centre of the space.

The building of the first phase of Knights Croft began in July 1968 and introduced elements of standardisation to the configuration of house terraces and planting schemes.[71] Allowing the houses to follow the contours of the land, together with the ingenious use of planting, made the use of standardised terraces undetectable (Fig. 5.13). Whilst still respecting the overall aesthetic that had been established, the design of each neighbourhood at this point followed Lyons's policy of experimentation and improvement. Deemed a medium density neighbourhood, Knights Croft did not include the K2N or K3N house type, but did include one new design, the single-storey K1A (Fig. 5.14). At an early stage in the building of New Ash Green, Lyons felt that provision had to be made for residents from an older age group; the K1A two-bedroomed bungalow was a response to this need. This lower-priced dwelling would contribute to Span's aim of encouraging the development of a balanced community that catered for the 'family in depth'.[72]

With Over Minnis completed and Punch Croft under construction, Span began building the first phase of the shopping centre. As a comprehensive development, there were plans to build a public house, old people's home, primary school, library, county clinic and church on an adjacent site to the north of the shopping centre and an office building and community building to the south. When complete, the shopping centre would consist of 48 units providing floor areas of 4,800 square metres for commercial use and 450 square metres for residential use (Fig. 5.15). With provision made for two large landscaped car parks, it was envisaged that the shopping centre would attract customers from New Ash Green and neighbouring areas, as Lyons described: 'We thought that the place could become a kind of out-of-town shopping centre, because there is very little good shopping for miles around. So we set out to achieve a wide range of good quality shops'.[73]

The concept of a fully-pedestrianised shopping street was a novel one for the time, as was the idea of shops at both ground and upper floor level. The shopping street, known as 'The Row', was flanked on the northern side by an arcade with Upper Street North, a second tier of shops, offices and restaurant (with open terrace) above. The shop units and a stair tower at the northern end of Upper Street North are intersected by a viewing tower, which gave residents a glimpse of the Village from its highest vantage point. The Row was divided on the southern side and leads to a block of studios accessed by stairs. To ensure the design of the shopping centre was in sympathy with the Village aesthetic, Lyons employed mono-pitch elements, soft stock and brindle engineering bricks,

Fig 5.13 Two terraces on Knights Croft (170–179), where intelligent landscaping made the use of standardised terraces virtually undetectable.

Fig 5.14 K1A bungalows were built on two designated areas within Knights Croft and were intended to be bought by residents from an older age group.

asbestos tiles and brushed aggregate walkways. Tom McKenna recalls how Lyons's sense of perfectionism manifested itself during the laying of the engineering bricks:

> He was very fussy, there was a lot of pulling down and putting back. But that was because there was a lack of skill on the part of those who were doing it, when I say lack of skill it was very new. Suddenly you're getting these weird shapes, bends and turns and the setting out baffled the contractors. Your setting out had to be done with such precision, the setting of those steps was mind-boggling.[74]

Eric Brindle was the first tenant in the shopping centre, opening the Village Pharmacy in 1969 and living with his young family in the maisonette above the shop.[75] To celebrate the official opening of the centre on 7th June 1969, Span organised 'Village Day',[76] hosted by the Radio 1 disc jockey, Peter Murray. Attractions included a children's fancy dress competition, rodeo show, flying display, Morris dancing, and Punch and Judy show, as well as various stalls run by residents (Fig. 5.16). Fireworks and two live bands provided the evening entertainment at a 'Dancing in the Street' party. By the end of 1969, the Village Pharmacy had been joined by an off-licence, greengrocer, supermarket, fishmonger, hardware store, newsagent and two banks.

Span in difficulty
Shortly after houses had been made available on Lambardes and Knights Croft in 1968, house sales in New Ash Green reached a new peak. But, as the year progressed, sales dropped as the country's economic slump and resultant mortgage squeeze continued to worsen. As a means of generating new sales, Lyons had to design a range of house types that mortgage lenders would find more appealing. To further rationalise house construction and control costs on Millfield (Zone 9), Jack Gostling, a director of Building Span, was appointed production manager. This meant that once Lyons had overseen the construction of the prototype houses, he was no longer in a position to make design amendments, although he did continue to supervise the layout and landscaping of the neighbourhood. The more uniform and formal arrangement of the 169 K2NA and K2NB houses on Millfield was similar to that used at Corner Green, Blackheath (1959), and were sold at just under £5,500. The houses were built using a brick cross-wall construction dispensing with the steel A-frame, window openings were reduced to a more conventional size and pitched roofs were introduced (Fig. 5.17). Whilst these houses could be deemed to represent a compromise on behalf of the architect, they were still of a high standard and relied upon New Ash Green's indigenous palette of colours and materials. Despite the earlier efforts made to increase house sales, news received by Span in May 1969 placed their hopes for the future development of New Ash Green in severe jeopardy. The GLC

Fig 5.15   The Row in the shopping centre, where the dense massing of angular forms was used to convey the impression of organic growth over a period of time.

Fig 5.16   New Ash Green Village Day 7th June, 1969, a social event organised by Span to celebrate the opening of the shopping centre.

Fig 5.17 Economic considerations gave the K2NB houses on Millfield a slightly more conventional appearance with smaller windows and pitched roofs.

Fig 5.18 The design of the 'D' range was Lyons's final attempt to encourage the sale of houses in greater numbers at New Ash Green.

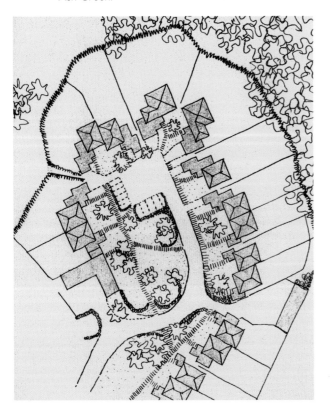

had decided not to purchase their first tenant neighbourhood in New Ash Green due to its own financial problems.[77] The GLC's decision not only added to Span's monetary concerns, it also clearly endangered its aim of achieving social balance. Driven by financial necessity as opposed to aesthetics, Span decided that new neighbourhoods would be restricted to no more than five house types, varying in cost from a bungalow to the detached house type at the top of the price range. Like the K range, the D range of houses was derived from the use of a basic floor plan with either a single or double-storey projection. The houses were of a more conventional construction with a hipped roof. A close examination of the typical layout plan produced by Lyons for the D range of house types proves how far he was prepared to modify the design principles established in the composition of the earlier Span-built neighbourhoods (Fig. 5.18). Road access is permitted to the very centre of these miniature communities, which minimised the size of the landscaped areas. Separate integral garages would be approached via individual driveways with each household given a much larger private garden.[78]

The mortgage squeeze of autumn 1969 hit New Ash Green badly as lenders regarded Span houses as too avant-garde and, therefore, a risky investment. With debts now standing at £2,000,000, Span's backers, Royal London, commissioned a report from the estate agents Connells, which criticised Span as misguided and ill-equipped to complete the development. The report was also critical of the design and the layout (only for the design conscious), which had led to the creation of insular communities. In seeking advice from an organisation guided purely by commercial and financial considerations, the relationship between Span and its backers had irrevocably changed and, in November 1969, Connells was given complete managerial control of New Ash Green. This led to the cancellation of 42 house sales and the withdrawal of the last remaining company offering mortgages there.

Believing all options to be now exhausted, Eric Lyons terminated his working relationship with Span in December 1969 and all building work in New Ash Green came to a halt. He commented in *The Evening News* on January 2nd 1970: 'I have the feeling of being at the end of an era'.[79] In *The Times* Lyons's described his decision as a 'reciprocal process', adding 'It's a wrench of course... There have obviously been differences of policy, and difficulties, but I feel that in the end I'd reached the end of the line. It comes too from my own unrest, I feel I've got a lot more to give. I want to find myself expanding into new fields'.[80] It was Lyons's status as 'consultant architect' that gave him the freedom to make this type of decision as he explained: 'I've always kept independent. I wanted independence so that I could always walk out. My independent judgement was part of my professional position'.[81] Span attempted to remain positive,

Fig 5.19   New Ash Green County Primary School, Eric Lyons and Partners, 1971. Lyons returned to complete Phase 1 of the School, his last architectural undertaking at New Ash Green.

indicating that New Ash Green would now be completed during 1977–80; however it was a difficult situation, summarised by Span salesman Mike Jaggard: 'No building society or Greater London Council will give mortgages... It is a vicious circle, we cannot build houses if people cannot get mortgages'.[82]

During this period the country was experiencing a national slowdown in house building. Connells announced that when building started again at New Ash Green, a more conventional style of design would be adopted. Bilsby and Townsend recognised the philosophical disparity between Span and those now dictating the future development of New Ash Green, and realised that their position was now untenable. With residents barely coming to terms with the loss of Eric Lyons, Bilsby and Townsend both elected to resign, giving up their directorships on the Span board. As a means of avoiding the appointment of receivers, Bilsby and Townsend were replaced by representatives from Royal London and, although Span did lose a large undisclosed amount of money, they were never declared bankrupt. Bovis Holdings Ltd bought New Ash Green for £2.65 million in January 1971 and its architects, Barton Willmore and Partners, produced a report that June, giving a clear indication of the organisation's future plans for the Village.

The form of the new neighbourhoods was to be more conventional in terms of design and planning with landscaped areas reduced in size. Furthermore, in promotional material produced by Bovis, the original concept underpinning Span's notion of a modern integrated community was underplayed (indeed Bovis unsuccessfully attempted to remove the residents' societies and Village Association). Despite this, there was a determination amongst the residents to do what they could to keep the 'dream' alive and in December 1970 a group formed the New Ash Green Amenity Society, an early newsletter outlining their position: 'The committee wants to see the village develop along the lines originally envisaged, to become a fully serviced community in the country'.[83]

The Span legacy

Even before the withdrawal of Eric Lyons and the resignations of Leslie Bilsby and Geoff Townsend, a social mix did exist and the design of the Village and residents' societies had engendered positive social interaction and a sense of pride and ownership. The Village was at its most vibrant during the 1970s as a result of the efforts of pioneering residents to uphold the concept and ethos that underpinned Span's vision. Those moving into the early Bovis-built neighbourhoods were also active participants in the social life of the Village, and trade at the shopping centre improved greatly with the arrival of the high-quality shops for which Lyons and Span had hoped. Working with another contractor, Lyons did, however, return to see the completion of his design for the first phase of New Ash Green's County Primary School in 1971 (Fig. 5.19).[84] A series

Fig 5.20 Aerial photograph – New Ash Green, July 1970, showing the scale of infrastructure work at various stages of completion.

of studies produced during the 1970s and 1980s confirmed that 'an integrated and relatively self-contained community' existed.[85] New Ash Green was now considered a fashionable place to live.

Span was a unique organisation; bold, idealistic and ambitious and, working in collaboration with Eric Lyons, they were able to utilise the expertise of one of the country's greatest domestic architects and creative thinkers. Accounts have implied that Span was not a commercially-minded operation, but it did adjust its designs and building program in response to the financial position at New Ash Green. Furthermore, the infrastructure costs incurred by Span were considerable; these included the building of new roads and laying an eight-mile sewer. An aerial photograph taken in 1970 illustrates the scale of infrastructure work at various stages of completion (Fig. 5.20). This included the second phase of the shopping centre; Lambardes, Knights Croft and Millfield; preliminary ground work had begun on the primary school and Manor Forstal neighbourhood; and roads and drainage had been installed on Redhill Wood. Perhaps Span would have survived the country's economic situation if they had been able to implement a more ruthless business-oriented contingency strategy without sacrificing their core values. Span were also victims of nefarious delaying tactics and the appalling economic situation that existed at the time. Due to mortgage problems or inability to sell houses, 226 people who had put down deposits for houses at New Ash Green had to withdraw. This demonstrates that Span was correct in its assumption that a market existed for the houses they were building at New Ash Green.

New Ash Green now has 24 neighbourhoods, far exceeding the number proposed by Span, and land sold to other developers has resulted in the use of architectural styles that have little or no relationship to earlier Span or Bovis houses. However, despite the changes that have occurred, New Ash Green still possesses a sense of community and continues to provide an agreeable environment in which to live. Don Allbury, an early resident, confirms that buying a house in New Ash Green represented more than a financial investment: 'The Village started as a concept to make the best place for people to live, work and bring up children without infrastructures being imposed on them from a previous society'.[86]

Many drawings exist of unrealised designs produced by Lyons for New Ash Green, although it is the drawing of Zone 14, Capelands, that provides the best clue to the next phase of development for the Village.[87] Lyons had intended to use the KL range of houses, first seen on Lambardes, arranged in various circular formations. The application of Lyons's policy of 'continuous improvement' leads one to speculate on the even greater levels of design excellence that would have been achieved.

Endnotes

1. *The Guardian*, 11 June 1971, quotes Eric Lyons from a 1968 interview.

2. Hessie Sachs and Beth Prince, *New Ash Green until March 1970*, Sociological Research Unit, University College London, 1970, pp. 27–28. Ernest Haynes had previously been invited to provide funding for a number of private housing projects. Haynes was already aware of Span's reputation and had been to see Parkleys in Surrey, where he immediately recognised the quality of the architecture and its landscaped setting. In 1962 one third of the equity of Span was acquired by Royal London and Haynes became chair of both Span Developments Ltd and Span-Kent (New Ash Green) Limited.

3. *A new village near Hartley Kent, New Ash Green*, Span publication, 1962, Section 1, Introduction. Northfield was designated as an area to be used for light industry. By 1966, Lyons had drawn a preliminary plan for the site and Span had begun negotiations with various companies. Span failed to receive approval from Kent County Council for the scheme.

4. *ibid.*, Section 2, The Community.

5. Geoff Townsend, interview with author, Angmering, September 1997.

6. *op. cit.*, Sachs and Prince, 1970, p. 44. (Appeal document S.R.L. Investments, 1964, p. 7).

7. It was these infrastructure costs that would ultimately contribute to Span's mounting debts and ultimate demise.

8. *op. cit.*, Sachs and Prince, 1970, p. 45. Representatives of the Kent County Council added that Span's intrusion into the proposed extension of the green belt would result in a 'moth eaten... green carpet'. New Ash Green planning permission enquiry, 7–10 July 1964.

9. Recognising the political implications of dealing with such a potentially controversial issue, Joseph refused to make a decision so close to the election.

10. Letter to Ashurst, Morris, Crisp and Co. from the Ministry of Housing and Local Government dated 26 November 1964.

11. *ibid.* This letter of confirmation also expressed the Ministry's belief that the benefits resulting from the development were likely to outweigh the disadvantages.

12. *op. cit.*, Sachs and Prince, 1970 p. 1, quoting from a BBC Home Service programme, 1964.

13. Ivor Cunningham, interview with author, Mill House Studio, East Molesey, 26 August 1997.

14. 'RDC threat to defy Housing Minister – Approval "Over My Dead Body"', unidentified local newspaper, 4 December 1964. A number of suggestions that were recorded on that day and eventually put into effect included delaying the legal process to allow the closure of internal roads to through traffic, to allow on-site construction work to be carried out more efficiently, and an insistence on procedural correctness that verged on the absurd. Drawings of neighbourhood plans, house types, the positioning of new roads and the main sewer for New Ash Green were scrutinised in minute detail and at great length.

15. Handwritten notes for an article 'Town and Around', 21 September 1967. Source unknown.

16. House of Lords (Hansard), *Development in Kent Area of Green Belt*, 21 December 1964, pp. 683–4.

17. Anthony Norton, *The Hartley and Ash Rural Preservation Society Minute Book* 1965, March 1965.

18. *ibid.*, Summary of meeting with Mr Reeves, 4 November 1965.

19. A number of photographs that accompanied the Memorandum were of areas surrounding the site Span had acquired and not the land they intended to build on.

20. *House of Commons, Official Report*, Parliamentary debates (Hansard), Wednesday 8 December 1965, volume 722, no. 23; Thursday 9 December 1965, Oral Answers, pp. 601–2.

21. Zone 1 was given the name Over Minnis.

22. 'Council Considers Masterplan for the New Village', *The Reporter*, 7 January 1966, p. 14.

23. 'Architect Welcomes inquiry on New Village', *The Daily Mail*, January 1966.

24. *Building* Interview, 'A New Lease for Lyons', *Building*, 18 October 1974, p. 92.

25. New Ash Green publicity brochure, Span publication, 1967, p. 3.

26. Prospective residents on Redhill Wood would be required to commission an architect from an approved panel to design their house. Panellists included Richard and Su Rogers, who had also been asked to design a Sports Pavilion for New Ash Green. It was to remain unbuilt.

27. *op. cit.*, 'The neighbourhoods Residents Society', New Ash Green publicity brochure, p. 10. See also Chapter 6.

28. The work of the Village Association was to be directed by the Council of Management, composed of six representative members and three consultant members, qualified in architecture, landscaping, planning, estate management or an associated field. *The Memorandum and Articles of Association of New Ash Green Village Association Limited* (September 1967) specified the formation of an Amenity Committee. This Committee, consisting of six members appointed by the Council of Management, was given the overall responsibility for assessing the viability of proposed alterations to buildings, landscaping, roads, paths and walls.

29. *op. cit.*, 'The neighbourhood Residents Society', New Ash Green publicity brochure, p. 10.

30. Caroline Moorhead, 'Building gardens with houses in them', *The Times*, 21 July 1975.

31. Eric Lyons, 'Domestic Building and Speculative Development', *RIBA Journal*, May 1958, p. 224. Lecture given at RIBA, 25 March 1958.

32. *op. cit.,* New Ash Green publicity brochure, p. 2.

33. Eric Ambrose (interview with Eric Lyons), 'New Ash Green, New Village, New Way of Life', *Ideal Home,* October 1967, p. 53.

34. *ibid.,* Denis Thomas (interview with Leslie Bilsby), p. 49.

35. The name New Ash Green, an amalgam of the names of the two former farms, can be cited as further evidence of an acknowledgement of the past.

36. Leslie Bilsby, 'Housing-Needs of the future in the private sector', *The Architects' Journal Information Library,* 15 May 1968, p. 1114.

37. *op. cit.,* Thomas (interview with Eric Lyons) p. 53. See Chapter 2 for a discussion of the Garden City Movement and also post-war new towns as 'self-contained and balanced communities'.

38. *The more we are together, Eric Lyons, the Architect and Suburbia,* BBC 1 programme, 4 May 1968. Director, Barrie Gavin.

39. *ibid.*

40. External changes to K range houses included modifications to window proportions, use of different brick, new door design.

41. Eric Lyons, 'Too often we justify our ineptitudes by moral postures', *RIBA Journal,* May 1968, p. 219. An address delivered at the RIBA, 6 February 1968.

42. John Donat (interview with Eric Lyons), 'Mid-Span', *Building,* 16 July 1976, p. 79.

43. Tom McKenna, interview with author, 1998.

44. In general terms, the use of a brick podium surmounted by a second storey clad in vertical wooden boarding was evident in houses designed in the 1950s and 1960s by the architects Leslie Gooday, Peter Moro, Basil Spence and Peter Womersley. These houses, like those at New Ash Green, would be open plan and light-filled due to the use of large areas of glazing. Needless to say there existed a recognisable idiom, although Lyons demonstrated how this type of house could be rationalised in its production and made more accessible to the general public.

45. For those who wished to pay, optional extras were available, such as the laying of woodblock floors, the plastering of internal brick walls to a smooth finish and the insertion of sliding glass panels into the kitchen storage/divider.

46. Eric Lyons, 'Architects' Pattern Books', The President's column, *RIBA Journal,* September 1976, p. 370.

47. *op. cit.,* Eric Lyons, 1968.

48. To avail themselves of the Span Shopping Service, residents would order groceries from a given list, the groceries would then be delivered to their house. This service is an early example of Span's wish build a good relationship with residents. Span had also discussed the idea of incorporating shops and accommodation for the elderly and council tenants into the early neighbourhoods. The shops on Over Minnis and nursery school on Punch Croft were the only examples of policy that would be abandoned.

49. Eric Lyons, 'Private Housing', *RIBA Journal,* May 1977, p. 182.

50. *op. cit.,* Eric Lyons, 1968, p. 219.

51. *op. cit.,* Sachs and Prince, 1970, p. 75.

52. The design of the pathways was considered at early sketch stage, with Lyons formulating the various configurations, which would lead people naturally to where they wanted to go.

53. *op. cit.,* Eric Lyons, 1968, p. 220.

54. *op. cit.,* Eric Lyons, 1976, p. 370.

55. *op. cit.,* Sachs and Prince, 1970, p. 23.

56. 'Eric Lyons: Architect President', *Architects' Journal,* 30 July 1975, p. 250.

57. The K2N was originally sold at a discount price of £4,700. Part of the deposit was paid through the owner agreeing to decorate the house with materials supplied by Span. The remaining part of the deposit was paid to Span at a rate of £6 per week over a six-month period. To qualify for this deal this had to be a first house purchase and the husband had to be 21–30 years of age.

58. *op. cit.,* Leslie Bilsby, 1968, p. 1111.

59. As a means of encouraging early sales Span offered a discount of £600 to buyers if contracts were exchanged by November 1967.

60. *op. cit., ,* Leslie Bilsby, 1968, p. 1111.

61. Brian Hardcastle, interview with author, 23 August 1997.

62. Jim Harbinson, interview with author, 28 July 1997.

63. Don Allbury, interview with author, 21 August 1997.

64. For the football team, Span provided the land, goal posts, pitch marking machine and demountable shed.

65. It is also interesting to note that when *The Argus* was redesigned for issue number 6 (October 1969), the title adopted the same typeface (Eurostile extended bold) that Span had used for the signage and publicity material for New Ash Green.

66. Margaret Burningham, interview with author, May 1998.

67. When Over Minnis and Punch Croft were put up for sale, houses could be bought on any part of each neighbourhood. This put pressure on Building Span who would then have to work simultaneously on a number of terraces at one time. To ease this situation, the Lambardes and Knights Croft neighbourhoods were both built in two phases.

68. Minor changes were made to the internal fittings and external detailing on the K2 houses at New Ash Green.

69. *op. cit.,* Eric Lyons, 1968, p. 219.

70. The larger KL house type had extras, such as woodblock floors and downstairs 'walk-in' shower unit fitted as standard.

71. This included the use of straight terraces consisting of one house type and the same number of houses. Another technique implemented was the use of repeated staggered terraces of mixed house types. On certain parts of the neighbourhood an individual terrace would be situated to an adjacent terrace in a mirror image arrangement. This method indicated a

rationalisation of the building programme, moving away from the use of the arbitrary composition of the terraces as seen on Punch Croft.

72. *op. cit.,* Sachs and Prince, 1970, p. 67. The parents of a number of the early residents at New Ash Green moved into the bungalows on Knights Croft.

73. Eric Lyons, 'New Ash Green village centre, Architect's account', *Architect's Journal,* 4 July 1973, p. 22.

74. *op. cit.,* Tom Mckenna interview, 1998.

75. Shop tenants became members of the Centre Society which shared similar responsibilities as the neighbourhood residents' societies. As a means of maintaining aesthetic standards, Span set up an advisory design panel for the shopping centre. Tenants had to consult and comply with their recommendations on the design of the façade of their shop.

76. The second Village Day was coordinated by a group of residents who had formed the Village Day Committee. New Ash Green Village Day has been an annual event since 1969.

77. The country's economic slump and subsequent credit squeeze contributed to the GLC's decision not to take their first allocation of 135 houses (Zone 6 Coltstead). The GLC's Finance Committee said that it was experiencing a shortage of money for new capital work and that the interest on which money could be borrowed was very high and would place a burden on the next generation of ratepayers. With the GLC having recently passed from Labour to Conservative control it has also been suggested that the newly-elected council was, in general, reluctant to participate in private building schemes.

78. A site near Lambardes was considered as the location for the first of the miniature communities.

79. Robert Langton, '"Village of the Future" Homes expert Quits', *The Evening News,* 2 January 1970, p. 9.

80. 'Lyons leaves Span', *The Times,* 1 January 1970.

81. *op. cit.,* John Donat, 1976, p. 82.

82. Mike Jaggard, 'New Ash Green Mortgages Ban?', *The Dartford and Swanley Chronicle,* 26 June 1970.

83. *New Ash Green Amenity Society Newsletter,* December 1970. A key member of this Society was Punch Croft resident and architectural historian, John Newman.

84. Disagreements over the sale price of the proposed site and government expenditure cuts had prevented the school from being built earlier. Externally the building relies on the features and materials common to the earlier Span-built designs, which included the use of mono-pitch roofs, soft stock brick and vertical wooden cladding. The assembly hall was crowned with a distinctive triangulated skylight. The interior exploits the principle of open plan with doorless classrooms facing onto central activity areas and enclosed reading bays. The design of the school was intended to create a friendly and humane environment, the single-storey building with low sweeping eaves giving an intimate scale, which would not overwhelm the pupils. Phase Two (unbuilt) of the school included a swimming pool and lodge.

85. *op. cit.,* Sachs and Prince, 1970, p. 184.

86. *op. cit.,* Don Allbury interview, 1997.

87. These drawings are part of the uncatalogued archive of the Eric Lyons Cunningham Partnership. The plan for Capelands (Zone 14) is on the same sheet as that for Lambardes (Zone 5): Drawing Number 1037/230 *Zones 5+14* by Ivor Cunningham, dated 27 May 1968.

CHAPTER SIX

Community and common
space: the role of
residents' societies

Barbara Simms

"The architects designed the landscape
hand-in-hand with the design of the
dwelling; and it was the integration of all
the elements...that created an ambience
and scale hitherto unknown in housing for
ordinary people. It created identity of place."

Eric Lyons

When Eric Lyons and Geoffrey Townsend resumed practice together in 1945, the depressed economic climate meant that private schemes were of little interest to most architects, many of whom were, by then, employed by local authorities to provide much-needed public housing.[1] Notwithstanding, Lyons and Townsend chose to pursue a vision of a new style of private estate development to provide 'affordable, well-designed homes in landscape settings, which would foster a village community atmosphere'.[2] Immersed in the euphoria of post-war visions of England – 'to provide pleasant homes for all in beautiful towns and villages and in noble cities, set against a thriving and unspoiled countryside'[3] – they set out their plans to create 'total environments'; buildings, planting, roads, car parks and children's play spaces integrated within 'a pleasant and stimulating background for day-to-day living'.[4] Lyons passionately believed that by providing a visual sense of community and involving people in their space – enclosed courtyards and garden squares, where children safely play and neighbours congregate; open plan rooms with picture windows to view and be viewed; and the segregation of pedestrians and cars to encourage residents to walk through the communal areas – he could provide a more positive and satisfying environment than that offered by traditional suburban housing.[5]

To safeguard the visual unity of the building exteriors and the open spaces according to Lyons's intentions, Geoffrey Townsend was determined to solve the problem of how the common parts of such schemes could be successfully maintained and managed. The resulting sense of community, engendered by mandatory participation in a residents' society, and the care of communal spaces

by an associated scheme of management, has been considered by some to be the greatest achievement of Span, its 'most important contribution to suburbia's design. Its benefits are both aesthetic and social… they have reminded us of the machinery by which communal gardens can be maintained in speculative development'.[6] This chapter considers the contribution of residents' societies and their schemes of management to the conservation of the design intention, character and sense of community on Span estates.

Designing a community

Eric Lyons was scathing about the modern movement's treatment of landscape – 'They had no philosophy about external space'[7] but, nonetheless, his belief in economic 'group living' may well have been stimulated by the social ideology of committed modernist Walter Gropius, with whom he worked in the mid-1930s in the architectural practice of Maxwell Fry.[8] Lyons would, undoubtedly, also have been aware of the well-publicised communal housing experiments in mainland Europe, particularly in Germany and Sweden,[9] and Fry's involvement in the MARS (Modern Architectural Research) Group, which in 1938 was planning an exhibition on how London could be refashioned into neighbourhood units with communal gardens. Furthermore, during the war years, Lyons's interest in housing design issues would most likely have been fuelled by the contemporary writings of the housing consultant Elizabeth Denby and the landscape architect Christopher Tunnard.

The visits of Denby and others to France, Germany and Austria contributed to the British enthusiasm for housing estates that

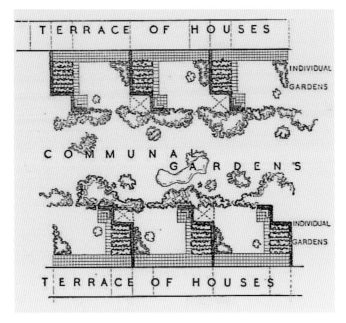

Fig 6.1 A detail of the layout of terraced houses, each with a private garden extending into communal gardens, as proposed by Christopher Tunnard.

garden, 'small enough to be worked by any owner', extending into communal gardens, reminiscent of the early 19th-century 'squares' on London's Ladbroke Grove Estate (Kensington), 'the germ of the idea of the Common-garden',[12] rather than their earlier, railed counterparts on the Bedford and Grosvenor Estates (see below).

From the mid-1940s, after the insecurity of the war years and post-war relocation of families, the concept of developing communities was fundamental to the design of new housing schemes in Britain. This was recognised in the 1944 Ministry of Health Report[13] and Patrick Abercrombie's key *Greater London Plan*,[14] which recommended planning new housing in neighbourhood units, without relinquishing the modernist vision of a new city that was 'clean, humane and beautiful'.[15] The Manual to the Housing Act 1949[16] provided guidelines on how 'unity and character are best achieved', suggesting the use of terraces, semi-detached houses and blocks of flats in low-density areas and a mixture of three-storey terraces and multi-storey flats and maisonettes in others.[17] The Ministry of Health even published advice on laying out gardens in the 'charming tradition of English cottage gardens'[18] and the landscaping of communal areas on estates, recommending the planting of trees, shrubs, and climbers and the provision of 'natural' open ground where children could play safely – the emphasis was on understanding space in terms of its many functions.[19]

Landscape architect Sylvia Crowe was concerned that the design intention for communal areas, often based on the English Landscape Garden model of 'an open stretch of grass and a few fine trees', was not always in harmony with residents' needs (somewhere for children to play and for 'adolescents and perhaps the father of the family' to mess about outside, for hanging the washing out of doors and sitting out in the summer), recommending that 'space division and sense of enclosure is essential'.[20] She proposed Scandinavian-style landscaping around flats as a model, perhaps influenced by her visit to Sven Hermelin's Star flats in Stockholm (Fig. 6.2), which she called 'a distinct form of garden art', that had 'caught the spirit and condition peculiar to its place and time' and made a 'distinctive contribution to the problems of creating a landscape for an urban democracy'.[21] Hermelin's broad masses of planting of a few species was in scale with the three-storey blocks, but he had also created an 'intimacy' by lavish planting, changes of level and ground patterning to divide the space. In the private sector, Crowe praised the 'continued and careful management' of communal gardens of London's Ladbroke Grove Estate, where 'trees and groups of shrubs effect a loose, informal space division which makes it possible to give a measure of separation to different uses without destroying the overall unity of design'. However, she cautioned against the lack of privacy, stating that a shared garden 'cannot supply all needs' and that residents will also seek out their own space, their own

incorporated flats with private balconies and communal amenities, including gardens, playgrounds, libraries and shops.[10] Denby was also inspired by the use of the traditional English garden square and terraced cottages with gardens as a model for new housing in Holland, Sweden and Germany. Promoted as the 'All-Europe working class house' at the Ideal Home Exhibition 1939, Denby hoped that the proposed offset terraces of flat-roofed, three-bedroomed houses with living room and kitchen, rear garden and open plan front, was a model for social housing in Britain that would facilitate the development of mixed class estates and create a sense of community in urban life.

Tunnard's seminal book, *Gardens in the Modern Landscape*, also addressed the issue of communal garden areas, proposing the (unexecuted) development of Claremont Landscape Gardens, Surrey, as a 'typical neighbourhood garden scheme' for 6,000 people.[11] Living accommodation was to be arranged in blocks of flats and terraces of houses, with facilities (shops, schools, cafes, library and social centre) to provide 'for the immediate needs of the neighbourhood unit'. The Claremont scheme also included private and communal gardens, allotments, play and sports areas, woodland walks and rides, a theatre and botanic garden, 'arranged as a related whole' linked by low maintenance landscape planting. A detail of the layout of the terraced houses (Fig. 6.1) shows each with a private 'glorietta'. Residents' desire for privacy was also considered by landscape architect Peter Shepheard, who suggested that 'what is needed... is a series of gradations in degree of privacy' from the living room through the private garden to the 'comparatively public, or at least, neighbourly aspect of the common [garden]'.[22]

From the early days of the new towns and in large-scale housing developments, despite government guidance on designing for cohesive and responsible communities, there had been indications that, although some provided 'a pleasant and neighbourly background for real community life',[23] others were neither providing scope for personal 'gloriettas', nor the more fundamental social support and communal facilities that had been envisaged. In a government publication of the early 1950s, Frederick Gibberd, architect and masterplanner of Harlow New Town (1946), reminded his readers (presumably planners and designers) of the basic principles of good housing design: 'the term "design" in connection with residential areas means the arrangement of the various parts – the houses, roads, paths and so on – in such a way that they function properly, can be built economically and give pleasure to look at'.[24] Reinforcing the disappointing findings of the Central Housing Committee Report 1948 that residents took 'little pride or interest' in the appearance of their housing estates, he stressed that each area must have its own identity to 'give the residents the feeling that it belongs to them'.

Maintenance and management

Closely allied to the issue of designing to encourage community and a sense of ownership was that of the maintenance of communal space. By 1948 this was uppermost in the minds of planners, particularly those involved in the design of local authority housing schemes – 'design and maintenance are inseparably related' stated T. F. Thomson[25] – confirming Peter Youngman's concerns in a talk given at the Housing Centre, London:

> It is... no use planning in terms of communal open space, first if you do not provide for the landscaping of that space, second if you do not provide communal maintenance. Without the first you get an unbearable dreariness, without the second you very quickly get a garden slum.... The problems they present must be solved, before ever aesthetics of design are considered.[26]

Sylvia Crowe expressed similar thoughts in an article the following year,[27] one of many on the topic published in the *Journal of the Institute of Landscape Architects*.[28] Peter Shepheard proposed that 'tenants in common' should be responsible for the maintenance of communal gardens and that it should have 'the character of a village green'.[29] Christopher Tunnard, writing on community gardens ten years earlier, had also focused on the need to consider a planned

Fig 6.2   At the Star Flats, Stockholm, Sven Hermelin created an 'intimacy' by lavish planting, changes of level and ground patterning to divide the space.

and sustainable maintenance scheme from the outset.[30] Viewing communal gardens as flexible and multi-purpose, he recommended planting 'of the simplest character for economy of upkeep':

> The whole of the upkeep could be carried out by the tenants or employees of the estate under the direction of a committee whose activities could be decided by the tenants themselves. The committee would have jurisdiction over the functions of the communal areas and the proper conduct of their users. Only co-operative effort can achieve the common garden and ensure its permanent value.[31]

Operating within the private sector, Eric Lyons and Geoffrey Townsend took as their model for the management of communal space neither European nor British social housing, but the London squares and the crescents and circles of Bath. Lyons often referred to the late 18th-century squares of the Duke of Bedford's estate in London's Bloomsbury, with their elegant terraced housing and shared gardens, as an influence on his design philosophy, but their management structure also proved an inspiration. Gardens in these squares were exclusively for residents' use, a precedent set in the 17th century to prevent the despoliation seen in residential squares with public access.[32] However, even in the 1680s the residents of both Soho Square and Golden Square, as part of their house leases,

Fig 6.3   The small development at Oaklands, Whitton, near Twickenham, was the first opportunity
for Lyons and Townsend to translate their ideas of communal management into practice.

were expected to contribute to the upkeep of the central gardens.
In Soho Square this amounted to ten shillings per annum 'towards
the makeing and keeping in repaire the Rayles, Payles, Fountain
and Garden in the middle of the said Square [sic]'; whilst in Golden
Square the lessees were expected 'to pay... for all charges in posts,
rayls, and other ornaments or materials fixed, or employed... for
dividing, distinguishing and adorning the same [sic]'.[33] However,
lack of regular maintenance over subsequent years resulted in the
residents' dissatisfaction with the condition of their squares and, in
St James's Square, a petition to Parliament for leave to present a bill
for its better maintenance.

The St James's Square Act 1726 was the catalyst for many garden
squares to apply for, and be granted, their own Acts and thus take
control of the design, maintenance and use of their communal space.
In Golden Square, its Act of Parliament 1750 authorised residents

to elect from their number thirteen trustees to 'inclose, pave, repair,
enlighten, adorn, and beautify [sic]' the square and to raise an annual
rate from each house.[34] Following these precedents, the Duke of
Bedford (building the Bloomsbury squares from 1776) also required
that speculative lessees of the land should be responsible for the
enclosure and planting of the garden squares. In the footsteps of
these Georgian landowners and property speculators, Lyons and
Townsend used the device of leasehold tenure and maintenance
of common space, through the formation of residents' societies, to
manage Span estates and enforce covenants to conserve
their character.

The role of residents' societies
The first opportunity for Lyons and Townsend to translate these
ideas of communal management into practice came in 1948 at
Whitton, near Twickenham, on a small site (later named Oaklands)

surrounded on three sides by the back gardens of houses. Here, Lyons altered an existing design for a row of 24 maisonettes and houses with individual plots, into four two-storey blocks of six flats with shared garden space between them. A contemporary article in *The Builder* notes that this scheme, with 'some communal amenities and responsibilities provided for' was 'one of the few post-war ventures of this nature carried out by private enterprise'.[35] A contemporary photograph shows one of the blocks, complete with family scene (Fig. 6.3), accompanied by a description of the amenities (living room with outlook over the common gardens, laundry-hanging spaces, fuel store, pram and cycle stores) and an explanation of the workings of what was the first 'Span' residents' society: 'The occupiers contribute a small sum which pays for the maintenance of the gardens and the cleaning of the common staircases, etc… [and] have their own committee which administers the expenditure. The gardens have been laid out, but the borders and tree planting will be put in this autumn'.[36] In the absence of any known English precedents, Townsend formed this first residents' society under the auspices of the Friendly Society Act, legislation introduced in 1793 'for the better support of poor persons'.[37]

Townsend would have been familiar with the concept and aims of Friendly Societies, which reached their peak in 1945 with 18,000 societies, embracing a wide range of activities, including building societies, savings banks and trade unions. A Friendly Society was a non-profit-making organisation, formed when a number (unlimited) of individuals joined together to achieve a common financial or social purpose. They were bound by rules devised by the members and which could be varied subject to a majority of members agreeing, based on one member one vote. When asked in an interview how Span had 'effected a revolution', Lyons's reply focused on the development of these self-regulating communities: 'We create neighbourhoods in which owners take a 99-year lease of their dwelling, become their own managers and do not rely on others to manage them. Although Span retains the freehold ground rent it does not interfere with the management of the estates'.[38] However, by retaining ownership of the land Span could ensure that the character of the estates was conserved by preventing alteration to the structure and external appearance of the houses.[39] Lyons described that being a Span owner involved:

> …*purchasing one share in a non-profit making limited company controlled by the Registrar of Friendly Societies. The tenants, as a Society, form their own managing committee which looks after the maintenance of the buildings and gardens…. Span residents can opt out of their 'responsibilities' merely by paying their subscription.*

The scheme developed at Oaklands formed the model for

subsequent Span developments: before any new housing scheme was launched on the market, an association was legally set up[40] and, as part of the sales documents, all purchasers became members.[41] To pre-empt potential purchasers' reservations concerning mandatory membership, early promotional literature emphasised the scheme's benefits: 'it makes sense that having planned a properly knit and integrated estate to which people come to live because they find it desirable, steps ought to be taken to keep it so. That is why all Span estates have a non-profit making Residents' Society or Association'.[42] Less prosaically, Lyons commented that Span estates had general appeal because residents were buying not only 'a living unit with a front door nobody else could enter without a search warrant, but also an insurance policy against mental isolation, physical defects, or even major structural failure and protection of the status quo unless all neighbours require a change'.[43] In practice, the residents' society entered into a covenant with Span and with the lessees to maintain the exterior of the properties by cleaning the windows on a monthly basis and repainting every three years 'so that the colours and materials used shall be the same as those originally applied or as approved by the estate owner'; to keep the grounds 'in good order and properly lighted', to renew walls and fences when necessary and 'to maintain the estate substantially in the form laid out at the completion of the development'.[44] Communal interior space, such as halls and stairways, was also maintained in blocks of flats.

Less well publicised, but incorporated into the lease, were the 'regulations to be observed' by residents. These were intended, according to Lyons, as restraints 'for the people, and not on them'[45] and not 'an attempt to make people fit into a communal pattern'.[46] Indeed, the restraints were probably no more draconian than those on many local authority developments or other private housing estates, with the important difference that Span residents themselves exerted day-to-day control over their enforcement. The regulations varied little from estate to estate and always included a general prohibition on anything that 'may cause inconvenience or annoyance' to other residents; contravention of bye-laws; and, significantly for the preservation of Lyons's concept of visual unity, that 'nothing shall be done that may alter the construction or external appearance of or damage the house or other part of the estate by the erection of structures or otherwise'.[47] Other restrictions included no loud music (or music at all outside the buildings); no car parking outside designated bays or garages; no driving off roads or car parks; no signs or advertisements to be displayed; no washing hung out at weekends or bank holidays or after 4 p.m. or more than 6 ft from the ground; single or family occupation only; and 'no person of drunken or immoral habits shall reside in the house'. (This last regulation was dropped from later leases!)[48] Additionally, at Fieldend, Twickenham, for example, the

"But, Michael, the highly literate, cultivated, superior kind of person who will buy these just wouldn't stare."

Fig 6.4   When the Span development at Templemere, Weybridge, was launched, the cartoonist
Mahood satirised the perceived lack of privacy in *Punch* magazine.

picture windows were not to be 'stopped up or obstructed other than by blinds or curtains'.[49]

Lyons saw the residents' societies as an opportunity for 'real participation by the sharing of responsibilities… The sense of ownership was tempered by mutual respect, and the shared responsibilities did not diminish the cash value of the individual's investment'.[50] Indeed, he emphasised that communal management had an economic benefit in that residents 'can obtain cheaper rates for such services as painting, porterage, window and staircase cleaning'.[51] Ivor Cunningham explained how the system worked:

> The residents would vote in a general committee who would be responsible for running the communal parts of the development and in particular the landscaped areas. Private roads and footpaths, children's play areas, external house painting, group house insurance, were more often than not included in the Residents' Association's terms of reference. Maintenance charges were established on a regular basis according to need.[52]

Many early estates held residents' society meetings at Span's offices at 18 Dryden Court, Parkleys, Ham Common: Lyons, Townsend

or Leslie Bilsby would attend and often chaired the meeting. The close association between Lyons and the residents in the early years was not solely a landlord-tenant relationship, but one that ensured residents understood the Span ethos and, most importantly, provided feedback on the success (or otherwise) of the estate design, facilities, maintenance and management.[53] Only when both Span and the residents were confident that a residents' society could manage the estate effectively did it officially assume control.

With the passing of the Leasehold Reform Act in 1967, 'that incredibly conservative measure… a positive handicap', according to Lyons,[54] residents of at least five years' standing were entitled to buy the freehold of their properties from Span on 999 year leases; the communal areas were vested in the residents' societies, which continued to maintain these areas. Geoffrey Townsend explained that when the legislation was first proposed Span:

> …made strong representations… to ensure the future maintenance of the estates through the existing Residents' Societies and this was eventually included in the legislation on the basis of registered Management Schemes approved by the High Court. These schemes regularised the positions of the Residents' Societies as a Management Committee and

*endorsed their power to enforce the payment of contributions
for maintenance and to enforce most of the covenants
originally enforceable by the landlords.*[55]

From the date of the Act, existing developments gradually
negotiated with Span Developments Ltd to buy their freeholds,
whilst new houses and flats were offered for sale as freehold
properties.[56] At New Ash Green, Span's 'village' community in Kent
(1969), a two-tier structure of management was implemented by
Span as a means of encouraging involvement and commitment in a
community of over 2,000 people. Each neighbourhood management
committee (residents' society) is responsible for its own landscape
whilst a Village Association, made up of the representatives from
the residents' societies, managed other communal spaces such as
the woodlands, commons, park and sports ground.[57] The exercise
of rights of way over these wider green spaces is subject to a
number of bye-laws (mainly relating to dogs, horses, cars, music
and litter), to ensure that they remain an attractive amenity for
residents; and, the prohibition that 'No tree or other plant shall be
cut, pulled up or planted'.[58]

Despite the publicised benefits of 'grouped community housing',[59]
design features embodying Lyons's visual sense of community
continued to attract criticism. In particular, lack of privacy, lack
of a private front garden, no parking immediately outside the
house and adherence to a 'book of rules' were frequently raised
in interviews and robustly defended by Lyons – 'people seem to
like [discipline] and accept it'; 'We [the British] enjoy gardens more
than gardening'.[60] Notwithstanding, when Templemere, Weybridge,
(1965) was launched, *Punch* magazine published a double page
cartoon satirising the perceived lack of privacy, attributed to the
large windows and close proximity of neighbours in Span terraced
houses (Fig. 6.4).[61]

Community, values and lifestyle

Lyons emphasised that, in addition to the financial and practical
advantages of shared responsibilities, communal management
would create an identity of place and give residents a sense
of pride in their development: 'The buildings overlooked the
common approaches and gardens; and it is because of everyone's
involvement, including the children, in their own place, that the
customary vandalism is not to be seen'.[62] It also became clear, as
more developments were built and residents' societies formed, that
communal management encouraged social integration and played
a positive and proactive role in the creation of communities. Lyons
was not alone in this belief – Brenda Colvin had earlier proposed
that 'Community gardens… may, if suitably designed, foster the
social unity of a group'.[63] Ivor Cunningham, joining Lyons in 1955,
brought with him knowledge of housing landscape projects in the

Netherlands and Sweden, as well as experience from working in the
landscape office of Colvin and Sylvia Crowe. In tune with Lyons's
concept of designing a total environment – 'The home landscape at
its best is a holistic approach to a living environment… A concept
which provides the psychological needs for security, a place for the
imagination to roam free and the instrument for keeping in touch
with the natural world's rhythms of growth, change and decay'
– Cunningham worked closely with him on the overall design of
all future Span developments.[64] His particular contribution was in
landscaping to create spatial divisions conducive to both private and
communal use.

In accord with the principles of many innovative post-war landscape
architects, Cunningham viewed plant material as a design element
to define space and encourage movement through the landscape.
Colvin stressed that plants should be considered an important part
of the structure itself, rather than mere decoration, and that they
should be used 'to define and separate one area from another',[65]
a concept explored in Cunningham's 'wall-to-wall landscape
carpeting'.[66] Initially conceived for an unexecuted design at Coventry
(1957), a 'romantic layout of curving paths, free forming groups of
plants and trees and grassed areas that overlapped and interlocked
with each other; the whole composition being framed by the house
fronts and the screened car parking areas', it was incorporated
into a scheme at Blackheath, later called Corner Green (1959).[67]
Cunningham reports that 'By facing the houses onto a pedestrian-
only green the landscape became the social as well as the spatial
focus of the estate'. A similar mastery of landscape design is seen
at Fieldend (1961), 'the most sylvan of all Span developments in
London',[68] where terraced houses with picture windows around
two informal green spaces also foster a sense of community. An
early resident recalls that 'Children used the common gardens as if
they were in an ordinary private garden. They all played together,
built camps out of garden chairs and set up "Old Toy Sales" to raise
money for Oxfam' (Fig. 6.5).[69]

The writer Nan Fairbrother applauded this general trend towards
housing planned, not as collections of separate units but as
integrated communities, welcoming the positive use of landscape
between houses, 'true spaces not gaps', 'intercommunicating
green enclosures with their own distinct identity as places'.[70]
She confirmed that design must develop 'from the forms most
appropriate for what the landscape will be used for' and argued
that communal landscapes must take into account not only the
needs of the users but also maintenance regimes. Fairbrother also
proposed that the emphasis should be on 'indestructible effects
– on broad massing and spacing, on clear planting of the right trees
and robust shrubs, on ground-modelling, the use of light and shade,
of enclosure, and open space, and vistas'. As seen in Cunningham's

Fig 6.5 An early resident at Fieldend recalls that children used the communal areas as if they were in an ordinary private garden, building camps and setting up 'old toy sales' to raise money for Oxfam.

detailing, for example, at Mallard Place, she suggested that small-scale effects and intimacy should be provided by hard landscaping, such as patterns of cobbles and setts, and by the 'self-renewing' patterns of plants rather than intensive maintenance (Fig. 6.6).

For its residents, however, Span represented more than an attractive housing scheme or even a community – it represented a lifestyle. Advertising was directed at 'the younger professional man, company administrator or business executive seeking a home to reflect his good taste and judgement' – and who earned '£1,000 a year or more';[71] 'people who work in advertising, broadcasting and television, journalism and law. School teachers, surgeons, executives, architects, surveyors';[72] and the T8 'town house' was built for people 'who like children and music and laughter, who like entertaining, good talk, Sundays that dawdle between *The Observer* and *The Sunday Times*, and better than average food'.[73] Others were more pragmatic, one describing a typical resident as 'a person of urban tastes… who prefers to buy roses from the florist rather than grow them himself, and who does not require a greenhouse, a workshop or an outdoor run for a boxer dog'.[74] Selling points reflected the desirability and financial astuteness[75] of owning an

architect-designed house in a 'good selling area… with shopping facilities nearby' and the practical advantages of a residents' society to maintain the open spaces, 'all the advantages of home ownership with the minimum responsibility for upkeep'.[76]

Many of the early Span residents were, indeed, architects, 'in most gratifying numbers' – Maxwell Fry's 'long suffering class of harried professional workers'[77] – although Townsend emphasised that they also had 'very ready sales to people with diverse backgrounds, and in all age groups, including quite elderly people, many of whom have courageously scrapped their furnishings accumulated over many years and started afresh with a fully contemporary interior'.[78] Others have suggested that these 'pioneers' were comparable to those of Bedford Park and Hampstead Garden Suburb in their 'exclusivity and their dependence upon a shared sense of values and community'.[79]

Span residents, however, shared more than values and community – they shared physical space and lived in closer proximity to each other than those living in turn-of-the-century garden suburbs: 'Span houses are usually grouped in enclosed courts; companionable, intimate, a little apart. Their residents can enjoy the neighbourly links, the casual visit, the occasional drink or, if they wish, complete privacy'.[80] An early resident at Parkleys (1956) fondly recounts 'social get-togethers' and car treasure hunts;[81] and memories of the 'early days' at The Lane, Blackheath (1964) include a subcommittee to create a play area, a 'mothers' committee, a points system for baby sitting and AGMs 'which were also social events' and 'provided an important glue'.[82]

Anecdotal evidence is supported by a study investigating the social networks formed by early residents at New Ash Green and on five Span estates in Blackheath.[83] Designed to evaluate the extent to which residential areas constitute communities, the study concluded that the majority of those sampled had established 'primary contacts', determined by activities such as babysitting (70 per cent of those with young children in New Ash Green and 60 per cent of those in Blackheath depended on each other for babysitting); inviting fellow residents for dinner (85 per cent in Blackheath); and turning to neighbours when ill (60 per cent in both samples). A subsequent study on New Ash Green confirmed that 'planning for community' facilitated local friendships and an active social life, but was particularly successful in providing for the needs of young mothers and their children.[84] Furthermore, a comparative study between four new speculative housing estates, two with residents' societies (including New Ash Green) and two without, also concluded that the level of communal activity and social interaction was higher on those estates 'that exhibited a system of communal management of common open spaces'.[85]

Even by the early 1960s many developers had realised that much of the attraction of Span developments lay in the communal gardens, and estates of terraced houses with communal spaces managed by the residents were built, for example, at Beckenham by Wren Properties (with John Brookes as landscape designer) and at Roehampton Vale, Croydon and at Ealing by Wates (with Derek Lovejoy as consultant landscape architect).[86] At Roehampton Vale (1960) the 40 houses and communal land, except for roads and parking areas, were sold freehold, the purchasers having rights of way over each others' sections of the common space.[87] Residents entered into a covenant to maintain, and not to enclose, their part of the garden and to pay a subscription (£21 per annum) to maintain the amenity areas. Although the formation of residents' associations on these estates was considered 'a focus for community feeling', the developers generally showed a lack of commitment to the concept of designing 'total environments' and little confidence in the residents to manage and maintain them. Kenneth Bland, chief architect for Wates described the complexities 'that await a developer whose declared aim is to help in making Britain a better place to live in', concluding that in a Dulwich scheme, where the residents 'are fortunate in having their communal landscaping efficiently looked after, without the bother of organising themselves into management associations', there was 'a lack of community'.

A 1965 article on new private estates also confirmed that, as on Span estates, 'residents are doing more than buying a home – they are buying a new kind of life' and 'see themselves as pioneers'.[88] At a Wren Estate at Rectory Green, Beckenham, a board of directors 'regulated life in close proximity to neighbours' becoming, at times, a 'morally effective' court of arbitration, laying down rules on behaviour such as car-parking, children's toys left on the lawn, the playing of musical instruments, bicycle-riding and noisy games. As with Span's committees of management, the management boards of the estate had access to legal powers when necessary, perhaps, for example, if residents break restrictive covenants relating to subletting. Interestingly, despite comments that 'activity is plentiful… housewives are never lonely… they can have coffee or go shopping together, or even babysit for each other', the article also reported that, on the estates considered, organised social activities decreased in popularity once people had settled in – 'you start off mixing like mad and then gradually it all tails off'.

In contrast, a recent article suggests that on Span estates the social 'glue' still works: 'Ever wished you lived somewhere where a sense of community still existed, where kids could play safely outside, and neighbours were friends, not strangers? Well, places like this do exist: they're called Span developments'.[89] Such is their popularity today that houses for sale on Span estates are quite rare and, indeed, many residents moved in when the houses were new (some

Fig 6.6   Cunningham's hard landscape detailing at Mallard Place creates intimacy by patterns of cobbles and setts and the 'self-renewing' patterns of plants.

bought off plan) and have stayed. *The Lane Handbook* notes that in 2004 the residents organised a party to celebrate the estate's fortieth anniversary, and included a display of photographs 'showing happy children playing and residents in their glamorous younger days' (Fig. 6.7).[90] There is also, it seems, a rediscovery of communal living on Span estates by a new generation:

> *Like the young people who bought the houses from advertisements in the quality papers in the 1950s and 60s, many [new residents] will find a congenial approach to living and will enjoy working with others to improve The Lane and to hand its unique qualities on to posterity. They will find, as well as complete privacy in their own house and walled garden, a safe, green environment and supportive neighbours that enrich their family life.*

Fig 6.7   In 2004, residents at The Lane, Blackheath organised a party to celebrate the estate's fortieth anniversary.

The future of Span estates

Residents' societies and their schemes of management are key to the conservation of the design intention, character and sense of community on Span estates.[91] Typically, as at The Lane (freehold since 1974), a scheme of management is drawn up and a committee of management elected at the AGM (here comprising eight members, including a chair, treasurer and secretary).[92] Committee members at The Lane have different areas of responsibility to ensure that all aspects of maintenance are covered, including gardening, road and pavement maintenance, exterior painting, lighting and window cleaning. Furthermore, and most importantly, The Lane Committee of Management now fulfils Span's original function of ensuring that the estate is maintained according to Lyons's design intention, providing guidance on alterations or repairs to homes to 'strive to keep to the original appearance in order to help maintain the original integrity'.[93]

A recent study considered the extent to which the residents' societies of three estates in the Richmond area (Parkleys, Fieldend and Mallard Place) have been successful in conserving Lyons's design intention.[94] At the time of the study, the Parkleys Residents' Society elected a committee of management of nine members (four for the garden, four for the buildings and one for the electrics), in addition to a treasurer, secretary and estate manager (to liaise with contractors), the two latter positions attracting some remuneration. A chair and vice-chair were elected from the Committee, which met every month. The four members of the Garden Committee each have responsibility for a defined geographical area, supported by one full-time gardener, contractors being employed for lawn mowing and tree work. Terms of reference include planning monthly maintenance of the gardens and the work of the gardeners, replanting and organising tree surgery, as necessary. The report concluded that the external appearance of the properties at Parkleys, repainted every three or four years, with repairs to woodwork, roof and windows, is consistent with the original, suggestions to replace wooden window frames by uPVC, for example, having been resisted. Details – such as paving, cobbles, gravel, Span signature mushroom-shaped garden lights and window boxes[95] – within the courtyards and gardens remain, although they are likely to require repair or replacement in the near future.

Although in theory all landscape is communal, in practice it is clear that residents use the gardens closest to their homes, many ground floor residents appropriating the areas outside entrances, windows and patio doors for exclusive use, despite covenants to discourage this (Fig. 6.8). The most dramatic changes on the estate have resulted from unchecked tree growth (Fig. 6.9) and replacement flower and shrub planting by a succession of committees of management. This has contributed to a shift from the original

Fig 6.8 Many ground floor residents customise the areas outside entrances, windows and patio doors, despite covenants to discourage this. Parkleys 2000.

Fig 6.9 Over time, unchecked tree growth can change the ambience of a garden area, reduce light to buildings and damage the structure. Parkleys 2000.

'carefully selected flowers, shrubs and trees in abundance set off by trim lawns'[96] to more contemporary groupings, although with a continuing emphasis on hardy, evergreen plants.[97] Furthermore, discussions with residents indicated that the sense of community and shared responsibility to care for their landscape, vital to the estate's success in its early development, was now lacking, with fewer families and an increasing number of retired or single people who preferred privacy to communal living.[98]

At Fieldend, the second estate considered in the study, the external appearance of the houses was also well preserved (although the colour of the paint used throughout changed from time to time), but the Committee of Management had been tolerant of alterations to the back of properties, extensions being common, and permission had been granted (as an experiment) for a back bedroom replacement uPVC window frame. At other estates, however, replacement windows are now routinely allowed (Fig. 6.10).[99] Furthermore, at Fieldend, it was clear from drawn curtains, blinds, shrubbery partitions and strategically placed plant pots that many residents craved greater privacy than Span's open plan interiors with large windows, glazed porches and communal front gardens were designed to allow (Fig. 6.11). Many original

trees, such as the plane trees in the garden square and the beeches in the access road, appeared to have outgrown their positions despite essential tree-work. A comparison of the original plans with existing planting also demonstrated a gradual transition from a simple modernist style, with trees set in grass with ground cover and a few sculptural shrubs, to massed shrub plantings serving to divide the communal space. There are still residents at Fieldend who have been there since the 1960s, who understand Span concepts, enjoy the communal lifestyle and appreciate the importance of encouraging new residents to take an active part in the residents' society. Here, the sense of community, despite a changing population, has evidently been preserved, demonstrated by the continued organisation of social events, children (now mostly teenagers) using the communal areas for football, and neighbours making informal calls on each other.

At Mallard Place, a residents' society has been constituted to encompass the needs of owners of both freehold houses and leasehold flats, a subgroup of a committee of management catering for the flat dwellers.[100] The sophistication and complexity of the original design at Lyons's last development has been conserved, but as there is a high turnover of directors on the Committee, it was reported that a determined effort is needed to secure representation from different parts of the estate and to encourage new residents to actively participate in management. In contrast to most Span estates, the courtyard design with the close proximity of cars and enclosed entrances to the flats, does not appear as conducive to social interaction; although the swimming pool provides a social focus, particularly for the gardenless residents of the flats and maisonettes.

Residents' societies and their schemes of management have undoubtedly contributed to conserving the original design intention on Span estates, although it is clear that covenants are not always strictly implemented, possibly because of cost implications or the undesirability of protracted disagreements with neighbours. However, in addition, statutory or non-statutory controls may have discouraged inappropriate changes. In December 1999, 457 of the 370,000 listed buildings in England were properties of the post-war period, including 31 housing developments, four of which were Span developments.[101] It is significant that 3–35 South Row, Blackheath, the first Span scheme listed in June 1996, was recommended as a reactive measure to prevent timber frame windows being replaced in uPVC, whilst the remaining three (Parkleys, Hallgate and Highsett 1), despite earlier recommendation, were not added until December 1998, all being examples of Lyons's late 1950s low-rise blocks based on a courtyard design.[102] However, despite nominal acknowledgement to 'setting', in practice listed building status gives inadequate protection to the total landscape design.

In recent years broader-based criteria have rightly increased the range of landscapes considered of historic significance, and the English Heritage *Register of Parks and Gardens*[103] currently includes two housing landscapes; the communal open space containing Victor Pasmore's Pavilion on the Sunny Blunts residential area, Peterlee, County Durham (1963) and the Barbican housing development, City of London, by Powell, Chamberlin and Bon (1963).[104] Conservation area status, to preserve local 'sense of place' rather than specific buildings or gardens, now also has been successfully established within the planning framework.[105] The first conservation areas were created in 1967 and there are now over 9,000 in England, the majority in urban areas, where the loss of the character of an area of historic significance is more widely recognised than in suburban or other housing landscapes.[106] In recent years, however, local authorities have seemed more appreciative of smaller 20th-century speculative developments.[107] Many Span estates are within conservation areas, notably those on the Cator Estate, Blackheath, but recognition of the special nature of Span housing schemes has been given by the designation of Fieldend, Parkleys and Mallard Place as conservation areas in their own right. Conservation area statements by a local authority

Fig 6.10 Although uPVC window frames are increasingly used to replace Span's original wooden frames, here the replacement frame is also wood.

commonly include valuable specification, covering improvement and protection of landscape setting, preservation, enhancement and reinstatement of architectural quality and unity, coordination of design and improvement in quality of street furniture, improvement of the highways and pedestrian convenience.[108]

To date there seems to be little formal or informal communication between bodies responsible for statutory or non-statutory controls or other forms of local protection, as confirmed by a local conservation officer: 'Despite being a conservation area, we rarely have anything to do with the... Span estates due to their Residents' Societies, which are entrusted to maintain standards'.[109] More effective integration of conservation controls might also encourage communication within an authority and improvement, for example, in repairs carried out in sensitive areas, such as the public roads on some Span estates. The emphasis on design aesthetics in development plans, design guides, supplementary planning guidance and urban design frameworks should also be welcomed as providing additional protection for areas vulnerable to change.[110] Participation and education as positive measures to prevent unwelcome changes in local character and practical suggestions for character enhancement are also strong themes in contemporary policy documents.[111] It is, therefore, encouraging to note the increasing number of residents' societies that are providing information on Span philosophy and its influence on the design of a development; encouraging residents to participate in management by increasing their understanding of its relevance; and ensuring that residents are aware of the covenants relating to alterations to property and procedures for dealing with infringements.[112] Furthermore, a Span handbook with suggestions on appropriate repair and replacement of hard landscaping materials, tree management and soft landscaping maintenance might usefully guide the decision-making of residents' societies.[113] Ideally, each scheme would benefit from a management plan to provide a statement of significance, a vision for the future and a planned scheme of conservation.

Lyons's designs were intended to facilitate social interaction and cohesion – 'to enable social exchanges to flourish'– whilst reinforcing the formal sharing of responsibilities.[114] Over the years the pioneering spirit of Span residents has lessened, social values have changed and the scheme of management is often regarded as a disadvantage, imposing restrictions on personal freedom. One New Ash Green resident, however, regards these obligations as benefits – 'you are an equal partner in your neighbourhood and you enjoy the same rights and responsibilities as everyone else living close by'[115] – whilst others are more critical – 'the residents' society works but as with all communal set-ups depends on the few with energy and enthusiasm to provide for the majority through goodwill'.[116]

Fig 6.11 Drawn curtains, blinds and shrubbery partitions indicate that today's residents crave greater privacy than Span's open plan interiors (with large windows and communal front gardens) were designed to allow.

Span Developments Ltd was a successful venture – its intimate courtyard designs, stylish functional planting of communal spaces and hard landscaping detail were highly influential in the second part of the 20th century. Lyons's innovative designs are now recognised by architectural historians, practitioners and those in related fields not only as part of the historic environment, but also as a model for future housing. Within a political climate more sensitive to heritage and the importance of conserving local character, local authorities are also now more proactive in considering protective measures for Span estates and preparing conservation area studies with specifications for the standard of work and appropriate materials to be used. The communal management of open space, through the formation and responsibilities of residents' societies, is one of Span's most important contributions to 20th-century housing and has assured it a place in the post-war housing debate. The obituary of Geoffrey Townsend, the innovator of Span's residents' societies, quoted the apposite words of a prospective resident when viewing the idyllic setting of uncompromisingly modern houses set around an informal lawn: 'This is how we should live'.[117]

Endnotes

1. See G. A. Jellicoe, 'Some Comments on Private Enterprise Housing', *Housing Review*, 5, 1954, p. 11; and R. Furneaux Jordan, 'SPAN. The Spec Builder as Patron of Modern Architecture' *Architectural Review*, February 1959, p. 120.

2. Ivor Cunningham, 'Span – The Total Environment', in Barbara Simms (ed), *London's Garden Suburbs. Community Landscape and the Urban Ideal*, (London: London Historic Parks and Gardens Trust, 2001), p. 54. Proceedings of a conference held 4/5 October 2000 at the Scientific Societies Lecture Theatre, London W1.

3. G. and E. McAllister (eds), *Homes, Towns and Countryside: A Practical Plan for London* (London: Batsford, 1945).

4. Geoffrey Townsend, *Architects' Journal*, 20 January 1955, pp. 72–3.

5. See Eric Lyons 'Building a Community', *Architectural Design*, September 1960, pp. 344–55.

6. Arthur M. Edwards, *The Design of Suburbia. A Critical Study in Environmental History* (London: Pembridge Press Ltd, 1981), p. 181.

7. Eric Lyons, *Building Design*, 17 August 1979.

8. See 'Max Fry. Inspirations, friendships and achievements of a lifetime in the Modern Movement', *Building*, 31 October 1975, pp. 52–8. See also Chapter 2 and Francis Yorke and Frederick Gibberd, *The Modern Flat* (London: Architectural Press, 1937), p. 13 for a residential scheme with communal landscaping and facilities at St Leonards Hill, Windsor, designed by Gropius and Fry.

9. An early example is Ernst May's innovative programme at Frankfurt–Romerstadt (1926). May's developments used prefabricated buildings and included communal facilities such as playgrounds and schools, but also paid attention to factors such as equal access to sunlight and air.

10. Elizabeth Denby, *Europe Rehoused*, 2nd edn (London: George Allen and Unwin Ltd, 1944), p. 263, 1st printed 1938.

11. Christopher Tunnard, *Gardens in the Modern Landscape* 2nd edn (London: The Architectural Press, 1950), pp. 138–58, 1st edn 1938.

12. Peter Shephard, 'The Small Private Garden: its Place in the Layout of Houses', *Journal of the Institute of Landscape Architects* 20, March 1951, p. 10.

13. Ministry of Health, *Design of Dwellings* (London: HMSO, 1944)

14. Patrick Abercrombie, *The Greater London Plan* (London: HMSO, 1945).

15. E. Goldfinger and E. J. Carter, *County of London Plan* (London: HMSO, 1945), p. 31.

16. M. Smith, *Guide to Housing* 1st edn (London: The Housing Centre Trust, 1971), p. 13.

17. Ministry of Health, *Housing Manual* (London: HMSO, 1949), p. 14.

18. Ministry of Health, *Our Gardens* (London: HMSO, 1948).

19. Ministry of Health, *The Appearance of Estates. Central Housing Committee Report* (London: HMSO, 1948).

20. Sylvia Crowe and A. Hedley Richardson, 'Landscape for Flats', *Journal of the Institute of Landscape Architects* 32, March 1955, p. 2.

21. Sylvia Crowe, *Garden Design*, 3rd edn (Woodbridge, Suffolk: Garden Art Press, 1994), p. 228. 1st published 1958.

22. *op. cit.,* Peter Shepheard, 1951, p. 11.

23. *op. cit.,* The Appearance of Estates, 1948, p. 271.

24. Frederick Gibberd, 'The Design of Residential Areas' in Ministry of Housing and Local Government, *Design in Town and Village* (London: HMSO, 1953), Chapter 2.

25. T. F. Thomson, 'Design and Maintenance of the New Town Landscape', *Journal of the Institute of Landscape Architects* 14, November 1948, p. 5.

26. Peter Youngman, 'Landscape Architecture and Housing', *Journal of the Institute of Landscape Architects* 13, April 1948, pp. 6–9.

27. Sylvia Crowe, 'The Upkeep of Open Spaces', *Journal of the Institute of Landscape Architects* 15, April 1949, p. 3.

28. See, for example, Brenda Colvin, Sylvia Crowe and H. F. Clark, 'Landscape Architecture in the New Towns. A Symposium', *Journal of the Institute of Landscape Architects* 18, July 1950, pp. 3–7.

29. *op. cit.,* Peter Shepheard, 1951, p. 11.

30. Tunnard's concept of communal gardens, 'controlled for the benefit of all', reflected a contemporary utopian desire to create a better world, an aspiration perhaps not incompatible with Lyons's more limited aim to extend the 'bourgeois values' of home ownership to 'ordinary people'. See Eric Lyons, 'Private Housing' in Muriel Emanuel (ed), *Contemporary Architects* (London: MacMillan, 1980).

31. *op. cit.,* Christopher Tunnard, 1950, p. 144.

32. For a history of London garden squares see Todd Longstaffe-Gowan, *The London Town Garden* (New Haven and London: Yale University Press, 2001), Chapter 8.

33. *ibid.,* pp. 188–9.

34. *Survey of London*, vols 31 and 32, St James Westminster, Part 2 (1963), pp. 145–46.

35. '"Oaklands," Whitton: Flats Built by Private Enterprise', *The Builder*, October 29 1948, pp. 502–4.

36. Bargood Estates was the development company for Oaklands with Lyons and Townsend as architects. The company, Span Developments Ltd, was not formed until 1957.

37. See also Industrial and Provident Societies Acts 1893 and thereafter. For a history of Friendly Societies see David Neave, 'Friendly Societies in Great Britain' in Marcel van der Linden (ed), *Social Security Mutualism: the comparative history of mutual benefit societies* (New York: Peter Lang, 1996).

38. 'The Span View of Neighbours', *Ideal Home,* January 1960, pp. 57–9. Eric Ambrose interviews Eric Lyons. Advertisements show that some properties were sold on 999 year leases. See, for example, those held at the London Borough of Richmond Local Studies Library.

39. At Highsett, Cambridge, Jesus College retained ownership of the land and at The Paddox, Oxford, the land was held by St Edward's School. Span held the head lease. See also Chapter 4.

40. The procedures for the setting up of residents' societies on Span estates were probably managed by the firm of Ashurst Morris Crisp & Co., who handled the company's legal matters.

41. Sachs reports that in 1952 Leslie Bilsby (before he joined Lyons and Townsend) had also set up an association of leaseholders to undertake the repair and maintenance of the buildings and gardens at The Paragon, a crescent of houses converted to flats with communal gardens in Blackheath. He had evidently modelled it on the Christian Brotherhood Friendly Society and the Scottish system of selling flats under covenants. Hessie Sachs, *A Study of New Ash Green,* Report of the Social Research Unit, Bedford College, London: Centre for Environmental Studies, 1971.

42. Undated Span Promotional Literature (late 1950s), RIBA Span Archive Box 3/1.

43. Eric Lyons in interview with Eric Ambrose, 'New Ash Green, New Village, New Way of Life', *Ideal Home*, October 1967, p. 50.

44. Lease Agreement Form between Span Developments Ltd and Weymede Residents' Society Ltd 1962, p. 3. The wording varies on some leases but the covenants are essentially the same.

45. Interview with Eric Lyons, *The Times*, 21 July 1975.

46. *op. cit.,* Span Promotional Literature (c.1960s).

47. *op. cit.,* Lease Agreement Form between Span Developments Ltd and Weymede Residents' Society Ltd 1962, p. 6.

48. *op. cit., Ideal Home,* October 1967, p. 49 gives examples from other Span developments.

49. Information taken from an explanation of the constitution of the Residents' Society and the Scheme of Management prepared for Fieldend residents by John Barney, 24 March 1999.

50. *op. cit.,* Eric Lyons, 1980, p. 495.

51. *op. cit., Ideal Home,* January 1960.

52. Ivor Cunningham 'Landscape for Housing', *Housing Today,* May 1990. The charge levied by the residents' societies varies according to housing, extent of communal landscaping and the type of planting. Undated Span Promotional Literature for the T8 house quotes 'about £25 per annum', for example, but at Highsett (Phases 2 & 3), Cambridge, the annual contribution in 1964 was £48 and New Ash Green promotional literature (c. 1969) quotes 'approximately £36' (by 1992 this had risen to £80 per annum).

53. Lyons considered that designing in the private sector took the architect 'closer to an understanding of users' preferences than volumes of social surveys' and prevented him from 'losing touch with the users'. See Eric Lyons, 'Architects in the Housing Market Place', *Building* 238, 18 January 1980, pp. 32–3.

54. Eric Lyons, 'Too often we justify our ineptitudes by moral postures', *RIBA Journal,* May 1968, p. 214. An address delivered at the RIBA on 6 February 1968. Lyons also stated that Span had considered giving up residents' societies when the Act was passed 'but they had conceived a way out'.

55. Personal communication from Geoffrey Townsend to Ivor Cunningham, 20 March 1991.

56. In 1995 Townsend informed Ivor Cunningham that the freehold of the last leasehold estate had recently been sold.

57. There is an additional annual subscription to the Village Association based on house size, which in 1969 was 10s. per 100 sq ft. Information from John Barr, 'Status Village', *New Society,* 30 October 1969, p. 68.

58. This last is also included in the lease for Mallard Place. See also Chapter 5, and Suki Pryce, 'A Dream Come True', *Horticulture Week,* January 16 1987, pp. 20–1 for further discussion of the role of neighbourhood societies and the Village Association at New Ash Green.

59. *op. cit.,* Eric Lyons, 1980.

60. *op. cit.,* 'The Span View of Neighbours', 1960.

61. *Punch,* 15 May 1965, p. 700.

62. *op. cit.,* Eric Lyons, 1980.

63. Brenda Colvin, *Land and Landscape* (London: John Murray, 1948), p. 211.

64. Ivor Cunningham, 'Landscape for Housing', *Built Environment* 21, 1 November 1995.

65. Brenda Colvin, 'Planting Design', *Journal of the Institute of Landscape Architects* 20, March 1951, p. 3.

66. Ivor Cunningham, *Spick and Span,* talk given at a seminar, Royal Botanic Gardens Kew, 7 March 1980.

67. Ivor Cunningham, 'A Span Site Revisited. Corner Green, Blackheath, London', *Landscape Design,* February 1982. See also Chapter 3 for further details of the Coventry scheme.

68. Bridget Cherry and Nikolaus Pevsner, *The Buildings of England. London 2: South* (London: Penguin, 1999), p. 552. 1st published 1983.

69. James Strike, *The Spirit of Span Housing* (London: Strike Print, 2005), pp. 53–4.

70. Nan Fairbrother, *New Lives New Landscapes* (London: The Architectural Press, 1970), Chapter 11, pp. 199–212.

71. Undated Parkleys Sales Brochure, Richmond Local History Centre, Ref LC10,008. The exact wording is '£1,000 a year or more is earned by as many as 85% of our purchasers'.

72. *Span – living with new ideas,* undated promotional literature 1960s (Private Collection).

73. *The Span T8 House*, undated Span Promotional Literature (Private Collection). It has also been noted that Span advertising was 'almost limited' to *The Observer* and *Sunday Times*. See *op. cit.*, R. Furneaux Jordan, 1959, p. 111.

74. *op. cit.*, Edwards, 1981, p. 178–9.

75. There was no mention of the likely difficulty in securing a mortgage for a property of modern design. Lyons criticised building societies as 'mostly stubborn opponents of modern architecture or any design idiom that is outside the grand old traditional style of pre-war spec building'. See Eric Lyons, 'Problems of Urban Development' *The Builder*, 201, 29 September 1961, p. 588.

76. *op. cit.*, un-dated Parkleys Sales Brochure, Richmond Local History Centre.

77. Maxwell Fry, 'The Speculative Builder', *House and Garden*, 12, June 1957, p. 35.

78. 'Men of the Year: Eric Lyons and G. P. Townsend', *Architects' Journal*, January 20 1955, pp. 72–3.

79. Gordon Millar, *Time Span: Eric Lyons and Span*, p. 15. Unpublished research 1991.

80. *op. cit.*, Span – living with new ideas, 1960s.

81. Personal communication, 19 April 2001.

82. *The Lane Handbook* (London: The Lane Residents' Society, 2005), p. 14.

83. Pilot study commissioned by Span to investigate the extent to which residential areas constitute communities. Sociological Research Unit, University College, London, 1966. Summarised in Barr, *op. cit.*, 1969, pp. 677–80.

84. *op. cit.*, Sachs, 1970.

85. B. R. Gates, *The planner and communal management of open space in new housing estates*, p. 15, unpublished thesis, Polytechnic of Central London, 1972.

86. Ivor Cunningham recounts a story of a conversation overheard between 'the directors of a well-known developing and building company' that took place in the show house at Corner Green, Blackheath, in 1959. They were debating the reasons for the success of Span and gradually realising that communal landscaping was a key factor. See *op. cit.*, Cunningham, 1982. See also Mary Gilliatt, 'Whatever is happening to England's green and pleasant land?', *House Beautiful*, July 1967, pp. 51–4 for discussion of estates by Span, Wates and Wren Properties.

87. Kenneth Bland, 'Layout and Provision for Maintenance of Private Enterprise Estates', *Housing Review* 15–16, 1966–7, pp. 98–105.

88. Michael Pearson, 'Top Estates for Top People', *Good Housekeeping* LXXXVIII/ 2, August 1965, pp. 56–60.

89. Claire Barrett, 'Span Houses', *Grand Designs* 13, March 2005, pp. 57–76.

90. *op. cit.*, The Lane Handbook (2005), p. 14.

91. See also Hugh Pearman, 'Spic and Span', *The Times* Style Supplement, 5 February 1995, p. 27.

92. The composition of the committee of management varies between estates and is determined by the residents. Information on The Lane is taken from *op. cit.*, The Lane Handbook (2005).

93. *op. cit.*, The Lane Handbook (2005), pp. 16–21.

94. Barbara Simms, *Landscape Conservation on Span Estates*. Unpublished dissertation for MA Conservation (Gardens and Designed Landscapes), Architectural Association, 2001.

95. Margaret Parker, 'Units of Comfort', *The Lady*, 17 January 1957, comments this was 'on the thoughtful assumption that every Englishman being a gardener at heart, window boxes would "grow" if not provided, so it is better to provide them in a good uniform design'.

96. Undated Span Promotional Literature, RIBA Span Archive Box 3/2.

97. A number of estates have, however, consulted Ivor Cunningham on suitable replanting.

98. Personal communication, April 2001.

99. The lifespan of uPVC windows is not as long as originally anticipated and they are impossible to repair. Even slight damage requires the replacement of the whole unit. See *Building Design*, 29 June 2001.

100. At Highsett, Cambridge, where there are also both flats and houses, there are separate residents' societies, as it is considered that their management and maintenance needs are different.

101. Heritage protection in England is under review (2006). See www.english-heritage.org.uk for current guidelines. The situation to date is as follows: Listing is a legal procedure to provide special protection to buildings of 'special architectural or historic interest', compiled by English Heritage under the Planning (Listed Buildings and Conservation Areas) Act 1990. Designation means that development proposals will require listed building consent before any repairs or alterations are made that might alter the 'special character' of the building. Listed building status is potentially of significance for housing landscapes in that the protection extends not just to the building itself but to its setting, 'an essential part of the building's character, especially if a garden or grounds have been laid out to complement its design or function'. See PPG 15 Part 1 Sections 2.16 and 3 and Annex C.

102. In total six examples of Span housing were recommended by English Heritage for listing in 1996, those still unlisted being Foxes Dale, Corner Green and Brooklands Park, all in Blackheath. Castle House by Eric Lyons for Southampton City Council was also recommended.

103. When English Heritage was created under the National

Heritage Act 1983, the compilation of a register of gardens and other land of special historic interest became part of its remit. Unlike listed buildings, inclusion on the Register does not provide additional statutory protection. It does, however, require local planning authorities to consider the safeguard of registered sites when assessing development plans and in their allocation of resources. *The Register of Parks and Gardens. An Introduction* (London: English Heritage, 1998).

104. There is an increasing consensus amongst amenity and heritage bodies that although the high profile of this non-statutory register in the local planning framework has ensured the protection of historic designed landscapes generally, statutory listing may be more effective. This was reflected in the recent recommendation to government that not only should a 'statutory duty of care' be introduced for owners of listed buildings, but also for owners of registered parks and gardens. English Heritage, *Power of Place. The future of the historic environment* (London: The Power of Place Office, 2000), p. 20.

105. Within a conservation area, the local authority has additional controls over demolition and trees, but not over minor developments (such as replacement doors, windows and external paint colour), usually given automatic permission as 'permitted development rights', unless an Article 4 direction is in force. They have responsibilities to protect trees and woodlands 'in the interests of amenity' by making Tree Preservation Orders. PPG 15 Part 1 section 2.24. See Charles Mynors, *Listed Buildings and Conservation Areas* (London: FT Law and Tax, 1995) for a detailed analysis of permitted development rights and Article 4 Directions.

106. There are notable exceptions such as London's Bedford Park and Hampstead Garden Suburb, areas that have been managed and protected since the 1960s although not without some loss of the original design intentions. See *op. cit.,* Simms (ed), 2001, Chapters 6–7.

107. Larkham reported that at the beginning of the 1990s 20 per cent of responding local authorities had designated 20th-century residential areas, some from the post-war period. A. N. Jones and P. J. Larkham *The Character of Conservation Areas* (London: Royal Town Planning Institute, 1993).

108. Conservation area status also gives additional protection for trees and could be useful in protecting those without existing Tree Preservation Orders, whilst their 'visual, historic and amenity contribution' is assessed. PPG 15 Part 1 Section 4.40.

109. Quoted in Catherine Bond, *Span – the protection of a post-war housing aesthetic*, unpublished Diploma in Conservation (Buildings) thesis, Architectural Association, 1999, p. 43.

110. Department of the Environment, Transport and the Regions, *By Design. Urban design in the planning system: towards better practice* (London: HMSO, 2000).

111. For example, see *Power of Place, op. cit.,* p. 31.

112. The Lane, Fieldend and New Ash Green are notable examples of this.

113. The Lane and New Ash Green provide this information.

114. *op. cit., Span – living with new ideas.*

115. Geoff Rogers, 'How the Village Works', *New Ash Green Villager* 1, October 1999, p. 2.

116. Personal communication, November 2004.

117. Obituary for Geoffrey Townsend, *The Times*, 2 October 2002.

"The test of good housing is not whether it can be built easily, but whether it can be lived in easily."

Eric Lyons

The core ingredients of Span are simple, even modest: an indivisible boundary between landscape and building design; the provision of attractive shared spaces; architectural design that allows the homeowner to be part of the shared space or separate from it; and management structures that sustain the immediate community over many years. The architecture provides the important elements of housing (a series of comfortable interior spaces with a view) with wit and attention to detail. Span is a home-grown response to providing housing in English suburbs that has been tested over 50 years. However, at a time when architects, developers and planners are looking for new, untested housing models, the findings from an objective evaluation of Span estates are particularly relevant. This chapter, therefore, compares housing demands in Lyons's time and now, and tests Span estates against the criteria given in a government-supported design guide, *Building for Life*, which promotes best practice to housebuilders.[1]

Recent appraisals of Eric Lyons's and Span's work come from many directions. The historic importance of the estates has been recognised by English Heritage and local authority conservation officers.[2] The aesthetic of 1960s and 1970s house designs and interiors means that Span regularly features in lifestyle magazines (Fig. 7.1)[3] and the schemes are considered to still hold valid lessons for the planning of interior and exterior spaces. The commitment to a social agenda, matched by design, intelligent marketing and the pursuance of development in the face of adversity, remains a guiding example for some contemporary architects and developers.[4] The houses have retained their values because the management of the

various sites has generally been able to maintain the original dense landscaping and delicate details that distinguish the estates.[5] The profile of the owners of Span houses also remains largely as that when first completed.[6] Lyons intended that Span's work would be relevant today:

By planning each project on its own merits, by creating a coherent architectural and natural pattern that retains fine old trees and acknowledges the need for stretches of grass, that provides the requirements for modern living – the garages and parking areas – without allowing them to intrude, we ensure that estates look mature from the outset and retain an informal dignity that will be pleasant still in fifty years.[7]

Lyons's long-term view of the continued viability of the estates has been vindicated. Span received the Historic Housing Design Award 2005, given to previous award-winning schemes 'that meet the current Sustainable Communities Plan of places where "people want to live… now and in the future"[8] [and] underlines why the enduring appeal of good design will prove the test of what these plans procure'.[9] A recent article places Span's success in the context of current housing needs:

Build – and sharpish – sustainable communities. And don't start moaning, 'We don't know what they look like'. Every week seems to bring some hot new architect with some hot new design, and some hot new developer with the cash to build it... The good news is these houses are being built.

Fig 7.1   Interior of a A3M-type terrace: Neil Bingham's house in Corner Keep (Corner Green Phase 2), Blackheath, 2006.

Fig 7.2   Guidelines for layout were given in *Community Layouts in Private Housing* published by the RIBA Housing Group.

The depressing news is that they're mostly reinventing the wheel, relearning all the stuff we forgot in the 1980s from the previous, post-war housing crisis, which, contrary to popular belief, didn't just carpet the land with concrete jungles, but built some magnificent, sustainable communities, such as... Eric Lyons's Span suburbs with a social conscience in Blackheath, South London... Sustainable communities are easy... The government wants them but says it can't afford them. Mass house builders can afford them but don't want them.[10]

In 1998 the Labour government defined a need for 4.4 million new homes by 2016,[11] with an annual target of 175,000 units per year.[12] This statement of required numbers coincided with the publication of *Towards an Urban Renaissance*, which outlined the need to revitalise urban areas by meeting the demand for housing on brownfield (abandoned industrial) sites.[13] The result has been a trend towards building high-density developments, on the assumption that the densification of our inner cities is the sustainable way to achieve the required numbers. The draft Planning Policy Statement PPS3 Housing establishes a benchmark of 30–70 dwellings per hectare, depending on whether the site is rural or urban.[14] Proposals in the Thames Gateway to achieve densities reaching 150–200 dwellings per hectare have met with cautious commentaries. The Commission for Architecture and the Built Environment (CABE) states that 'there should be a recognition within PPS3 that density is about intensity of use, about functions and services supporting the housing component – that it's more about optimising land use and about the spatial planning of neighbourhoods'.[15] The emphasis on urban regeneration has been subsequently balanced, either through published commentary or policy, with an acknowledgement of the need for landscaped suburban development to achieve sustainable communities.[16]

Span as a housing model

Span's agenda was to provide high-quality architecture as competition to the mundanity of the product offered by volume house builders.[17] The work was supported by commentators, such as Ian Nairn, and by the architectural establishment.[18] The Royal Institute of British Architects (RIBA) Housing Group published the pamphlet *Community Layouts in Private Housing* (Fig. 7.2), using 10 examples of private developments, built between 1955 and 1968, to promote successful layouts as solutions to developers' perceived concerns over the financial viability of communal schemes.[19] Three Span estates were cited: The Priory, Blackheath (1955), Templemere, Weybridge (1964), and Holme Chase, Weybridge (1966). In particular, the document promoted managed estates and stated:

Recent years have brought many new influences to bear on the design of private housing estates. Perhaps the two most important of these have been the tremendous increase in car ownership, with its benefits and disadvantages, and the tendency of middle class estates to be built to much higher densities than hitherto (and particularly on the fringe of Britain's larger cities), mainly but not entirely as a result of pressures arising from green belt policies... Until recently, a man in the higher income group would normally have expected to buy a detached house standing in its own grounds... For people wishing to live reasonably close to major city centres, the only new house at a comparable price is in a development of a much higher density than would hitherto have been acceptable to people at this income level. Consequently it has been necessary to find methods of making higher density developments more attractive to people whose natural inclinations are towards a completely different home environment. For people such as these, the conventional pattern of houses arranged along street frontages has tended to become decreasingly acceptable as densities of buildings and cars have increased.[20]

The foreword by C. Douglas Calverley, then chair of the National Home Builders Registration Council (NHBRC), summarised the issues for his registered members: 'customers who once expected a quarter-acre plot now have to live at a density of ten or more to the acre. But they have to be given a product that will satisfy them at a price they can afford to pay'.[21] The foreword, however, was not a full endorsement of the RIBA's proposed solutions:

Many of us [developers] have shied away from this because of the legal and maintenance problems, because of the cost, and because we have been doubtful if our customers would like a communal garden however attractively landscaped... The houses shown were built at prices that meant they could only be sold to the top 20–25 per cent of the market. The RIBA are convinced that the techniques shown can be used in lower priced estates to combine high density with schemes that are attractive in appearance. Certainly it is true that with the present land shortage it would be most helpful if more house buyers could be weaned away from the notion that a terraced house is in some way an inferior product.[22]

Contemporary commentators show that the opposition between design intentions for housing promoted by architects, or their supporters, and the work of volume housebuilders remains unresolved.[23] Any appraisal of the validity of Span as an exemplar must be qualified by its impact on the housing market of the time. The Span project was modest: 2,134 houses and flats in 73 developments.[24] As a comparison, four non-Span, social housing schemes by Lyons for London boroughs, completed within eight

Fig 7.3   Aerial photograph from 1957 from Span archive assessing future development sites.

years of each other, provided 1,567 dwellings.[25] During the 1950s, some 230,000 new homes a year were constructed in the United Kingdom. This increased to 300,000 a year in the 1960s, but then fell to 260,000 a year in the 1970s and to 180,000 a year in the 1980s. From 1991 to 2004, more than 1 million new dwellings have been completed in total.[26]

Span offers an attractive model for developments of around 40–60 dwellings, but the impact of such models on the required number of houses will be small unless the ideas are embraced more widely by those building in great volume for the private and low-cost housing markets. The intention of the 1969 RIBA Housing Group pamphlet was to show that the techniques of the 10 examples could be used in lower-priced developments to combine high density with schemes that are attractive in appearance, even though the examples shown 'could only be sold to the top 20 to 25 per cent of the market'.[27]

The Span estates were generally built in attractive existing gardens in affluent London boroughs or southeast towns (Fig. 7.3).[28] The sale market was, and still is, almost exclusively white and middle class; the latter celebrated in Span's own marketing.[29] However, the model of ownership of the communal areas (through payment of maintenance rather than purchase) and the architectural intention are not invalidated as an appropriate wider model by these factors. Neither is the relevance of Span today linked to the strength of its, now, fashionable, image.

Fig 7.4a   T15 house at The Lane 1964.

Fig 7.4b   T15 house at Brooklands Park 1964.

The study

Span estates need to be tested against current design guidelines to evaluate the success of the built schemes. A useful assessment tool for this purpose is the *Building for Life* criteria, an initiative which promotes design excellence and celebrates best practice in the house building industry. Supported by the government as the standard for the design quality of new homes, CABE and the House Builders Federation have developed 20 questions that reflect current policy guidance. It is intended that developers should use these questions – which consider criteria under the main headings of character; road, parking and pedestrianisation; design and construction; and environment and community – as a basis for writing development briefs, with a view to speeding up planning approvals and winning local community support. Housing schemes that meet 14 of the 20 criteria are eligible to apply for silver standard recognition, whilst schemes that meet 16 or more are considered to be gold standard.

Ideally, to consider Span as a relevant housing model for today, a generalised, representative scheme needs to be established from the completed 73 estates. However, despite the apparent repetition of plan types, layout principles and details, each of the estates is varied because of site constraints and the numbers of dwellings. Many estates with street frontages and little or no common land have houses that have been altered and extended, individually or severally, in ways not found in larger estates, where the frontages are required to be consistent or unchanged. Larger estates, with sufficient scale of communal land for shared involvement in the overall management, have gone through periods of reduced, or even no maintenance, only to be revitalised by changes in the committee of management of the residents' society or through increased contributions.[30] This study, therefore, takes the 20 questions that form the *Building for Life* standard as the criteria against which Lyons's generic design rationale for Span estates can be evaluated.

The *Building for Life* questions

The 20 questions are discussed in detail in the *Building for Life* standard guide *Delivering great places to live*, together with the policy guidance that shaped them (see below).[31] The questions (organised according to the four sections – character; road, parking and pedestrianisation; design and construction; and environment and community) are listed below, together with key points from policy guidance and explanation of the issues (by CABE). Span's performance against each criteria is demonstrated by examples from selected Span estates.

Character

1. Does the scheme feel like a place with a distinctive character?
PPS 1 (sustainable development):*'key objectives should include*

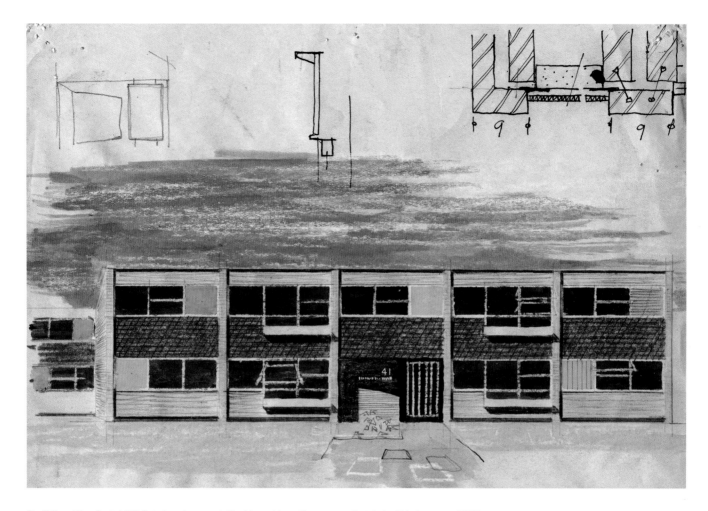

Fig 7.5   The first ABC flat development: Parkleys, Ham Common, sketch by Eric Lyons c. 1955.

ensuring that developments respond to their local context and create or reinforce local distinctiveness'; **CABE summary:** *'how a neighbourhood looks affects how residents feel about where they live... this not only needs architecture of a high standard but a strong landscape strategy... A design with strong character needs to be supported by strong ideas. These ideas may be about reflecting contemporary society or about responding to local patterns of development and landscape'.*
Span score: Yes.

Twenty-five flat and house types were used for the 73 Span developments, each developed in response to the contemporary lifestyle. The ABC flat, as an example, was used on nine estates; three in Blackheath, two in Cambridge, the others in Ham Common, Twickenham, Hove and Beckenham. Of the three in Blackheath (Hallgate, Hall 1 and The Priory), Hallgate is finished in white weather boarding to reflect the predominant character of

Blackheath Park, early 19th-century villas. The Priory and Hall 1 are both finished in boarding and clay tiles possibly intended to reflect the character of the surrounding 1930s housing. The colours and the disposition of blocks in the grounds give them their distinctive character. The Lane and Brooklands Park use the same house type (T15), finished identically, with a similar relationship to Blackheath Park. Photographs of the houses can be confused, but not when seen in their setting (Figs. 7.4a and 7.4b). As a qualification, the planning relationship with the wider context and surrounding buildings is described under Questions 5, 10 and 11.

2. Do buildings exhibit architectural quality?
PPS 1 (sustainable development): *'good design ensures attractive, useable, durable and adaptable places and is a key element in achieving sustainable development';* **CABE summary:** *'architectural quality is about being fit for purpose, durable, well built and pleasing to the mind*

119

Fig 7.6   Windows at Parkleys, Ham Common, in a photograph by Eric Lyons c. 1957.

Fig 7.7   Signage at Mallard Place designed by Minale Tattersfield for Span.

and eye... *planners, developers and design teams should ensure that a significant proportion of home buyers have their spirits lifted by what is on offer... Good architecture is less to do with a particular style and more to do with the successful co-ordination of proportions, materials, colour and detail'.*
Span score: Yes.

The architectural quality of Lyons's estates was recognised on completion, and subsequently. Those schemes with communal areas are defined by the care of the landscaping and planting schemes. All schemes show a wit and enjoyment in the design of the fundamental requirements of a house; how it reads as part of a whole, the composition of the individual unit, how it touches the ground and defines a permeable boundary between shared and private space, arrival at the house and entry, movement through the house and provision of light.

CABE cites the example of windows which 'need to be arranged to look good but also to work for views and light inside the house'. All Lyons's schemes show a fascination with window pattern. The ABC flats (Fig. 7.5) use windows to reflect the size of room within, but the composition of a whole block is maintained by glazing bars, which maintain the strong horizontal plane of the tile hanging (Fig. 7.6). This is reinforced by window boxes. On the other hand, the strong composition of squares used in the design of the T15 house (Figs. 7.4a and 7.4b), predominate over a recognition of how we inhabit a room; the wide glazing bar restricts views of the gardens when seated. As a further qualification, the developments were generally built cheaply so as to be affordable.[32] The results are that many elements are not durable (such as the T7/8 porches) but the residents' societies have ensured that details survive through maintenance.

3. Are streets defined by a well-structured building layout?
PPG 17 (planning for open space): *'local networks of high-quality and well-managed open space help to create urban environments that are attractive, clean and safe'.* **CABE summary:** *'streets, homes, gardens, places for leisure and parking must be carefully arranged. A successful layout should be characterised by a framework of interconnected routes which define "blocks" of housing, open spaces and other uses. Streets, squares, courts, mews, circuses and avenues are tried and tested layouts which successfully achieve this'.*
Span score: Yes.

The majority of the Span estates are 'island' developments in existing gardens or on undeveloped land with limited frontages to existing street patterns. The scale of the developments (up until New Ash Green) meant that the role of the street within an estate was subservient to the decision to focus all blocks on a single

Fig 7.8   Span demonstrates that the assessed character of existing buildings can inform contemporary design without having to be replicated in historic details or forms. Southrow as viewed from the heath, Blackheath.

vehicle-free space or series of spaces, as at Fieldend. Vehicle access is relegated to the perimeter of the site.

4. Do the buildings and layout make it easy to find your way around?
PPG 3 (housing): *'applicants… should be able to demonstrate how they have taken account of the need for good layout and design'*.
CABE summary: *'a neighbourhood that is easy to get around tends to feel safer and more secure. It will have a clear network of streets, courtyards and alleyways that are interesting, welcoming and people friendly'*.
Span score: Yes (qualified).

As with Question 3, the criteria appear to be directed to developments larger than Span estates, on which identity of an individual house or apartment is clearly directed. Eric Lyons took great care with the design of corners, vistas, change of scale and paths. Complex estates (such as The Priory) are signed through maps. The scale of the estates makes them understandable in the

same time it would take, for example, to find a house on a typical suburban street (Fig. 7.7).

5. Does the scheme exploit existing buildings, landscape or topography?
PPG 15 (planning and the historic environment): *'new buildings do not have to copy their older neighbours in detail. Some of the most interesting streets include a variety of building styles, materials and forms of construction, of many different periods, but together forming a harmonious group'*; **CABE summary:** *'new housing should respond to and reinforce locally distinctive patterns of development, landscape and culture'*.
Span score: Yes.

Whilst this repeats observations made under Questions 1 and 2, as an example, an appraisal of the Blackheath Park conservation area (which contains 22 Span estates), if carried out today, would define the modern buildings as contributing to the uniqueness and character of the area. For those considering new housing in

Fig 7.9   Visitor parking bays at Holme Chase, Weybridge, 2006.

conservation areas today, Span demonstrates that the assessed character of existing buildings can inform contemporary design without having to be replicated in historic details or forms (Fig. 7.8).

Road, Parking and Pedestrianisation

6. Does the building layout take priority over the roads and car parking?

PPG 3 (housing): *'local planning authorities should… place the needs of people before ease of traffic movement in designing the layout of residential development'.* **CABE summary:** *'the building layout should be the priority in any new housing development… the rigid application of highway engineering standards for roads, junction separation distances and turning circles can create an environment which is unpleasant and difficult to use, especially for pedestrians'.*

Span score: Yes.

Span went further by prioritising landscape as the driver for the building layout. The limited size of most developments and their centralised communal gardens, means that the landscape and buildings dominate the road layouts. Ivor Cunningham states that one of the principal reasons for working on the private Cator Estate in Blackheath was that the developments were not then required to meet the local authority's highway standards, which were in danger of destroying the careful balance between house, communal area and access.[33] In any housing scheme, making provision for cars has a critical impact on the making of place. Span's priorities were clear and well-intentioned, but it must be acknowledged, however, that sharp, blind bends and remote parking courts cause concerns amongst residents today. Our understanding of these concerns now can be addressed simply by increasing visual connection and overlooking – an enhancement of Span thinking (Fig. 7.9).

7. Are the streets pedestrian, cycle and vehicle friendly?

PPG 3 (housing): *'local planning authorities should seek to reduce car dependency by facilitating more walking and cycling';* **CABE summary:** *'in a low speed environment, pedestrian, vehicular and cycle routes need not necessarily be segregated… a good streetscape will offer direct connections and crossings that are convenient and easy to use'.*

Span score: Yes (qualified).

On Span estates vehicle speed is managed through the configuration of roads and materials, although residents over time have voiced concerns that some motorists may consider that the roads accessing garage courts are solely for vehicles. Neither is CABE's requirement that routes should be *'well lit, feel safe and make it easy for users to find and follow a route'* fulfilled on all estates.[34] For example, The Plantation feels unsafe for some residents at night. This is, however, not a fundamental design fault because lighting can be improved without changing the scheme.

8. Is the car parking well integrated and situated so it supports the street scene?

PPG 3 (housing): *'focus on the quality of the places and living environments being created and give priority to the needs of pedestrians rather then the movement and parking of vehicles'.* **CABE summary:** *'car parking is one of the most difficult challenges in housing design... At roughly 30 to 50 dwellings per hectare, limiting parking squares and courtyards to 10 spaces will help avoid visual dominance. On-street parking can bring activity to the street and have a traffic calming effect'.* **Span score:** Yes (qualified).

CABE's comments incorporate conflicting demands, i.e. provide on-street parking to calm traffic, but ensure that the fronts of properties are not dominated by cars. The provision of parking facilities at Span estates varies. For example, The Priory (43 dwellings per hectare) has two parking courts (one for 29 vehicles, the other for 13); Fieldend (25 dwellings per hectare) has 49 garages in three courts (the largest being a single run of 25, the smallest of eight); The Lane (57.9 dwellings per hectare) has 42 garages in three courts (11, 12 and 19); and Templemere (14.6 dwellings per hectare) has 90 garages in seven courts (the largest being 21 and the others varying from six to 14).[35] Later developments use the more successful, smaller Templemere courts.

The CABE recommendation is to limit areas of parking that might otherwise 'freeze' the use of large parts of a development area and become unsightly. Span garage courts were always designed as integral components of the estates (Fig. 7.10), but some schemes, for example Corner Keep (Corner Green Phase 2), Blackheath, have dominating parking areas, probably as a result of limited plot areas and restricted access. Whilst the cited examples fail, the body of Span work shows the development of the court principle as a component of the layouts. CABE also requires that *'any development should avoid large areas of unsupervised garage court parking'.*[36] Even courts of 10 garages on a limited plot (for example, The Hall, Blackheath) are remote and are, therefore, prone to vandalism (Fig. 7.11).

9. Does the scheme integrate with the existing roads, paths and surrounding development?

PPS 1 (sustainable development): *'high quality and inclusive design should create well mixed and integrated developments which avoid segregation and have well planned public spaces';* **CABE summary:** *'Designing well-connected layouts depends on the local context (including local security issues) and how the development relates to existing areas'.* **Span score:** Yes.

When building in urban settings Span integrated developments into the existing town form as, for example, in the creation of shops at Parkleys, which links the new development with the existing High

Fig 7.10 Parking is organised as shared garage courts on the perimeter of the site, 2006.

Fig 7.11 Parking at Holme Chase, 2006.

Fig 7.12 Children can still enjoy free play. The improvised dens are called Tree 1, Tree 2, Tree 3 etc, Corner Green, Blackheath, 2006.

Street. Other estates, such as Highsett 1, Hallgate, Spangate and Southrow are aligned with existing frontages. Crucially, they are not gated or isolated; access and even stair halls are open to the street, with thresholds to private spaces implied through materials rather than locked barriers. The connection of the estates to streets is handled at the scale of the surrounding developments, by presenting houses to the street (as, for example, at Fieldend and The Lane) unless the access to the site is too narrow (as at The Plantation and Streetfield Mews). Such permeable connections, however, are unlikely to be built now, because of local security issues. Access to the cited examples at Blackheath remains protected only through overlooking or by the addition of security grilles on individual apartment doors. This does not invalidate the principles and intent of the designs, which are consistent with CABE's recommendations. In an area with a high crime rate, the planting could provide good hiding spaces for muggers; the parking courts would then appear threatening. It is, therefore, suggested that design factors alone cannot provide the protection, but rather the creation of a community that not only maintains an estate, but can support those who live there.

10. Are public spaces and pedestrian routes overlooked and do they feel safe?
PPG 17 (planning for open space): *'in identifying where to locate new areas of open space… carefully consider security and personal safety, especially for children'.* **CABE summary:** *'Developments should be planned in a way that makes sure buildings overlook all public spaces, roads and footpaths to increase surveillance. Windows and doors opening onto all streets and footpaths can provide greater security for users. Bay and corner windows will provide views in different directions, as well as bringing more light into people's homes. Blank gable walls facing onto public spaces should be avoided'.*
Span score: Yes.

All Span communal spaces are overlooked by houses and flats. Blank gable walls are used in many schemes, but when they occur within groups of housing the spaces are overlooked by other units. Visiting Span estates one is always conscious of being visible. However, there are instances (Brooklands Park for example) where, on a limited site area, blank gables are against the garage courts making the garages prone to vandalism or theft.[37] This was addressed in later schemes.

Design and construction
11. Is the design specific to the scheme?
PPS 1 (sustainable development): *'design which is inappropriate in its context, or which fails to take the opportunities available for improving the character and quality of an area and the way it functions, should not be accepted'.* **CABE summary:** *'The design of individual homes and entire neighbourhoods should be specific to context, based on an understanding of the way the local area looks and works… It is not about style. A good*

design should make best use of the land, provide value and create successful places with character, variety and identity'.
Span score: Yes (qualified).

These points have been demonstrated in Questions 2 and 5. As a qualification, it is worth noting the number of times particular house types and materials are repeated. Fieldend, Corner Green Phase 1 and The Plantation all use the same house type and materials: it is the landscaping and layouts that make the designs specific to each scheme.

12. Is public space well designed and does it have management arrangements in place?
PPG 17 (planning for open space): *'new open spaces should improve the quality of the public realm through good design'.* **CABE summary:** *'If this is well designed it will result in a pleasurable place that will be popular and well used. This brings with it economic, social, environmental and cultural benefits...Too often, public space is the area left once buildings have been planned... A maintenance plan needs to be in place from the start to guarantee long-term success'.*
Span score: Yes.

Chapter 6 outlines the structure of the Span maintenance arrangements in place at purchase and landscape planning as indivisible from the architecture of the buildings.[38] The structure provides 'ownership' of maintenance of shared space for residents and is a flexible model for other forms of tenure, where the need to maintain the collective space, rather than a need to maintain value, is realised. As a result, Span estates are designed to encourage the development of a community and are 'pleasurable… popular and well-used' places. For example, at Corner Green Phase 1, the relationship of the house porches to the landscaping allows children to come and go as they wish and, if required, to be supervised by one household. The communal spaces encourage children's 'play and adventure, or for reflection and learning', as recommended by CABE (Figs. 7.12 and 7.13).[39]

13. Do buildings or space outperform statutory minima, such as the Building Regulations?
PPG 3 (housing): *'local planning authorities should promote the energy efficiency of new housing where possible'.* **CABE summary:** '
• *Good space standards contribute to the long-term flexibility and future proofing (able to accommodate changing lifestyle demands) of a home.* • *For various aspects of building performance, including energy efficiency, the higher levels of achievement under Ecohomes or other equivalent standards are relevant reference points.* • *Good sound insulation between homes is important, especially for schemes where there are lots of houses close together. The biggest effect on privacy is sound coming through dividing walls'.*
Span score: Yes (qualified).

Fig 7.13   The design of the front porches with their double doors means that children can come and go as they please, as seen here at Corner Green, 2006.

The constant refinement and development of the house and flat plans demonstrates not only that Span was exceeding the space standards recommended at the time of construction, but also that great efforts were made to provide complex three dimensional space. The relevant standards were provided by the Ministry of Health's *Housing Manual* 1949 and the Parker Morris standards.[40] These introduced requirements for storage that were incorporated into Span house planning (although most residents today would comment that this provision does not meet the needs of long-term ownership or current purchasing patterns). The *Housing Manual* provided sample plans, like many other design guides of the time; rooms are indicated as cellular or traditional (fully enclosed with doors) (Fig. 7.14). Span brought modernist free space planning, '3 dimensional space', (see endnote 3) to a mass market by the use of sliding panels (or lightwells); one is always aware of a space beyond, which creates an impression of even more generous space within a small house (Fig. 7.15). Regulations or recommendations in guidelines were seen by Lyons as a necessity, but not the completion of a design: 'the design process is not just problem solving: that is the easy part'.[41]

Span met the Building Regulations requirements for conservation of heat and power and sound separation at the minimum standards of the time.[42] The sound transfer between the 1960s house types, for example, is not acceptable today and insulation in many house types is non-existent. CABE recommends that 'well-designed homes will excel in some, if not all, of these areas',[43] and it is clear that some Span estates do not meet this criteria. However, by achieving current standards, would the schemes be radically different or impossible to build? There is no doubt that all the built designs could be reproduced now and achieve present standards without affecting the appearance or organisation of the original designs.[44]

14. Has the scheme made use of advances in construction or technology that enhance its performance, quality and attractiveness?
CABE summary: *'Advanced building technology can help improve quality and reduce defects in construction, improve health and safety on site and improve the environmental performance of a home... Examples of systems that are considered as advanced forms of construction include prefabricated elements such as "thin joint blocks" (glued brick panels), fast track foundations or advanced methods of cladding'.*
Span score: No.

The Span house and flat designs could now be constructed by the currently recommended methods and techniques (including prefabricated bathrooms and toilets). Elements such as window and door framing and porches were, at the time, prefabricated off site, but the construction was generally traditional, with wet trades (poured foundations, masonry walls and plaster). Construction did develop to embrace lightweight steel frames for faster erection during the

Fig 7.14   An example of an urban terraced house published in *The Housing Manual* 1949.

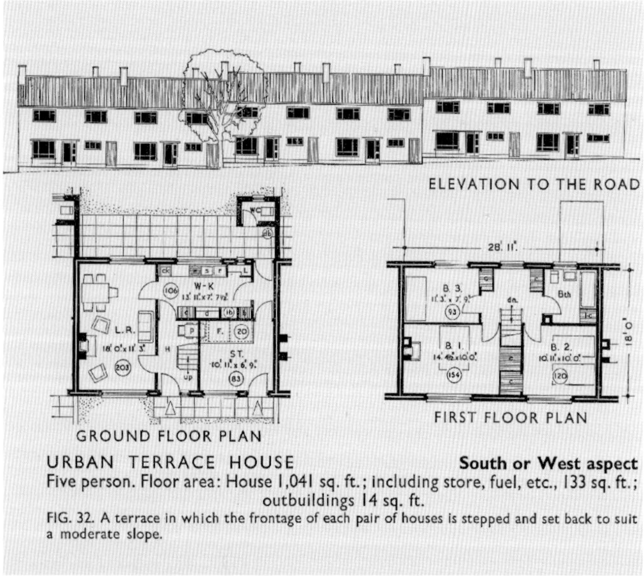

Fig 7.15   A diagram describing ideas for open plan space and connected rooms was published in *Homes for Today and Tomorrow* (1961).

Fig 7.16   Flats above the local shops at Parkleys, 2006.

period when Span estates were being built. The *Building for Life* criteria, however, does not consider the use of tried (and improved) methods, such as panel systems, as against untried technological advances. Nor is there a reflection on cost. Volume housebuilders use some prefabrication techniques, but generally use the same construction methods used by Span.[45]

15. Do internal spaces and layout allow for adaptation, conversion or extension?
CABE summary: *'The main consideration is adaptability. For houses, the design could accommodate a downstairs toilet, wider doorways, level entrances and allow for a lift or stair lift to be fitted in the future. The potential to extend back or upwards, or to open up between rooms to allow open plan living, is valuable, as is garden space and the space to allow a conservatory to be added'.*
Span score: 'Yes.

Because most of the estates are in high-value locations, there is a large price jump to the next band rating. This, combined with the high level of satisfaction amongst residents and changing needs through long tenure, has led to many examples of rear extensions and adaptations, generally achieved without losing the clarity of the original design. It would also be possible to adapt the house plan and layouts to accommodate much larger expanding units. As the estates are small, they are generally designed for one household type with two or three bedrooms. As an example, one group of 16 houses in Blackheath has two end terraces extended by 50 per cent to make larger family houses, seven houses have had living room extensions and five have been adapted with downstairs bathrooms and bedrooms for elderly or disabled residents.

The residents' society's rules prohibit business operations within houses. Whilst this was intended to reduce traffic and disturbance, working patterns are changing. The house types have flexible living room spaces that can be used for home working, which, on a small scale, could achieve the level of inhabitation and security once provided by housewives.

Environment and community

16. Does the development have easy access to public transport?
PPG 13 (transport): *'local planning authorities should actively manage the patterns of urban growth to make the fullest use of public transport'.*
CABE summary: *'For smaller developments, public transport connections within a 400-metre radius or five-minute walk would be sufficient'.*
Span score: Yes (qualified).

Span sites were carefully chosen for access to public transport connections into urban centres (Fig. 7.16). In some cases the exceptions are, not surprisingly, a reflection of a particular area's current public transport provision. Weymede and Grasmere (Byfleet) and Templemere (Weybridge) are located in car-dependent suburbs, although bus services stop near the estates. In other cases, the available land was outside the current understanding of a five-minute neighbourhood walking distance (for example, The Plantation, Blackheath), but within a 10-minute walking distance acceptable for urban areas. The largest development, New Ash Green, generated bus links to connect the village to train stations.

17. Does the development have any features that reduce its environmental impact?
CABE summary: *'There is a wide variety of ways that housebuilders can reduce a scheme's effect on the environment. This question relates to the overall development where site-wide environmental approaches have been adopted (environmental design for individual houses is covered in number 13). Features may include: • using alternative and renewable energy schemes • promoting recycling • using sustainable drainage systems • reducing construction waste • prioritising brownfield development • increasing biodiversity'.*
Span score: Yes (qualified).

The emphasis on high density and shared space in the suburban schemes demonstrates their sustainable intent. Likewise, the use of infill land, brownfield sites, market gardens or the grounds of single houses, was sustainable.[46] The design thinking that saw the total integration of two apparently different disciplines, building and landscape design, could encompass the integration of environmental systems (such as photovoltaics or grey water recycling), thereby continuing the evolution of Span's work.

18. Is there a tenure mix that reflects the needs of the local community?
PPG 3 (housing): *'there should be greater choice of housing and that*

Fig 7.17   Marina, Villamoura, Portugal, drawn by Robert Voticky 1979.

housing should not reinforce social distinctions. The needs of all in the community should be recognised, including those in need of affordable or special housing'. **CABE summary:** *'The percentage of affordable housing should be based on an assessment of the area in question. Successful development fully integrates the tenure mix avoiding differentiation between individual dwellings and parts of the scheme based on their tenure'.*
Span score: Yes (qualified).

Span's agenda was to provide housing in good locations for people who could not otherwise afford to live there. The size of the estates meant that this was a modest proposal that could not cater for all sectors of society. It is worth noting that the demographics of the Blackheath Cator Estate were changed in part by the 22 Span estates and, more significantly, by a number of Lewisham and Greenwich council housing developments constructed before and at the same time as Span. The issues of social integration were addressed at a wider planning policy level that, as evidenced by PPG3, is now changing.

The current requirement to provide affordable homes to the same standard as those sold at full price can make small-scale development less viable. It is impossible to assess if current policy would have changed Span's business model.[47]

19. Is there an accommodation mix that reflects the needs and aspirations of the local community?
PPG 3 (housing): *'local planning authorities should… provide wider housing opportunity and choice and a better mix in the size, type and location of housing.* **CABE summary:** *'A good mix of housing types and sizes is important in creating a basis for a balanced community. Even comparatively small developments can have a wide mix of types of property. Also, a mix of housing types and uses can create more attractive residential environments with greater diversity in building forms and scales'.*
Span score: Yes (qualified).

Span's performance against this criteria is a reflection of the size of development and the changing demographics noted by CABE: 'Since 1971, the average size of household has declined from 2.91 persons to 2.31, whilst one-person households have grown from 17 per cent to 31 per cent'.[48] The small-scale Span developments probably addressed the contemporary demographics and the company acknowledged changing patterns in its later developments, with a mix of units (for example 15 houses and five flats at Streetfield Mews) and various sizes of units for different age groups at New Ash Green. CABE recommends that 'Layouts should aim to reduce possible tensions between families, older people and students for example by considering the different activities of

these groups and maintaining privacy between them'.[49] The variety of tenure and mix of ages and family types reflected in current ownership of Span houses is an indication that the schemes satisfy the recommendations.

The nature of Span's commercial model meant that small developments provided a mix within an existing area, developed over time with evolving ideas. This is part of its success. Where Span did try to provide a new community at New Ash Green, the variety of the various phases and zones did not provide sufficient differentiation and architectural diversity (even when seen with the later Bovis housing). However, as explained in Chapter 5, the intention was to provide diversity within a larger county framework.

Span was an evolving project. Lyons's Vilamoura masterplan for the town centre area on a 120-hectare site around a marina, shows a much richer diversity of urban form and character, probably as a result of what was learnt at New Ash Green (Fig. 7.17). The latter was an assemblage of layouts and forms that had previously been tested in individual developments, where diversity was provided by existing buildings. The realisation of play and diversity learnt in Portugal directly feeds into the complex forms of Mallard Place.[50]

20. Does the development provide for (or is it close to) community facilities, such as a school, parks, play areas, shops, pubs or cafés? **PPS 1** (sustainable development): *'good design should contribute positively to making places better for people'.* **CABE summary:** *'Appropriate community facilities and services, such as open spaces, crèches, day-care and health services, local pubs and other places for residents, are important in this framework'.*
Span score: Yes.

The locations of small developments were chosen for easy access to existing centres and facilities.[51] The exception is provided by New Ash Green (see Chapter 5), which fulfills this criteria because all the recommended facilities were integral to the masterplanning from its inception.

The success of Span

The *Building for Life* questions have proved a valuable tool in assessing Span projects, which are seen to achieve a gold standard, according to the scheme's criteria of excellence. The Span estates were developed in the same policy environment of housing demand as today, the designs being driven by a sensitivity to the needs for good housing and shared spaces. Lyons's practice, therefore, can be said to have created, or at least developed, the same design approach now recommended by CABE. The ultimate validations are that the houses have retained their value, all remain desirable places to live, and have kept their intended character; the schemes are as inspiring

to designers and residents today as they were when first built. Span's poor score regarding construction, might demonstrate that good building technology alone does not make good architecture or, more importantly, a good home. In Lyons's own words, 'the test of good housing is not whether it can be built easily, but whether it can be lived in easily'[52] and 'technology is not a substitute for design and neither is research'.[53]

These qualifications are, in part, an acknowledgement that the principles by which Lyons worked were refined over 36 years, through observation of what was successful. His practice not only adapted and developed schemes throughout the company's life, but also drew on non-Span housing work; the office and Lyons's house were also test beds for ideas, forms and materials.[54] Lyons even continued his commitment to affordable design after having apparently 'disappeared' at New Ash Green: 'the fact that Span folded was a badge of honour and a reflection of the worthiness of their projects'.[55] Where present day standards are not met on the built estates, they could be achieved on a hypothetical new Span estate, without altering the character or principles of the design. The varied, developing stylistic character of Span estates between 1948 and 1984 also shows that the image, style or appearance of a development is irrelevant to the quality of a home or shared space: the most difficult element of design is to think about content rather than surface.

The quest for successful housing is a constant search for the new: new patterns, images and technologies.[56] Whilst the *Building for Life* document reveals a greater understanding of place and community than was evident, for example, in the Parker Morris Report, there still needs to be careful study of a body of work, such as Span's refinement of house plans. Furthermore, reflection on how communities can continue to be sustained through legal structures, independent of the physical aspects of a scheme, would also be valuable. Whilst management is probably the most important strand of the Span project, the success and continued relevance of the schemes is also due to a fortuitous working relationship between the individuals involved. Architecturally, this is represented by a landscape design philosophy that did not just specify planting, but actually took over the house layouts and, ultimately, the house planning. This was matched with a sensibility that architecture is no more than the setting for the activities within it and around it. Image must be divorced from an assessment of the projects: 'people are perfectly clear about their prejudices, but not their needs'.[57]

Lyons fused modernist and vernacular traditions to achieve what the practice believed reflected life in contemporary England. The functional requirements of privacy and efficiency could be matched with a need for well-planned space. The modernism of Lyons's training provided the design intent to solve technical problems efficiently. The models for shared space and planning were taken from Georgian London and 18th-century landscaping: a balance between ordered arrangement that worked (the Georgian square) and the notion of an Arcadian, often architectural, landscape. This meant that the work was outside the perceived architectural mainstream of pure modernist housing, such as that commissioned by the London County Council. The success of Span was in understanding the value of good design, that time invested in design would benefit the developer and the long-term interests of the neighbourhood, and that by initiating a residents' management structure the impermanence of construction would be safeguarded long after the architect's role was completed.

ENDNOTES

1. *Building for Life* is a scheme led by CABE and the Home Builders Federation. It is supported by the Civic Trust, Design for Homes, English Partnerships and the Housing Corporation. See www.designforhomes.org. The authors are grateful to CABE commissioner Dickon Robinson CBE for his suggestion to evaluate Span against these criteria.

2. Of the 73 completed Span developments 35 are in conservation areas and four are listed (Hallgate and 3–35 Southrow, Blackheath; Highsett 1, Cambridge; Parkleys, Ham Common). Two of the listed buildings, Hallgate and Southrow are amongst seven schemes refused planning consent but won on appeal; amongst eight schemes which received Housing Design Awards and amongst six which received Civic Trust awards.

3. *Grand Designs* 13, March 2005, pp. 57–81.

4. Two examples are provided by Graham Morrison, Allies and Morrison Architects, and Stephen Proctor, Proctor and Matthews Architects. Morrison worked in Lyons's practice 1976–1978. The experience gave him the confidence to consider his own practice's development of their office building. It also provided him with an understanding of the enjoyment of the human needs of architecture as well as a search for an English modernism (interviews with authors March and April 2006). Proctor first encountered Span's work at Blackheath when planning his practice's housing scheme at Greenwich Millennium Village Phase 2 (completed in 2001). For him the body of work demonstrated the potential for high-density housing with attractive shared spaces. The practice has been inspired by Span's work to undertake a housing development scheme in Harlow (interview with authors March 2006).

5. The average cost of a terraced house in the UK in the first quarter 2006 was £143,512; in Greater London the average was £326,039. A terraced T7, T8 or T15 house in Blackheath could have sold for £320,000 to £360,000; Corner Green Phase 1 T8 houses were marketed at £3,850 to £3,950 (it was one of these that was sold as the millionth private post-war house in

December 1959 for £4,300, *Daily Express*, 7 December 1959). The average UK house price in 1960 was £2,784. London weighting and comparison of the average house measured against a terraced house make comparisons difficult but the conclusion that the Span houses have retained their value is inescapable. These figures are based on information provided by the Economic and Social Research Council and the Land Registry of England and Wales, and published by the BBC (current data; figures updated 8 May 2006 and based on sales January to March 2006).

6. 'Between 80 per cent and 90 per cent of the owners of our properties are drawn from the professional, administrative and executive classes. The younger professional man, the middle class buyer – call him what you will – is a special case. His financial status is sometimes potential rather than actual. But he will have absorbed, almost without thinking, the tradition of thrift, the sense of community, duty towards his family that make him the best possible kind of buyer in terms of stability and security'. Span Developments, marketing brochure for the Hall Phase 2 and companies profile c1957, p. 13.

7. *ibid*, p. 7.

8. A fuller definition is provided on the website www.communities.gov.uk/communities, which says: sustainable communities are those that 'meet the diverse needs of existing and future residents, are sensitive to their environment, and contribute to a high quality of life. They are safe and inclusive, well planned, built and run, and offer equality of opportunity and good services for all.'

9. Historic Housing Design Awards 2005 (www.designforhomes.org); historic award for Mallard Place. The award was supported by a brief description: 'The success of the concept is still evident today and the visionary approach to effective long-term estate management by a residents' association has served residents well and maintained the quality of environment that they enjoyed at the start... Think Span, think 1960s. Flat roofs, glazed porches, painted timber, formica worktops and parquet floors. Those who know a little about Span assume it all ended in tears with New Ash Green, the end of the decade and of a vision. Mallard Place was completed in 1984 and won a Housing Design Award and a Civic Trust Award in 1985, five years after Eric Lyons died. Surviving partner Ivor Cunningham says he and Lyons had a "Damascene moment" after they won a competition to design an Algarve resort. They thought their Vilamora so much fun that they wanted to repeat the vibrant designs in Britain... Here is a scheme built at just under 58 homes to the hectare, with one- and two-bed flats, two, three and four-bed houses, Kew-like planting, charming architecture and unparalleled amenity. Local agents say people queue to pay over the odds to live here. Anyone seeking an irresistible higher

density model need look no further'.

10. Tom Dyckhoff, 'Build Homes, not just Houses', *Sunday Times, Inside Out Magazine,* 1 April 2006, p. 120.

11. Department of the Environment, Transport and the Regions (DETR), *'Planning the Communities of the Future'*, 23 February 1998.

12. UK Parliament Memorandum, DETR H04, 1998.

13. *Towards an Urban Renaissance: Final Report,* (London: Urban Task Force, 1999). The number of houses required and discussion of strategies for meeting the demand closely parallels the housing demand identified during and shortly after the Second World War. This is discussed at length in Nicholas Bullock, *Building the Post-War World* (London: Routledge, 2002), p. 151, Chapter 7, 'Preparing for Reconstruction'.

14. Office of the Deputy Prime Minister, February 2006; PPS3 is proposed to replace Planning Policy Guidance note PPG3 'Housing', March 2000 with two updates January 2005.

15. Jan-Carlos Kucharek, 'Happiness per Hectare', *RIBA Journal,* 113/ 5, May 2006, p. 65.

16. *ibid.* Richard MacCormac, architect and former President of the RIBA, suggests that 'the suburb is the aspirational English way of living. We are keen on testing whether it's possible to meet the sustainable housing agenda using the suburban housing idiom'.

17. The introduction to an unpublished Span corporate identity brochure (RIBA archive reference SPAN 2/2 dating from 1966 or 1967), explains the evolution of the company's approach as 'not conceived as a conscious act in the first instance, it was basically an amalgam of three needs – building – landscape – architecture... the earliest efforts were directed to achieving housing – in an economical form at a price competitive with the common market but with design and environment as the quality "the others hadn't got" (and still haven't got!)'.

18. Ian Nairn, *The more we are together: Eric Lyons, the architect and suburbia,* BBC television documentary.

19. The pamphlet is described as 'circulated by the National House-Builders' Registration Council'. The NHBRC is the forerunner of the National House Builders Council (NHBC). There is no copyright, pressmark or date of publication. The date of 1969 is assumed from examples quoted and that it was catalogued in the RIBA library in 1970.

20. *ibid.* p. 2.

21. *ibid,* p. 1.

22. *ibid,* p. 1.

23. 'The prognosis is clear: if Britain's attempts at tackling its housing crisis are to succeed they will necessarily involve the provision of new suburban development on a significant scale. This raises a major challenge for a profession [architecture] long since persuaded of the suburb's fundamental deficiencies. However sniffily they might view the prospect, the need for British architects to reclaim the ideal from the clutches of Barratt and Wimpey has never been more pressing'. Ellis Woodman, *Building Design,* 14 October 2005, p. 20. The perception that the housing provided by housebuilders is inferior or inappropriate can be summarised by Lyons's own observations: 'I can't think of anything more incongruous than a man in drainpipe trousers getting out of a new Ford Consul and walking into a mock Tudor house' (1961, quote provided by Ivor Cunningham). Such anecdotal observation is as true today and is supported by the plethora of design guides produced by CABE and government to promote improved housing design.

24. It is worth observing that the energy required to plan and deliver 73 individual developments (not counting a small number taken to detailing planning) with all the attendant risks, costs and delays over a 34 year period is a remarkable achievement. The office of Eric Lyons completed 2,057 dwellings for Span: the remainder was provided by four other practices (Andrews Emerson and Sherlock; Calderhead and Scoble; R. Towning Hill and Partners; and Gooday and Noble) for seven developments.

25. World's End (742 flats) by Eric Lyons Cadbury-Brown Group Partnership for the Royal Borough of Kensington and Chelsea (1963–1979); Mayford (183 flats and a children's home); Oakley Square, Camden for St Pancras Borough Council (1963–1971); Urban Community, Westbourne Road (268 houses, 132 flats) for LB Islington (1969–1976); high-density low rise-housing, Copenhagen Street (242 dwellings) for the London Borough of Islington.

26. UK Parliament Memorandum by DETR H04, 1998.

27. *op. cit., Community Layouts in Private Housing,* p. 1, foreword.

28. Developments largely confined to the southeast. See Gazetteer.

29. 'On a small estate in Blackheath are three doctors, several company directors, an analytical chemist, a bank official, several architects, an accountant, a lecturer in economics, two journalists, an advertising executive, a nuclear engineer, a lecturer in physics, a principal scientific officer, four civil engineers, two surveyors, a senior oil executive, a solicitor and two civil servants. This pattern is repeated on each development'. Hall Phase 2 marketing brochure, 1957, *op. cit.,* p. 3.

30. Based on comments from members of various residents' societies; information provided by Rosemary Clements, chair of the Hall Residents' Society, November 2005; observations by the authors as shareholders of the Brook Park Residents' Society. The delays to completing maintenance or the quality of work at particular times have not affected the overall character of any of the estates. Another example is the 24-unit Span development at The Paddox, Squitchley Lane, Oxford (1965), the focus of a study to assess the success of housing schemes. It was found that the active involvement of residents on the Committee was dependent on the scale of repairs required (and by extension

the scale of costs involved), the number of absentee landlords (at the time of the study there were five) and the ability to rely on the work of a minimum of six Committee members. A Paddox resident also noted that had the estate been built to its original intended size (53 units), there would have been five times as many candidates for a Committee of the same size addressing the same maintenance issues, albeit at a larger scale. This finding is repeated through comments made by chairs of residents' societies on other estates today. Nicholas Smith, *Studying Housing Success*, dissertation Department of Town Planning, Oxford Polytechnic January 1985; taken from Section 3 'The Human response to the Scheme'. See also James Strike, *The Spirit of Span Housing* (London: Strike Print, 2005), Chapters 6 and 7 for the pressures faced by a typical residents' society and the ways society rules could be enforced more strongly as the pressures on change increase.

31. *Delivering great places to live: 20 questions you need to answer* (2005) is available to download from www.buildingforlife.org or can be obtained from CABE free of charge.

32. Ivor Cunningham points out that, whilst detailed costings are not now available, the local authority projects by the practice for London boroughs were built to a more expensive and better standard than those for Span (conversation with the authors).

33. Ivor Cunningham's presentation to CABE Space tour of Blackheath, 18 October 2005.

34. op. cit., *Delivering great places to live*, p. 10.

35. The density of the Templemere estate is distorted by the retention of woodland: excluding this area the density is 21 dwellings per hectare.

36. op. cit., *Delivering great places to live*, p. 11.

37. At Brooklands Park the site conditions meant that the courts are open to the street.

38. See Chapters 3 and 6.

39. op. cit., *Delivering great places to live*, p. 15.

40. Ministry of Housing and Local Government, *Homes for Today and Tomorrow*, (London: HMSO, 1961).

41. 'The Architect's Approach to Architecture', *RIBA Journal*, 6 February 1968.

42. The need to see the Building Regulations as a minimum that should be exceeded is now a fundamental aspect of all new regulations.

43. op. cit., *Delivering great places to live*, p. 16.

44. As an example the high proportion of glazing in the T15 house (The Lane and Brooklands Park, Blackheath) exceeds the current standards set in draft Part L1A (conservation of heat and power 2006). This requires that the maximum area of windows and doors is to be 25 per cent of floor area or if less the exposed façade area. The glazing in the T15 is 34.8

per cent. The regulations are for reference and performance is measured through loss, gain and consumption. The design would still be achievable but the design time and costs of measures to compensate for the architectural intent could be cost prohibitive for a developer.

45. We will have to await the outcome and assessment in use of the ODPM's £60,000 house competition to see if the CABE recommendations are appropriate. Volume housebuilders achieve the ODPM cost threshold through experienced management and the repetition of standard details.

46. The 16 units of Brooklands Park, for example, were constructed in the grounds of two villas, 42 and 44 Blackheath Park.

47. As an indication of the likely impact the 22 Blackheath estates are within the London Borough of Greenwich. The authority's Unitary Development Plan requires that 35 per cent of new homes are affordable (SH5) developments of 15 units or more or for sites in excess of 0.5 hectares (H16). Fourteen of the estates (including The Hall phase four which qualifies on site area) would now have to comply.

48. Office for National Statistics (2004) quoted by CABE in *Building for Life*, www.designforhomes.org.

49. op. cit., *Delivering great places to live*, p. 22.

50. Current thinking for large developments addresses diversity by designing it into the masterplan. A recent model promoted by CABE is the Leidsche Rijn masterplan for 30,000 dwellings outside Utrecht, by Kees Christiaanse Architects and Planners. Variety was provided by parcelling district plans with set rules, but the architectural language was provided by different practices designing approximately 140 houses each.

51. The Blackheath estates remain popular because they are in the catchment area of Brooklands State Primary School. 'Britain's most exclusive schools (400 yards away and you're out)', *The Observer*, 13 July 2003.

52. 'Test of Good Housing', *The Sunday Times*, 10 November 1969.

53. 'Managing without Design', *RIBA Journal*, September 1966, p. 459.

54. Lyons added a Parkleys ABC flat to Mill House in 1955, converting the majority of the old house into flats.

55. Interview with Dickon Robinson, April 2006.

56. op. cit., 'Build Homes, not just Houses', p. 120.

57. Eric Lyons, *Punch*, 17 January 1962. It is worth noting the summary of Span's work in Edward Jones and Christopher Woodward, *A Guide to the Architecture of London* (London: 1983), p. 393 reference XII: 'Whilst the layouts have been widely and successfully copied, Lyons' architectural style, with its attempts to extend the range of materials usable for houses (by such means as tile hanging and weather boarding), later degenerated, and was perhaps partly responsible for the present ubiquitous Pixie style'.

1956 MILL HOUSE (LYONS'S HOUSE)

Mill House, East Molesey: view of entrance screen.

Mill House, East Molesey: view of living area.

Mill House, East Molesey: detail of the kitchen.

Mill House, East Molesey: view from garden.

Mill House, East Molesey: view from front
entrance towards dining platform and garden.

Parkleys, Ham Common: first floor shared landing to flats over shops.

Parkleys, Ham Common: view of shop unit on Upper Ham Road.

1956 PARKLEYS, HAM COMMON

Parkleys, Ham Common: entrance to Marlowe Court.

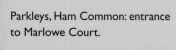

The Priory, Blackheath: flat entrance with hard landscaping materials used in lobby.

1956 THE PRIORY, BLACKHEATH

The Priory, Blackheath: junction between flats around an entrance.

The Keep, Blackheath: T2 houses with exposed gable walls at offset between two defined areas of communal landscaping.

1957 THE KEEP, BLACKHEATH

The Keep, Blackheath: three T2 houses. Porches and colour schemes define the individual house within the whole.

The Hall, phase 2, Blackheath: communal landscaping and playground.

1958 THE HALL, PHASE 2, BLACKHEATH

The Hall, phase 2, Blackheath: T2 houses fronting communal landscaping and playground.

The Hall, phase 2, Blackheath: T2 houses fronting Foxes Dale.

Hallgate, Blackheath: view of
west gable on Foxes Dale.

1958 HALLGATE, BLACKHEATH

Hallgate, Blackheath: view looking
north back to entrance to the Hall
off Blackheath Park under Hallgate.

Hallgate, Blackheath: view of
entrances to flats in passageway
between Blackheath Park and
The Hall. *The Architect in Society*
sculpture (Fig. 1.1) faces the
Hallgate lettering.

HALLGATE

1960 HIGHSETT 1, CAMBRIDGE

Highsett phase 1, Cambridge: flats' entrance in the east range of the quadrangle.

Southrow, Blackheath: view from the open northwest corner on Pond Road with the maisonettes on the left and apartments on the right.

1963 SOUTHROW, BLACKHEATH

Southrow, Blackheath: view from the Heath of the main entrance to the flats and quadrangle.

Southrow, Blackheath: view looking south of the maisonettes.

Southrow, Blackheath: entrance to courtyard and flats off the Heath.

1965 HIGHSETT, PHASE 3, CAMBRIDGE

Highsett phase 3, Cambridge: view of entrances to R22-type houses
on the west edge of the development.

Holme Chase, Weybridge: view of entrances to E1, E2, E3
house types (west side of the development).

Holme Chase, Weybridge: entrance to E2/E3 houses
on south side of development.

1966 HOLME CHASE, WEYBRIDGE

Holme Chase, Weybridge: view from central
communal garden looking southwest.

1967-9 NEW ASH GREEN, KENT

New Ash Green: Knights Croft, (Zone 3). Houses from the K2
range, looking northwest.

New Ash Green: Knight's Croft, (Zone 3),
central path dissecting courtyards composed of
K1A bungalows, view looking east.

New Ash Green: Knight's Croft, (Zone 3),
K1A bungalow, view looking southeast.

New Ash Green: Over Minnis, (Zone 1). Houses from the K2 range. View from North Ash Road looking northwest.

New Ash Green, Kent: (Zone 5) Lambardes, KL1 house type. View looking south.

Corner Keep (Corner Green Phase 2), Blackheath: view of A and B type houses looking east, seen from Corner Green.

Corner Keep (Corner Green Phase 2), Blackheath: view of B2MX-type house looking south.

1979 CORNER KEEP (CORNER GREEN PHASE 2), BLACKHEATH

Mallard Place, Twickenham: view of W1 and N1 type houses looking east.

1984 MALLARD PLACE

Mallard Place, Twickenham: view of communal pool
and frontages to the River Thames.

Mallard Place, Twickenham: view of dining and living areas in a W1 type house.

INTERIORS

Corner Keep (Corner Green Phase 2), Blackheath: view of living room and
kitchen looking towards garden in an A3M three-storey house.

Lambardes (Zone 5), New Ash Green: interior of a KL4 type house.

Knight's Croft (Zone 3), New Ash Green: view of living
area and kitchen screen in a type KIA bungalow.

Parkleys, Ham Common: flat in Dryden Court.

Parkleys, Ham Common: flat in Dryden Court with original
fireplace. The Tecta chair was designed by Eric Lyons.

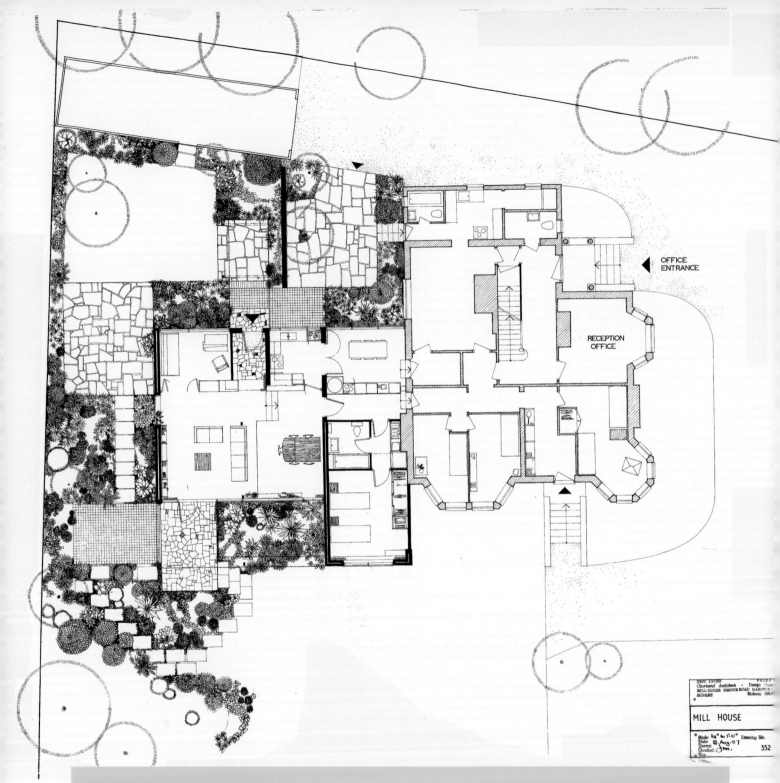

OFFICE
ENTRANCE

RECEPTION
OFFICE

MILL HOUSE

352

1957 MILL HOUSE (LYONS'S HOUSE)

Design for alterations and additions to Mill House, East Molesey, Surrey, 1957c. In 1956, Eric Lyons added a one-storey addition to the turreted 19th-century Mill House which had been the family residence and office since 1944. In this ground floor plan, Lyons shows the arrangement of furniture, dense planting and paving.

Dates given are correct as far as can be ascertained and missing data is indicated by a question mark.

Eric Lyons Partnerships

Eric Lyons & Geoffrey Townsend (EL&GPT)
Eric Lyons (EL)
Eric Lyons & Partners (EL&P)
Eric Lyons Cunningham Partnership (ELCP)
Eric Lyons Cunningham Metcalfe (ELCM)

Partners

Eric Lyons: 1945–80	EL&GPT, EL, EL&P, ELCP
Geoffrey Townsend: 1945–53	EL&GPT
Ivor Cunningham: 1962–2003	EL&P, ELCP, ELCM
Gilbert Powell: 1962–71	EL&P
Warner Baxter: 1968–72, 1978–81	ELCP
Anthony Butler: 1968	ELCP
Richard Lyons: 1972–85	ELCP
John Metcalfe: 1991–94	ELCM

Eric Lyons Cadbury-Brown Group Partnership: 1967–79

Eric Lyons, Jim Cadbury-Brown, Ivor Cunningham, John Metcalfe, Betty Cadbury-Brown

Ivor Cunningham Landscape Design: 1985–2004

Ivor Cunningham

Span Companies

Eden Residential Construction: 1948–51   Director: Geoffrey Townsend

Bargood Estates: 1951–60   Directors: Geoffrey Townsend, Henry Cushman (Alliance Building Society Agent)

Townsman Investments: 1953–60   Directors: Geoffrey Townsend, Henry Cushman

Hampton Cross: 1953–?   Directors: Geoffrey Townsend, Henry Cushman

Foxdale Property Investments: 1954–?   Directors: Geoffrey Townsend, Leslie Bilsby

Priory Hall: 1954   Directors: Geoffrey Townsend, Leslie Bilsby

Span Developments Ltd: 1957–64   Directors: Ernest Haynes (Royal London Insurance), Geoffrey Townsend, Leslie Bilsby

Building Span: 1964–?   Directors: Geoffrey Townsend, Leslie Bilsby, Frank and Jack Gostling (E. Gostling Builders)

Span Kent: 1964–70   Directors: Ernest Haynes (Royal London Insurance), Geoffrey Townsend, Leslie Bilsby, Frank and Jack Gostling (E. Gostling Builders)

Span Environments: 1976–84   Directors: Geoffrey Townsend, Leslie Bilsby, Frank and Jack Gostling (E. Gostling Builders)

Mill House Studio Staff

Architects:

John Sheldon (1945–9)
Jack Howe (late 1940s)
Geoffrey Scoble (1949-58)
William Pack (?–1955)
John Bednall (?–1956)
Fred Hughes (?–1956)
Kenneth Wood (?–1956)
John Kerss (?–1958)
Ivor Cunningham, later partner (1955–62)
Iain Langlands (1956–?)
John Malyan (1956–?)
Ronald Jones (1956–7)
Robin Butterell (1957–9)
Warner Baxter, later partner (1959–68)
Ivor Plummer (1961–2)
Martin Marquiston (1961–3)
Robin Matthews (1961–3)
Keith Blowers (1963–?)
Judy Bratt (1967–8)
Louis Hawkins, student (1967–8, 1972–3)

Adrian Hills (1967–9)
Michael Chester (1967–70)
Bera Sehmi (1967–72, 1976–79)
Brian Pugh (1968)
Neil Carr-Jones (1969–70)
Rodney Whittaker, student (1969–70)
Harold Saunders (1969–71)
Martin Habell, student (1970–1)
Noel Jordon (1970–1)
Leo Morgan (1970–1)
Paul Gibbons (1970–2)
Richard Lyons, later partner (1970–2)
David Chamberlain (1971–2)
Anthony Lyons, student (1971–2)
Royston Summers (1971–2)
Michael Paul, student (1972)
Dennis Pitt (1972)
James Wood (1972)
Mary Hackett (1972–3)
Anthony Wright (1972–4)

Alex McEwan (1972–5)
Martin Sapetto (1973)
Christopher Maguire (1973–4)
David Spence, student (1973–4)
Andrew Thomas, student (1973–4)
David Thomas (1973–5)
Robert Springett (1973–6)
Roger Evans (1974)
David Short, student (1974–5)
Peter Lankilde (1975)
Robert Studd, student (1975–6)
Bob Bailie (1975–7)
Graham Morrison (1975–8)
Malcolm Thomas (1975–8)
Robert Voticky (1975–8)
Michael De Fries, student (1976–7)
David Davis, student (1976–7)
Brian Redfearn (1976–7)
Thomas Pike (1977)
David Adams (1977–8)
David Ahern, student (1977–8)

Bryan Allum (1978)
Andrew Murdoch (1978–9)
Roger Whiteman, student (1978–9)
Ray Jones (1979)
Fergus Kirkham, student (1979)
Kevin Ryan (1979)
David Tooth, student (1979–80)
Matthew Hucklesby, student (1980–1)
Mario Suakay (1980–1)
David Rowley, student (1981–2)
Paul Cook, student (1982–3)
Gillian Wilson (1982–3)
Gill Casemore (1983)
Steven Pollock (1984–5)
Roy Tighe, student (1985–6)
Mark Nolan (1986–7)
Perry Barnes (1986–91)
Andrew Pritchard (1986–91)
John Metcalfe, later partner (1986–91)
Andrew Comber, student (1987–8)
Greg Watts (1989–?)

Also (dates unknown): James Calderhead, Roy Christie, John Clarke, Leo Curtis, John Darbourne, Geoffrey Darke, Edward Grogan, George Jackson, Len Jacobs, Heather Jones, John Kimber, Julian Lincoln, Philip Lindsey-Clark, Thomas Poplett, Alex Redhouse, Peter Sizman, Norman Starratt, Michael West (student)

Landscape architects:	Michael Brown (1960–61), Preben Jakobsen (1961–9), Crispin Downs (1987–90)
Quantity surveyors:	John Budgen (1959–?)
Secretaries:	Brenda McLaughlin (1969–70), Penny Lewis (1970–2), Jane Walton (1972–?), Penelope Cooke (1971), Susan Cracknell (1972), Jill Baker (1972–3), Swava Oleksowicz (1973), Philippa Ramage (1973), Rosemary Thompson (1973–5), Phyllis Sturtivant (1973–87), Elizabeth Almond (1976–9), Pamela Champion (1975), Penny Elmes (1975–6), Elizabeth Fraser (1976–7), Anne Third (1979), Janet Taylor (1979–82), Pauline Amendt (1987–92). Also Barbara Fermor, Sally Porter, Gill Sleven (dates unknown).
Book keepers:	L.E. Battersby (1973–9), E. Marshall (1979–80)
Tea makers:	Eve Smith (1964–8), Fred Molyneux (1968–80)

ORIGINAL DRAWINGS

Fig 9.1 **1944 HORNING SAILING CLUB**
Unexecuted design for chalets, Horning Sailing Club, Norfolk, 1944, drawn by Eric Lyons. Near the end of the Second World War, Lyons and Geoffrey Townsend rejoined in partnership and optimistically began designing for peacetime with such projects as these chalets which accompanied their design for a large sailing clubhouse.

Fig 9.2 **1952–3 UPPER HAM ROAD**
Design for shops and flats, Upper Ham Road, London, 1952. In this coloured chalk perspective, Lyons playfully advertises his partnership with Townsend on the side of a bus passing by the commercial row fronting their first large estate of Parkleys.

Fig 9.3 **1957 HIGHSETT CAMBRIDGE**
Design for Highsett, Cambridge, 1957. To preserve as much of the original planting as possible, Lyons proposed a 15-storey tower block for the second stage of Highsett. Although this was refused planning permission, the collegiate-style quadrangles of flats and maisonettes were granted.

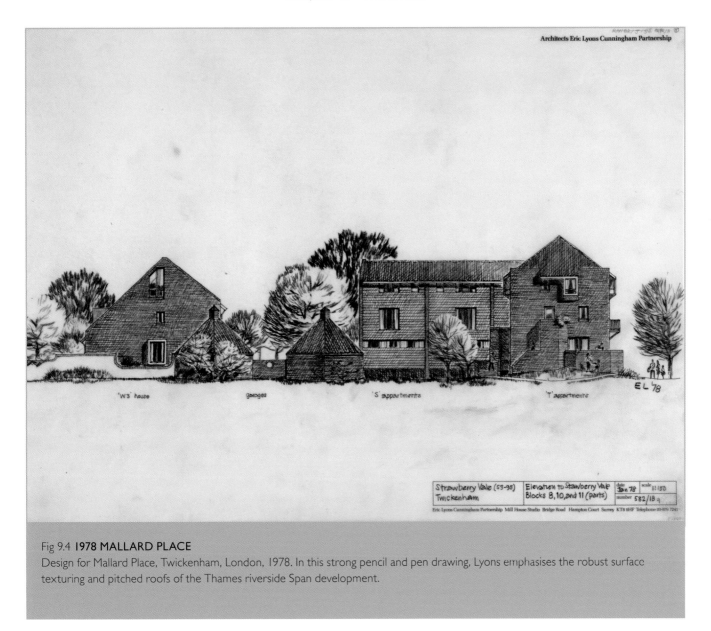

Fig 9.4 **1978 MALLARD PLACE**
Design for Mallard Place, Twickenham, London, 1978. In this strong pencil and pen drawing, Lyons emphasises the robust surface texturing and pitched roofs of the Thames riverside Span development.

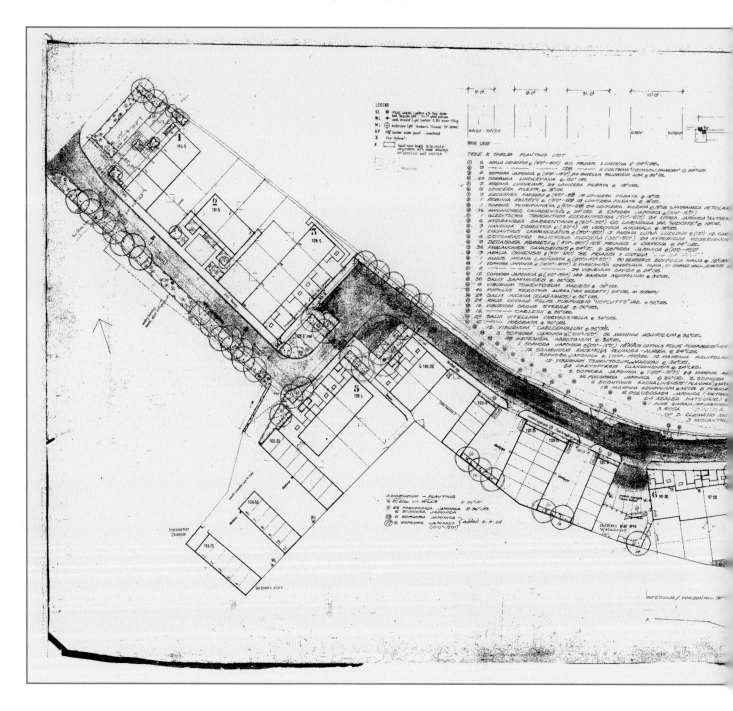

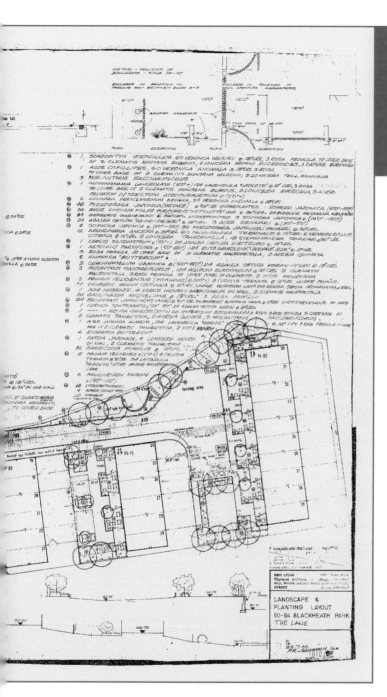

Fig 9.5 **1963 THE LANE, BLACKHEATH**

Plan for landscaping, The Lane, Blackheath, London, 1963, drawn by Preben Jakobsen. Nothing was left for chance in Span planting schemes. During the 1960s, Jakobsen, who had trained in his native Denmark and at Kew Gardens, made a strong contribution to Span's dynamic relationship between architecture and nature.

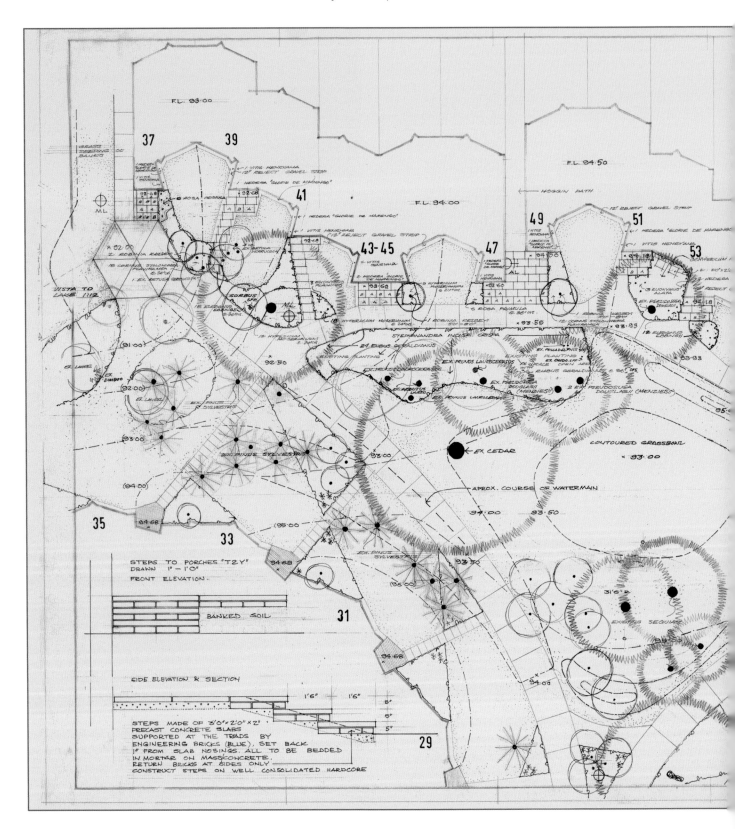

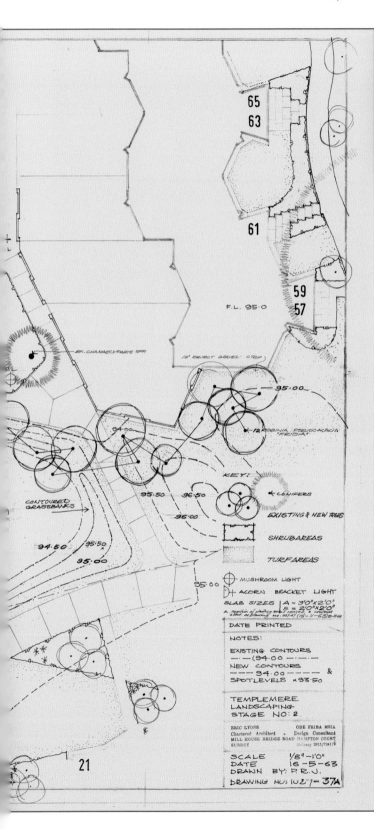

Fig 9.6 1963 TEMPLEMERE, WEYBRIDGE
Plan for landscaping, Templemere, Weybridge, Surrey, 1963, drawn by Preben Jakobsen. Templemere was an important model in establishing a new movement in corporate landscaping, influencing a new generation of landscape architects with its artistic approach to structural planting.

FURNITURE/PRODUCT DESIGN

Fig 9.7 (above) and **Fig 9.8** (below) Between 1946 and 1949, Lyons created the Tecta range of furniture, manufactured by the Packet Furniture Limited. Many pieces were laminated bentwood, and could be demounted for ease of shipping and storage.

Fig 9.9 The audio 'midget speaker' designed by Lyons for Celestion, which went into production in the late 1940s.

Fig 9.10 A battery charger manufactured by the McMurdo Instrument Company and designed by Lyons in the late 1940s. Lyons also created exhibition stands for the company.

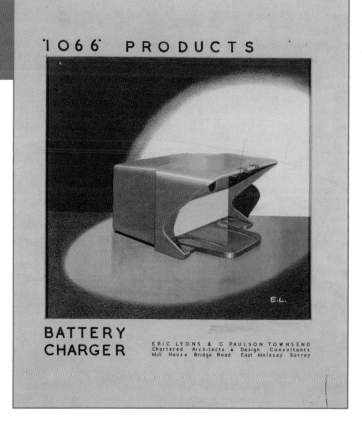

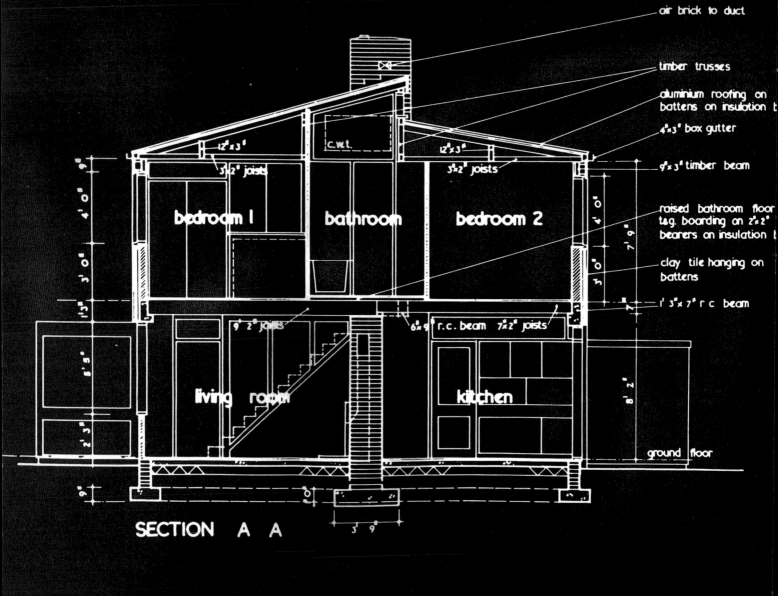

air brick to duct

timber trusses

aluminium roofing on
battens on insulation t

4"x3" box gutter

9"x3" timber beam

raised bathroom floor
t&g. boarding on 2"x2"
bearers on insulation t

clay tile hanging on
battens

1'3"x7" r.c beam

12"x3"

3½2" joists

c.w.t.

12"x3"

3½2" joists

bedroom 1

bathroom

bedroom 2

9' 2" joists

6"x 9" r.c. beam   7½2" joists

living room

kitchen

ground floor

SECTION   A A

Section through T2 house from a Span marketing brochure for The Hall, phase 2 (c. 1957)

Key	
h	houses
f	flats
s	shops
R	refused planning consent; won on appeal
A	RIBA Architecture Award
H	Housing Design Award
com	Highly Commended Housing Design Award
C	Civic Trust Award
L	Listed

CHAPTER TEN

GAZETTEER

Compiled by Ivor Cunningham, and Research Design

Built projects by Eric Lyons
(later, Eric Lyons Cunningham Partnership)

[I] Indicates image. See pages 197-198

Completed	Address	Client	Description
1945	18 Matham Road, East Molesey	Major H. A. Whyle	Addition to house
	393 Katherine Road, Forest Gate, E7	Messrs Keen (Watford) Ltd	Conversion; dwelling over shop
	193/7 Kneller Road, Whitton	-	War damage repair to maisonettes
	2, 4, 14 & 16 Bramley Close, Whitton	-	War damage repair to maisonettes
1946	26–36 Orme Road, Coombe	-	War damage to houses
	Station Road, Hayes	Hygenic Homes Ltd	14, 3B terraced houses
	54 Long Lane, Smithfield, EC1	A. A. Fisher Ltd	Alterations to office and shop
	319 Green Street, E13		
	20 & 22 Plashet Gre., E6	A. A. Fisher Ltd	New factory
	5 Bell Street, Edgeware Road, NW1	A. A. Fisher Ltd	War damage repair to shop
	Marlow Court, NW9	A. A. Fisher Ltd	War damage repair to shop
	28 Plashet Street, E6	A. A. Fisher Ltd	War damage repair of offices, 1st floor flat
	311–321 Pinner Road, Harrow	A. A. Fisher Ltd	War damage repair of six terraced houses
	104 Lordship Lane, Stoke Newington	A. A. Fisher Ltd	War damage repair to shop
	124 Dalston Lane, Hackney, E8	Messrs. Keen (Watford) Ltd alterations	Butcher's shop and warehouse;
	Temple Bar House, 23–8 Fleet Street, EC4	Blakes (Norfolk Broads) Holidays	Alterations to showroom
	Couchmore Avenue, Portsmouth Road, Esher	H. & B. Kingston Ltd	15 houses on 3 acres
	Couchmore Avenue, Portsmouth Road, Esher	G. E. Price (H. & B. Kingston Ltd)	Cottage alterations
	Emberfield, Broom Road, Teddington	G. Bridgewater	House additions
	174/6 Kingsbridge Road and 143/5 Seymour Road, Morden	-	War damage repairs to two pairs of semi-detached houses

Completed	Address	Client	Description
	120–122 Heath Road, Twickenham	Percy Bullock	War damage repairs to shop
	'1066' Battery Charger	McMurdo Instrument Co. Ltd	Product design; Lyons designed at least two other products for McMurdo: a speaker and a radio
	29 Mortimer Crescent Worcester Park	-	War damage repair
	Tyssen Street, Dalston, E8	Messrs G. A. Reed & Co. Ltd	Extension to moulding shop of plastics factory
	44 Norland Square, Kensington, W11	Edward A. Thomas	Alterations
	Embassy Snack Bar, Ashburnham Road, SW10	J A Hickman	Alterations
1947	Chalcott Estate, Church Road, Long Ditton	H. & B. Kingston & Esher UDC	22 semi-detached houses
	127 Ryden Road, Walton on Thames	H. & B. Kingston & Esher UDC	Completion of house started before war
	Wolsey Drive, Walton on Thames	H. & B. Kingston & Esher UDC	Completion of bungalow started before war
	85 Whitton Road, Twickenham	Mr E. Gostling	Conversion of flats
	16 & 17 Upper Brook Street, W1	Messrs Dalrulzion Trust Ltd	Conversion of six flats and caretaker's flat
	Bentley Road, Dalston, E8	Messrs L. Herve Ltd	Factory alterations
	71 Burdette Road, Bow, E3	Mr Fisher	Conversion of maisonette over existing shop
	30 The Island, Thames Ditton	W. Hartnell	Alteration and bathroom extension
	65 Parkway, Camden Town, N1	S. Subiotto	Workshop extension and bathroom
	85 Whitton Road, Twickenham	E. Gostling Ltd	New store and workshop
	170 Broom Road, Teddington	B. V. Lawton	Conversion into flats
	Co. Cork, Eire	Geoffrey Bishop	Cottage alterations
	86 Hampton Road, Twickenham	G. P. Townsend	House and flat conversion
1948	85 Cole Park Road, Twickenham	H. H. Thomas	War damage repair to house
	Jasper Lodge, Palace Road, East Molesey	R. Jones	Conversion of stable into house
	78 Hurst Road, East Molesey	S. Wooderson	House
	80 Chrisp Street, Poplar, E14	A. A. Fisher Ltd	Shop alterations and additions
	Roebuck Road, Surbiton	Messrs Constructex Ltd	Factory alterations
	40 Nelson Road, Whitton	P. Bullock	Alteration to shop and flat
	56 & 57 Nevem Square, Earls Court, SW5	Edward Thomas	Conversion of two terraced houses into flats
	30 Roehampton Gate, SW15	W. Leigh–Williams	War damage repair to house
	84 Brook Street, W1	AageThaarup	Upper floor conversion
	The Barn Site, Morden	–	Estate office
	Exhibition stand	McMurdo Ltd	Product design
	Oaklands, Twickenham	Span	
1949	Oaken Drive, Claygate	Messrs J. & W. Woodhead	Two houses
	14 Strawberry Hill Road. Twickenham	C. H. Oliver	Conversion of upper floor into flat
	Thursley Corner, Thursley	Edward Thomas	Alterations to cottage
	72/80 Hounslow Road, Feltham	Eden Residential Construction Co.	Conversion of five terraced houses
	Furniture	Tecta	Product design: at least 12 chair designs, a sideboard and a table

Completed	Address	Client	Description
1950	11 Lower Teddington Road, Kingston	E. Berent	Conversion of house into flats
	28 Lennox Gardens, SW1	Mrs E. Thomas	Conversion of house into five flats
	RECMF exhibition stand	McMurdo Ltd	Product design
	Hill Farm Road, Pulborough	S. G. & A. Mason (Pulborough) Ltd	House alteration
	Elmsleigh House, Staines Road, Twickenham	Twickenham BC	Eight old people's flats
	Chatsworth, 50 Strawberry Hill Road, Twick.	Mr Lavender	House
	13–17 Jameson Road, Bexhill on Sea	Span	
	Longmead Road, Thames Ditton	Esher UDC	Houses and flats
	Eden Court, Station Road, Ealing	Span	
1951	Box Corner, Twickenham	Span	
	Onslow House, Richmond	Span	
1952	Temple Bar House, 23/8 Fleet Street, EC4	Blakes (Norfolk Broads) Holidays	Alterations to showroom
	Dysart Avenue, Kingston	N. Haveland	House
	Chesham Avenue, Bromley	Mr Houseden	House
	31 Wolsey Road, East Molesey	S. Fermor	Conversion of stable into house
	Cavendish Court, Richmond		
	Hampton Road, Hampton Hill		
1953	Rydens Road, Walton on Thames	–	House
	Albermarle Street, W1	Blakes (Norfolk Broads) Holidays	Shop
	Ham Farm Road, Ham Common	Dr D. Cussen	House
1954	36 Davies Street and 25 Brook Mews, W1	Aage Thaarup	Two showrooms
	Third Cross Road, Twickenham	Span	
1955	Domus, 81 Broad Lane, Hampton	Mr Rowlands	House
	Sandpits Road, Petersham	Span	
	Campbell Close, Twickenham	Span	
1956	Walpole Gardens, Twickenham	G. P. Townsend	House
	Mill House, Bridge Road, East Molesey	Eric Lyons	House extension
	Parkleys, Ham Common	Span	
	The Priory, Priory Park, Blackheath	Span	
1957	West Hill, Highgate, N6	Soviet Trade Delegation	Flats
	55 Avenue Road, St Johns Wood, NW8	Mr & Mrs Rose	House
	Hall 1, Foxes Dale, Blackheath	Span	
	T3 Houses, Foxes Dale, Blackheath	Span	
	Priory Park, Blackheath	Span	
	The Keep, Morden Mews, Blackheath	Span	
1958	The Cedars, Teddington	Span	
	Cambridge Road, Teddington	Span	
	Thurnby Court, Twickenham	Span	

Completed	Address	Client	Description
	Hall 2, Foxes Dale, Blackheath	Span	
	Hallgate, Blackheath Park, Blackheath	Span	
1959	Olympia, Kensington, W14	National Union of Teachers	Exhibition (with Leslie Gooday)
	Howard House, Pevensey Road, Bognor Regis	Bognor Regis, UDC	Old people's home (50 flats + warden); H; demolished 1980
	Princes Road, Kew	Span	
	Corner Green, Pond Road, Blackheath	Span	
1960	Park Gate, Somerhill Road, Hove	Span	
	Victoria Drive, Wimbledon	Span	
	Highsett 1, Hills Road, Cambridge	Span	
	Drosier Road, Cambridge	Span	
	West Oak 1, The Avenue, Beckenham	Span	
1961	Walton Road, West Molesey	Molesey Football Club	Pavilion
	Fieldend, Teddington	Span	
	Rayners Rd, Putney	Span	
	Westrow, Putney	Span	
	Applecourt, Newton Road, Cambridge	Span	
	West Oak 2, The Avenue, Beckenham	Span	
1962	The Hamlet, Corbishley Road, Bognor Regis [1]	Bognor Regis UDC	Old people's home (34 flats + warden); H; demolished 1980
	Pitcairn House, Mare Street, Hackney, E8 [1]	LCC	93 flats
	Pirbright Camp, Surrey	War Office	94 married soldiers' houses
	The Plantation, Morden Road, Blackheath	Span	
	The Farm, Putney	Span	
1963	Parkrow, Lee Road, Blackheath	Span	
	Southrow, Blackheath	Span	
	Highsett 2, Hills Road, Cambridge	Span	
	The Verneys, Old Bath Road, Cheltenham	Span	
1964	Friars School, Webber Street, Southwark, SE1 [1]	LCC	Primary school
	Albion Street, Bermondsey, SE16	LCC	Primary school
	Mill House, Bridge Road, East Molesey	Eric Lyons	Office extension (major building)
	Spangate, Blackheath Park, Blackheath	Span	
	The Lane, Blackheath Park, Blackheath	Span	
	Brooklands Park, Blackheath	Span	
1965	Castle House, Castle Hill, Southampton	Southampton BC	72 flats in 14-storey building
	Highsett 3, Tenison Ave, Cambridge	Span	
	The Paddox, Squitchey Lane, Oxford	Span	
	Templemere, Oatlands Drive, Weybridge	Span	
	Brackley, Queens Road, Weybridge	Span	

Completed	Address	Client	Description
	Castle Green, Weybridge	Span	
1966	St Clare Works, Holly Road, Hampton Hill Area 77 South, Harlow New Town [I] Chertsey Centre Development Chertsey UDC (Planning proposal) Weymede, Byfleet Holme Chase, St George's Avenue, Weybridge Cedar Chase, Taplow	E. Gostling (Builders) Ltd Harlow Development n Corporation Span Span Span	Office 216 houses and flats on 4.8Ha @ 149p/Ha Scheme for new road pattern, car parking, refurbished and new shopping and housing (shop front facelift by Kenneth Wood)
1967	Dryden House, Newton Road, Cambridge [I] Hall 4, Foxes Dale, Blackheath Parkend, Blackheath Park, Blackheath Grasmere, Byfleet Over Minnis, New Ash Green, Kent	Trinity College Span Span Span Span	Nine flats and laundry for graduates; H
1968	Punch Croft, New Ash Green, Kent	Span	
1969	Knights Croft, New Ash Green, Kent Lambardes, New Ash Green, Kent Millfield, New Ash Green, Kent Shopping Lane , New Ash Green, Kent Westfield, Ashtead , Surrey Marsham Lodge, Gerrards Cross	Span Span Span Span Span Span	(uncompleted) (uncompleted) (uncompleted) stage I
1971	Pirbright Camp, Surrey [I] Mayford, Oakley Square, Camden, NW1 [I] New Ash Green, Kent Marina Area (phase 1), Vilamoura, [I] Algarve, Portugal	Ministry of Public Buildings and Works St Pancras BC (later LB of Camden) Kent CC Lusutor SARL	193 married soldiers' houses on 4.9 Ha @ 183p/Ha 183 flats and children's home on 1.61 Ha @ 409p/Ha Primary and infant schools (1st stage built) Competition entry selected for building 1st stage
1973	40 Acres Road, Canterbury	County Developments Co. (Canterbury) Ltd	House and mews flats (1st stage built)
1974	Chertsey Centre Housing Wates House, University of Surrey, Guildford Phase 1, Vilamoura, Algarve, Portugal	Chertsey UDC University of Surrey Lusutor SARL	155 houses and sheltered home (30 flats + warden on 2.72Ha) Staff and social building (limited Flats and shops by marina (part built – work stopped by revolution)

Completed	Address	Client	Description
1975	Walsingham Lodge, Ferry Road, Barnes SW13	Workhouse Trust	15 bungalows and sheltered home (30 flats + warden); Highly commended Housing Award
1976	Westbourne Road, Islington, N9 [1]	LB of Islington	268 houses, 132 flats, sheltered home (30 flats + warden), community centre, medical centre and five shops on 5.9Ha
	Caledonian Road, Islington, N9	GLC	42 houses and 35 flats on 0.94Ha @ 254p/Ha
1978	Holm Walk, Blackheath Park, Blackheath	Span	
1979	Delhi Street, Islington, N1	LB of Islington	110 houses, 132 flats on 2.76Ha @ 373p/Ha
	Fieldend, Telford	Telford Development Corp.	193 houses, 54 flats and 1 shops on 8.15Ha @ 138p/Ha
	Aqueduct Village, Telford	Telford Development Corp	Masterplan for new village (including Fieldend, above). 11 houses built by Fairclough Building Ltd
	World's End, Kings Road, Chelsea, SW10	Chelsea BC (later LB of Kensington)	744 flats, children's home, play school, primary and infants' school, church, shops, supermarket, offices, community centre and boys' club (with H. T. Cadbury-Brown and Partners)
	Corner Keep (Corner Green Phase 2), Blackheath	Span	
1980s	Phase 1, Vilamoura, Algarve, Portugal	Lusutor SARL	Flats and shops by marina (contd)
1982	Birchmere, Pond Road, Blackheath St. Michael's, Randell's Pond, Islington, London N1	Span LB Islington	Completion phase of the Delhi Street Estate (1979)
1984	Mallard Place, Teddington Streetfield Mews, Blackheath Park, Blackheath	Span Span	

Total numbers of dwellings (excluding Span): Single houses: 11; houses: 1316; Flats: 1685; 3012 dwellings in 26 schemes.

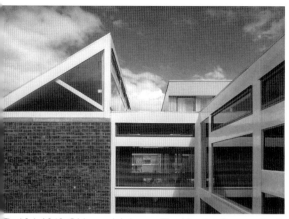

Fig 10.1 **1962** Old people's home, The Hamlet, Bognor Regis.

Fig 10.2 **1971** Married soldiers' housing, Pirbright Camp, Surrey.

Fig 10.3 **1962** Pitcairn house, Hackney.

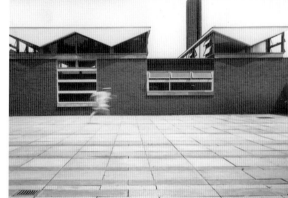

Fig 10.4 **1964** Friars School, Webber St, Southwark.

Fig 10.5 **1965** Castle House, Southampton.

Fig 10.6 **1966** Housing, Area 77 South, Harlow New Town.

Fig 10.7 **1967** Dryden House, Trinity College, Cambridge

Fig 10.8 1971 **Mayford, Oakley Square, Camden: model.**

Fig 10.9 **1971** Competition model, Vilamoura phase 1.

Fig 10.10 **1974** Wates House, University of Surrey, Guildford.

Left: Fig 10.11 **1974** Wates House, University of Surrey, Guildford.

Right: Fig 10.12 **1976** Westbourne Road, Islington.

Key	
h	houses
f	flats
s	shops
R	refused planning consent; won on appeal
A	RIBA Architecture Award
H	Housing Design Award
com	Highly Commended Housing Design Award
C	Civic Trust Award
L	Listed

Span Housing by Eric Lyons (later, Eric Lyons Cunningham Partnership) and others

[I] Indicates image. See pages 204-205. Site areas and densities added where known.

District	Date	Scheme	Dwellings	Type	Site area Ha (acres)	Density units/Ha	Notes
Richmond/ Twickenham	1948	Oaklands, Twickenham	24f				
	1951	Box Comer, Twickenham	6f				
	1951	Onslow House, Richmond	4f (+ 4s)				CA
	1952	Cavendish Court, Richmond [I]	8f		0.08 (0.20)	100	CA
	1952	Hampton Road, Hampton Hill	5h	TI	0.12 (0.30)	50	
	1954	Third Cross Road, Twickenham	6h	TI			
	1955	Sandpits Road, Petersham	5h	TI	0.12 (0.30)	42	CA
	1955	Campbell Close, Twickenham	20h	TI	0.42 (1.05)	48	
	1956	Parkleys, Ham Common	175f (+ 6s)	ABC	3.24 (8.00)	52	L[1] ; CA[2]
	1958	The Cedars, Teddington	19h	T2	0.58 (1.44)	33	CA
	1958	Cambridge Road, Teddington	14h	T2	0.43 (1.07)	33	
	1958	Thurnby Court, Twickenham	27f	ABC	0.57 (1.40)	47	
	1959	Princes Road, Kew	8h	T7/T2	0.12 (0.30)	42	CA
	1961	Fieldend, Teddington	51h	T7/T8	2.06 (5.10)	25	H, C, CA[3]
	1960	Beech Row, Ham Common by Gooday and Noble	10h				
	1984	Mallard Place, Twickenham	45h + 57f	N+W/S F+T	1.76 (4.35)	58	H , C, CA[4]
total: 16 schemes; 301 flats, 183 houses (484 dwellings), 10 shops							
Ealing	1950	Eden Court Station Road, W5 3HX	15f				
Bexhill on Sea	1950	13-17 Jameson Road, TN40 1EJ	9f				

District	Date	Scheme	Dwellings	Type	Site area Ha (acres)	Density units/Ha	Notes
Blackheath	1956	The Priory, Priory Park	61f	ABC	1.42 (3.52)	43	CA[5]
	1957	Hall 1, Foxes Dale	44f	ABC	1.15 (2.84)	38	
	1957	T3 Houses, Foxes Dale	3h	T3	*		
	1957	Priory Park	4h	T2	*		
	1957	The Keep, Morden Mews	44h	T2	1.38 (3.42)	32	
	1958	Hall 2, Foxes Dale	41h	T2	1.46 (3.61)	28	
	1958	Hallgate, Blackheath Park	26f	ABC	*		R, C, L[7]
	1959	Corner Green, Pond Road	23h	T7/T8	0.67 (1.66)	34	
	c. 1959	Morden Road by Andrews Emerson + Sherlock	6h				
	c. 1959	Morden Mews by Andrews Emerson + Sherlock	5h				
	1962	The Plantation, Morden Road	34h	T7/T8	0.97 (2.40)	35	
	1963	Parkrow, Lee Road	9h	T9/T10/T11	0.21 (0.52)	43	
	1963	Southrow	10h + 23f	Q maisonettes	0.61 (1.50)	54	R, C, L[8]
	1964	Spangate, Blackheath Park [I]	17f	Q	0.54 (1.33)	31	
	1964	The Lane, Blackheath Park [I]	39h	T10/T15	1.05 (2.60)	37	H, C
	1964	Brooklands Park	16h	T15	0.57 (1.40)	28	R
	1967	Hall 4, Foxes Dale	13h	R	0.73 (1.81)	18	
	1967	Parkend, Blackheath Park [I]	19h	T2AX	0.51 (1.26)	37	
	1978	Holm Walk, Blackheath Park	10h	A/B	0.46 (1.15)	22	com
	1979	Corner Keep (Corner Green Phase 2)	10h	A/B	0.32 (0.81)	31	
	1982	Birchmere, Pond Road	6h	Mews	0.19 (0.47)	32	
	1984	Streetfield Mews, Blackheath Park	15h + 5f	Mews	0.65 (1.60)	31	R

total: 22 schemes; 176 flats, 307 houses (483 dwellings)

District	Date	Scheme	Dwellings	Type	Site area Ha (acres)	Density units/Ha	Notes
Hove	1960	Park Gate Somerhill Road, BN3 1RL [I]	47f		0.52 (1.30)	90	H

District	Date	Scheme	Dwellings	Type	Site area Ha (acres)	Density units/Ha	Notes
Wimbledon/ Putney	1960	Victoria Drive, Wimbledon	6h	T8			
	1961	Rayners Rd, Putney [I]	13h	T8	0.37 (0.91)	35	C
	1961	Westrow, Putney	12h	T8	0.38 (0.95)	32	
	1962	The Farm, Putney	8h	T7	0.22 (0.55)	36	

total: 4 schemes; 39 houses

District	Date	Scheme	Dwellings	Type	Site area Ha (acres)	Density units/Ha	Notes
Cambridge	1960	Highsett 1, Hills Road CB1 2DX	37f	ABC	0.61 (1.50)	61	CA, L[8]
	1960	Drosier Road CB1 2EY	6h	T2	0.18 (0.45)	33	CA
	1961	Applecourt, Newton Rd CB2 2AN	24f	ABC			
	1963	Highsett 2, Hills Road	17h	T7/T8	0.59 (1.45)	29	H, CA
	1965	Highsett 3, Tenison Avenue	31h	R22	0.71 (1.75)	44	H, A, CA

total: 5 schemes; 61 flats, 54 houses (115 dwellings)

District	Date	Scheme	Dwellings	Type	Site area Ha (acres)	Density units/Ha	Notes
Beckenham	1960 1961	West Oak 1 West Oak 2 The Avenue, BR3 5EZ	12f 21h	ABC/T8	1.44 (3.50)	8	
colspan total		total: 2 schemes, 12 flats, 21 houses (33 dwellings)					
Cheltenham	1963 c. 1964	The Verneys Old Bath Road, GL53 7DB Park House 131 The Park, GL50 2RG by Towning Hill and Partners	8h[9] 32f	C1	0.53 (1.30)	15 G	CA
colspan total		total: 2 schemes, 32 flats, 8 houses (40 dwellings)					
Bristol	1964	Pitch and Pay Park (ph 1) Julian Road, Sneyd Park, BS9 1JY by Towning Hill and Partners	14h[10]				
Oxford	1965	The Paddox Paddox Close, Squitchey Lane, OX2 7LR	24h[11]	R22	1.68 (4.14)	14	R
Kensington W14	1965	Buckley House [1] 96 Addison Road, W14 8DE by Andrews Emerson + Sherlock	10f				
Weybridge/ Byfleet	1965 1965 1965 1966 1966 1966 1967	Templemere, Oatlands Drive Brackley, Queens Road [1] Castle Green Weymede, Byfleet Holme Chase, St George's Ave Lakeside, Oatlands Drive by Calderhead and Scoble Architects Grasmere, Byfleet	65h 46h 22h 120h 62h 19h 11h	T2Y/L1 T16/T17 T2AB T2A/R E1/E2 K	4.45 (11.00) 1.91 (4.72) 0.88 (2.17) 5.06 (12.51) 2.32 (5.74) ?	15 24 25 24 27	H, C H H
colspan total		total: 7 schemes; 345 houses					
Buckingham	1966 1969	Cedar Chase, Taplow Rectory Road, SL6 0EU Marsham Lodge, Gerrards Cross, Marsham Lane, SL9 7AB	24h 14h[12]	C30 C30	1.55 (3.83) 0.95 (2.34)	15 26	H, CA R
colspan total		total: 2 schemes, 38 houses					

District	Date	Scheme	Dwellings	Type	Site area Ha (acres)	Density units/Ha	Notes
New Ash Green	1967	Over Minnis	33h (+3)	K			
	1968	Punch Croft	140h	K	6.15 (15.20)	23	
	1969	Knights Croft (uncompleted)	117h[13]	K	7.45 (15.20)	25	
	1969	Lambardes (uncompleted)	36h[14]	K			
	1969	Millfield (uncompleted)	64h[15]	K	5.34 (13.20)	32	
	1969	Shopping Lane – stage 1	8f (+35)[16]				
		total: 6 schemes, 8 flats, 390 houses, (398dwellings), 35 shops, 7 studio workshops					R[17]
Ashtead	1969	The Marld [1] Westfield, KT21 1RH	40h	K	2.27 (5.50)	18	com, CA
		GRAND TOTAL: 73 schemes, 662 flats, 1,463 houses, 48 shops: 2,134 dwellings					

[1] Listed Grade 2 in 1998
[2] Designated as its own conservation area
[3] Designated as its own conservation area 2005
[4] Designated as its own conservation area; the project received a Housing Design Award on completion and a Historic Winner's Award in 2005
[5] All Blackheath projects are within the Blackheath Park conservation area
[6] Listed Grade 2 in 1998
[7] Listed Grade 2 in 1996
[8] Listed Grade 2 in 1998
[9] 15 houses originally planned
[10] Phase 2 (a further 30 terraced houses) was built by another developer (Chivers Ltd) and this scheme received a Housing Design Award
[11] 53 houses originally planned
[12] 25 houses planned: the remainder were built by another company to the Span designs
[13] Knights Croft: 183 proposed; remainder constructed by Bovis
[14] Lambardes: 57 proposed; remainder constructed by Bovis
[15] Millfield: 169 proposed; remainder built by Bovis
[16] Phase 2 included a further 18 shops and three apartments but was not executed
[17] Overall plan refused planning consent and won on appeal

Fig 10.13 **1960** Park Gate, Hove (left).

Fig 10.14 **1964** The Lane, Blackheath.

Fig 10.17 **1964** Spangate, Blackheath (below).

Fig 10.15 **1952** The Lane, Blackheath.

Fig 10.16 **1961** Rayners Road, Putney.

Fig 10.18 **1965** Buckley House, Addison Road, Kensington.

Fig 10.19 **1965** Brackley, Weybridge (below).

Fig 10.20 **1969** The Marld, Westfield, Ashstead, Kent.

Fig 10.21 **1967** Parkend, Blackheath (right).

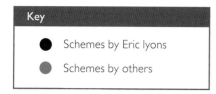

Key

● Schemes by Eric lyons

● Schemes by others

LOCATION PLANS, SITE PLANS
AND HOUSE TYPES

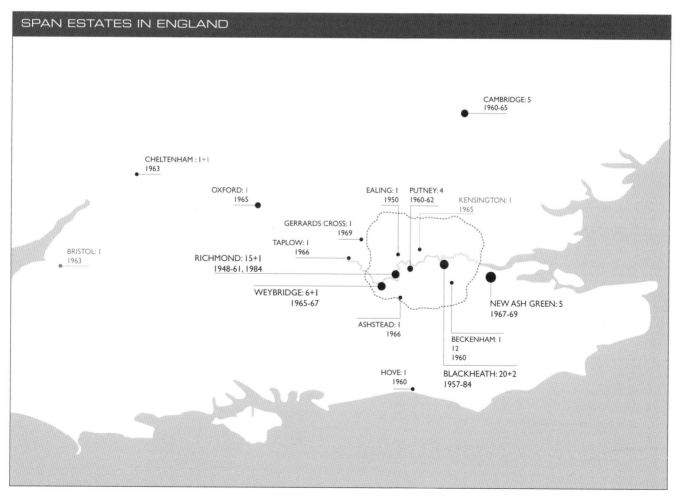

SPAN ESTATES IN ENGLAND

CAMBRIDGE: 5
1960-65

CHELTENHAM : 1+1
1963

OXFORD: 1
1965

EALING: 1   PUTNEY: 4
1950   1960-62   KENSINGTON: 1
1965

GERRARDS CROSS: 1
1969

TAPLOW: 1
1966

BRISTOL: 1
1963

RICHMOND: 15+1
1948-61, 1984

WEYBRIDGE: 6+1
1965-67

NEW ASH GREEN: 5
1967-69

ASHSTEAD: 1
1966

BECKENHAM: 1
12
1960

HOVE: 1   BLACKHEATH: 20+2
1960   1957-84

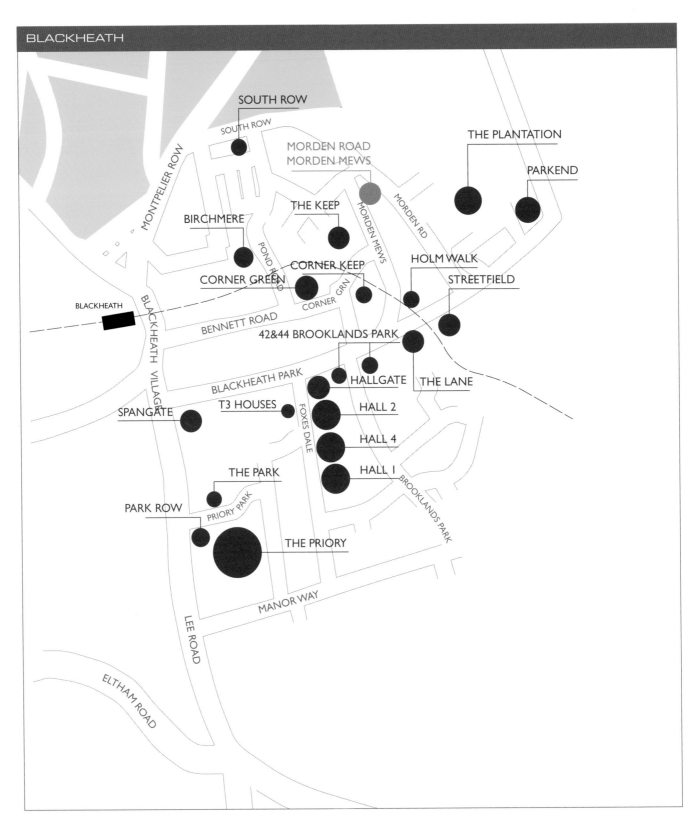

SOUTH ROW

SOUTH ROW

MORDEN ROAD
MORDEN MEWS

THE PLANTATION

PARKEND

MONTPELIER ROW

THE KEEP

MORDEN MEWS

MORDEN RD

BIRCHMERE

POND ROAD

CORNER KEEP

HOLM WALK

STREETFIELD

CORNER GREEN

CORNER GRN

BLACKHEATH

BLACKHEATH VILLAGE

BENNETT ROAD

42&44 BROOKLANDS PARK

BLACKHEATH PARK

HALLGATE

THE LANE

SPANGATE

T3 HOUSES

FOXES DALE

HALL 2

HALL 4

BROOKLANDS PARK

THE PARK

HALL 1

PARK ROW

PRIORY PARK

THE PRIORY

MANOR WAY

LEE ROAD

ELTHAM ROAD

BLACKHEATH

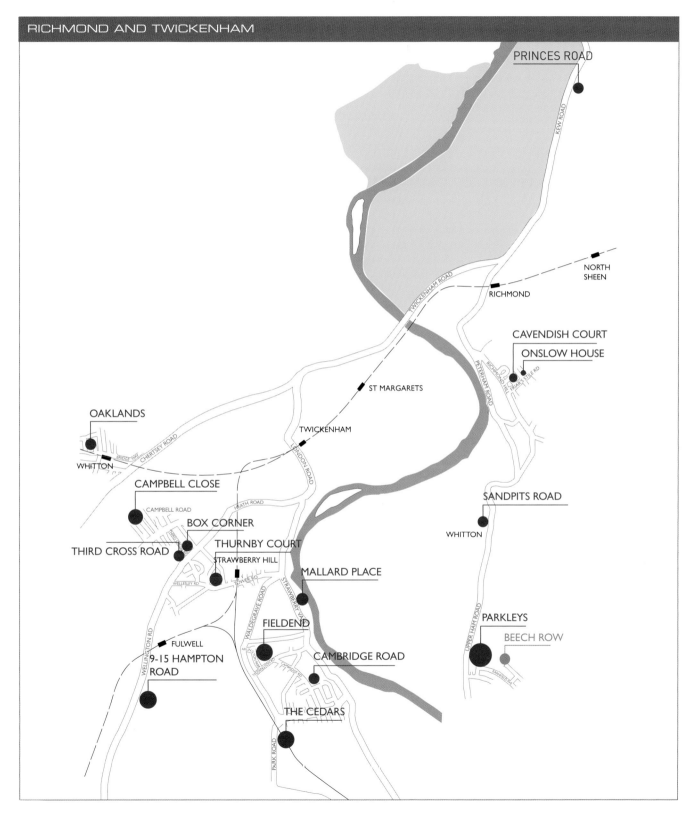

RICHMOND AND TWICKENHAM

PRINCES ROAD

KEW ROAD

NORTH SHEEN

RICHMOND

TWICKENHAM ROAD

CAVENDISH COURT

ONSLOW HOUSE

PETERSHAM ROAD

RICHMOND HILL

FRIARS STILE RD

ST MARGARETS

OAKLANDS

CHERTSEY ROAD

BRIDGE WAY

WHITTON

CAMPBELL CLOSE

CAMPBELL ROAD

HEATH ROAD

LONDON ROAD

SANDPITS ROAD

WHITTON

BOX CORNER

THIRD CROSS ROAD

THURNBY COURT

STRAWBERRY HILL

WELLESLEY RD

TOWER RD

MALLARD PLACE

STRAWBERRY VALE

UPPER HAM ROAD

PARKLEYS

BEECH ROW

WALDEGRAVE ROAD

FIELDEND

WELLINGTON RD

FULWELL

9-15 HAMPTON ROAD

CAMBRIDGE ROAD

THE CEDARS

PARK ROAD

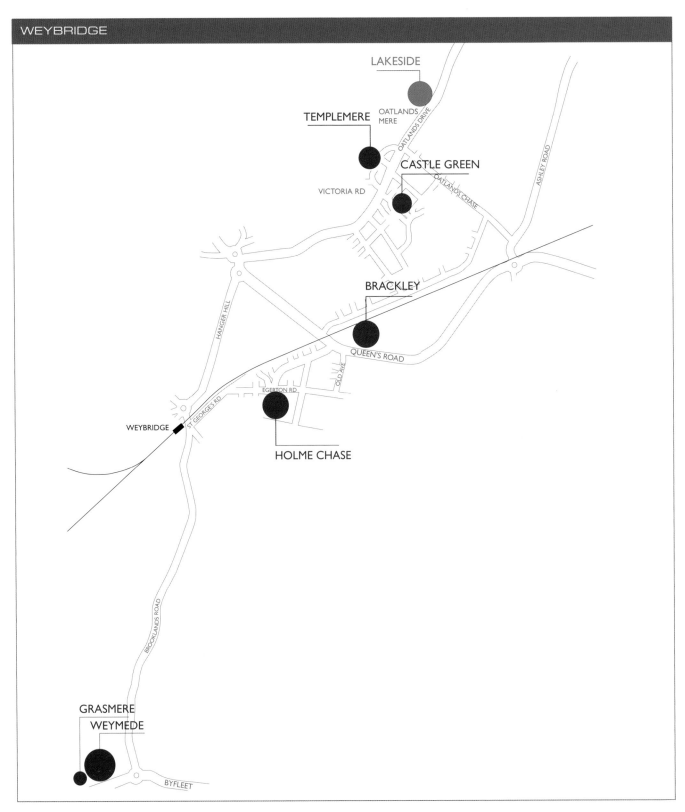

WEYBRIDGE

LAKESIDE

TEMPLEMERE

OATLANDS MERE

CASTLE GREEN

OATLANDS DRIVE

ASHLEY ROAD

VICTORIA RD

OATLANDS CHASE

BRACKLEY

HANGER HILL

QUEEN'S ROAD

OLD AVE

EGERTON RD

ST GEORGE'S RD

WEYBRIDGE

HOLME CHASE

BROOKLANDS ROAD

GRASMERE

WEYMEDE

BYFLEET

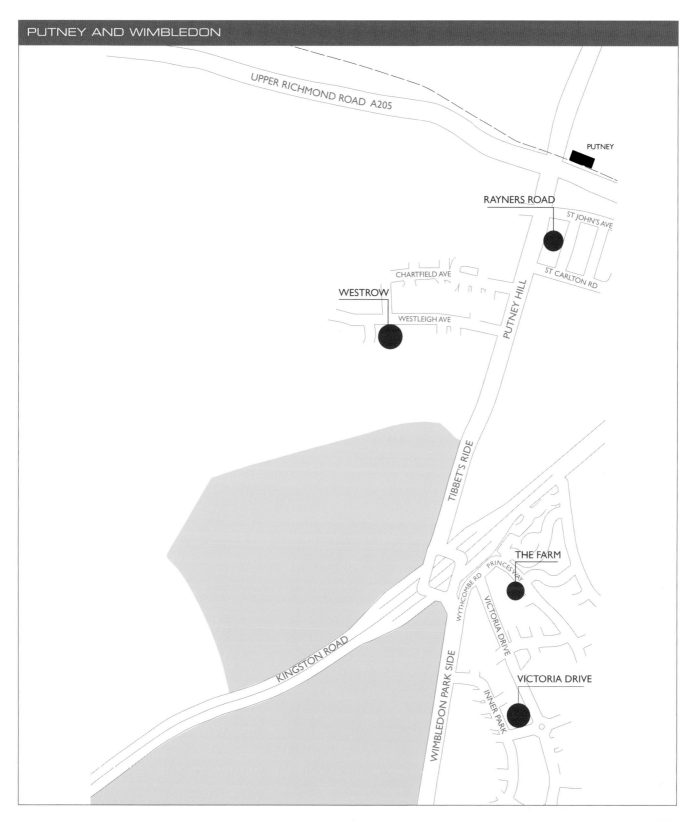

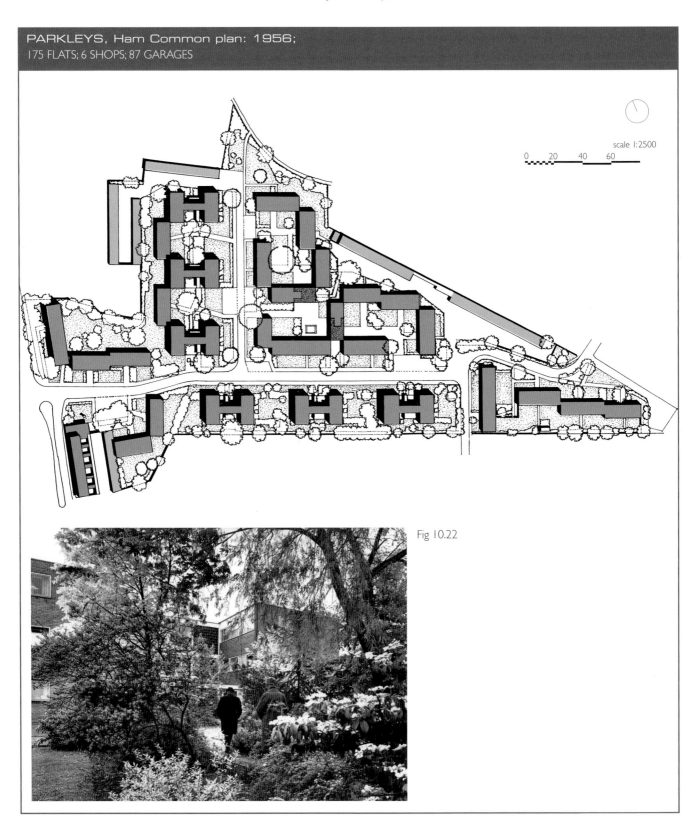

PARKLEYS, Ham Common plan: 1956;
175 FLATS; 6 SHOPS; 87 GARAGES

scale 1:2500

0   20   40   60

Fig 10.22

THE PRIORY, Blackheath plan: 1956;
61 FLATS, 41 GARAGES

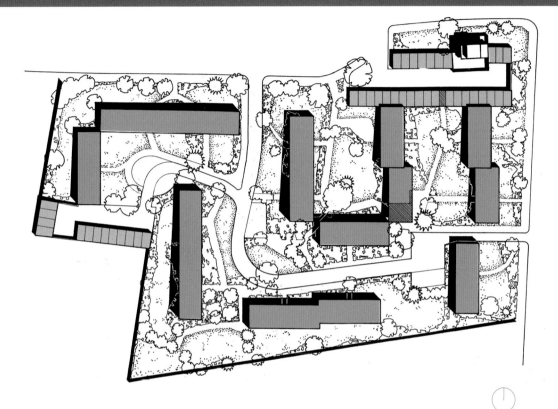

scale 1:2500

0   20   40   60

Fig 10.23

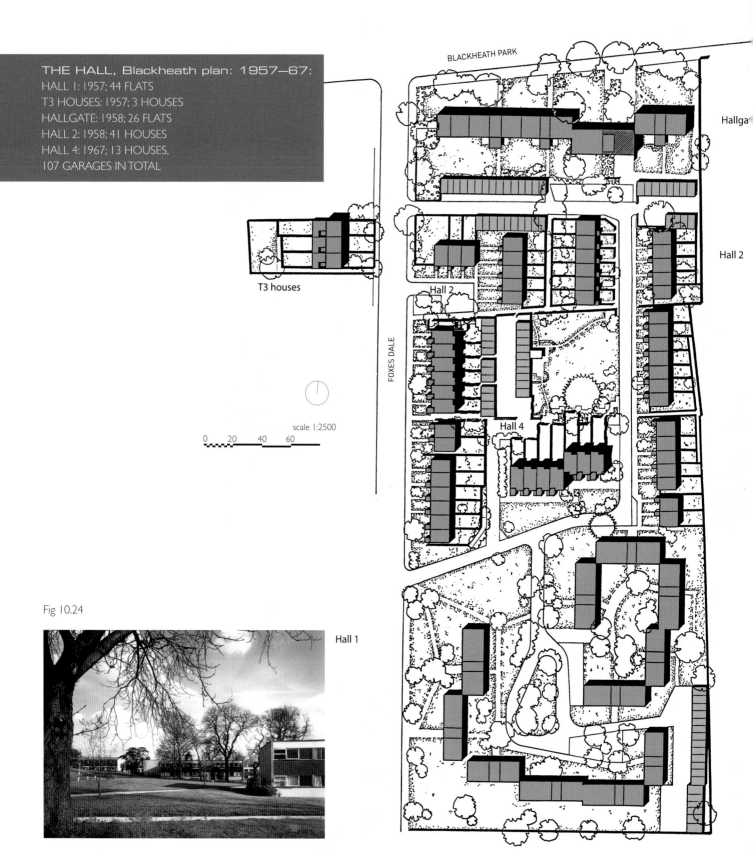

THE HALL, Blackheath plan: 1957–67:
HALL 1: 1957; 44 FLATS
T3 HOUSES: 1957; 3 HOUSES
HALLGATE: 1958; 26 FLATS
HALL 2: 1958; 41 HOUSES
HALL 4: 1967; 13 HOUSES,
107 GARAGES IN TOTAL

BLACKHEATH PARK

Hallga

Hall 2

T3 houses

Hall 2

FOXES DALE

scale 1:2500

0   20   40   60

Hall 2

Hall 4

Fig 10.24

Hall 1

CORNER GREEN, Blackheath plan: 1959;
23 HOUSES; 21 GARAGES

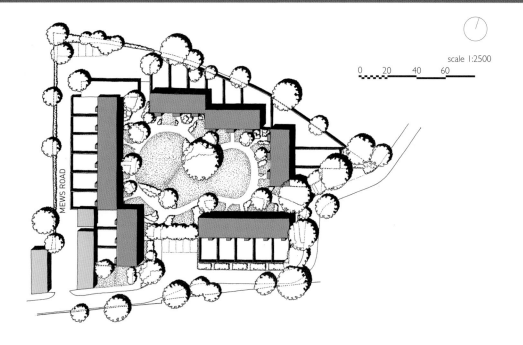

MEWS ROAD

scale 1:2500

0   20   40   60

Fig 10.25

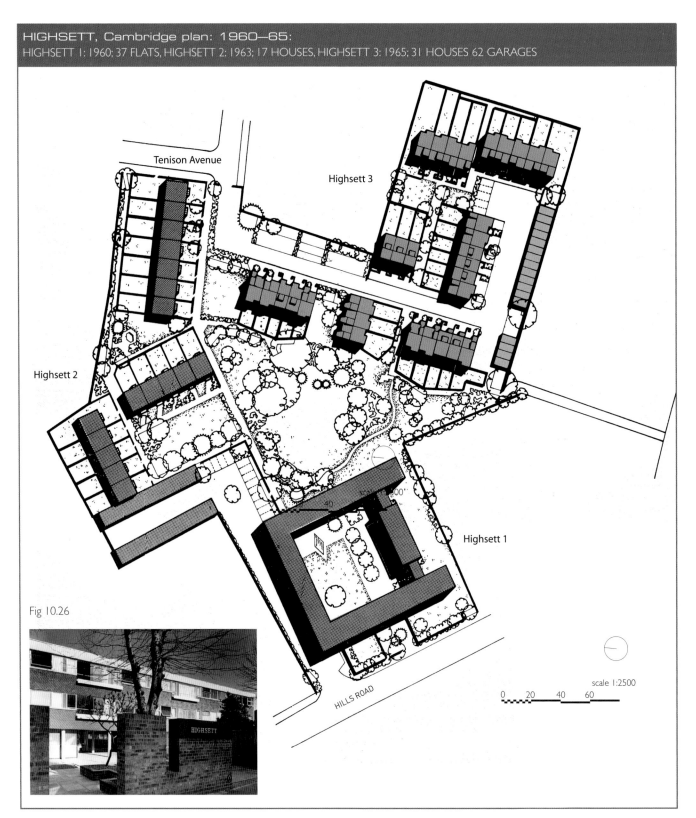

HIGHSETT, Cambridge plan: 1960—65:
HIGHSETT 1: 1960; 37 FLATS, HIGHSETT 2: 1963; 17 HOUSES, HIGHSETT 3: 1965; 31 HOUSES 62 GARAGES

Fig 10.26

FIELDEND, Teddington plan: 1961
51 HOUSES; 49 GARAGES

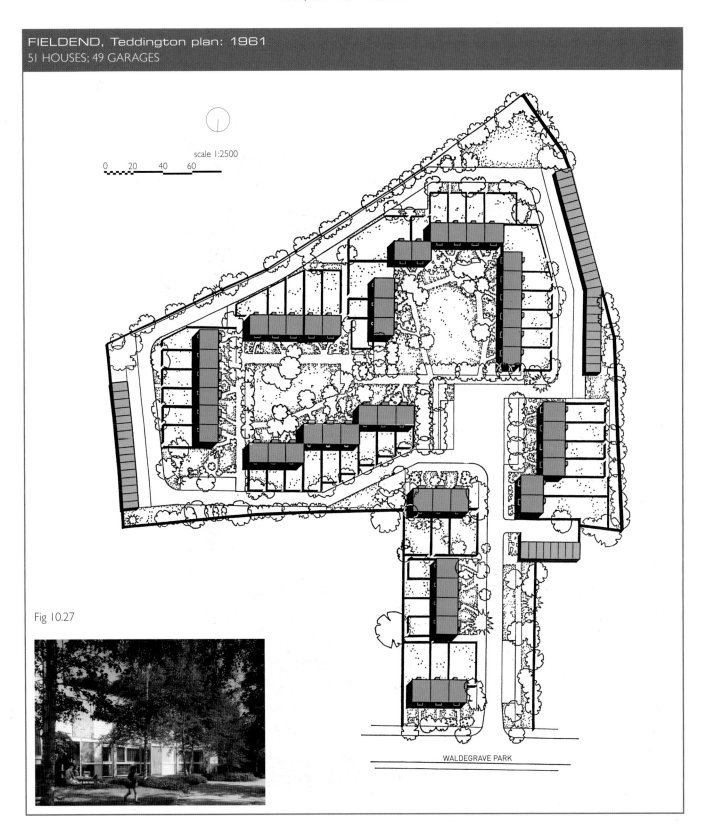

scale 1:2500

0   20   40   60

Fig 10.27

WALDEGRAVE PARK

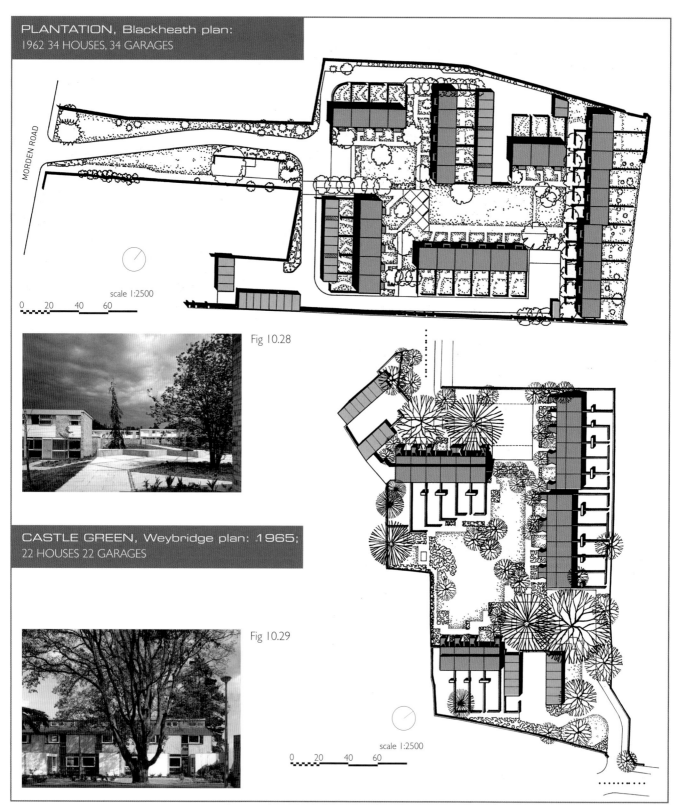

PLANTATION, Blackheath plan:
1962 34 HOUSES, 34 GARAGES

MORDEN ROAD

scale 1:2500

0   20   40   60

Fig 10.28

CASTLE GREEN, Weybridge plan: 1965;
22 HOUSES 22 GARAGES

Fig 10.29

scale 1:2500

0   20   40   60

PADDOX, Oxford plan: 1965;
24 HOUSES, 24 GARAGES

Fig 10.30

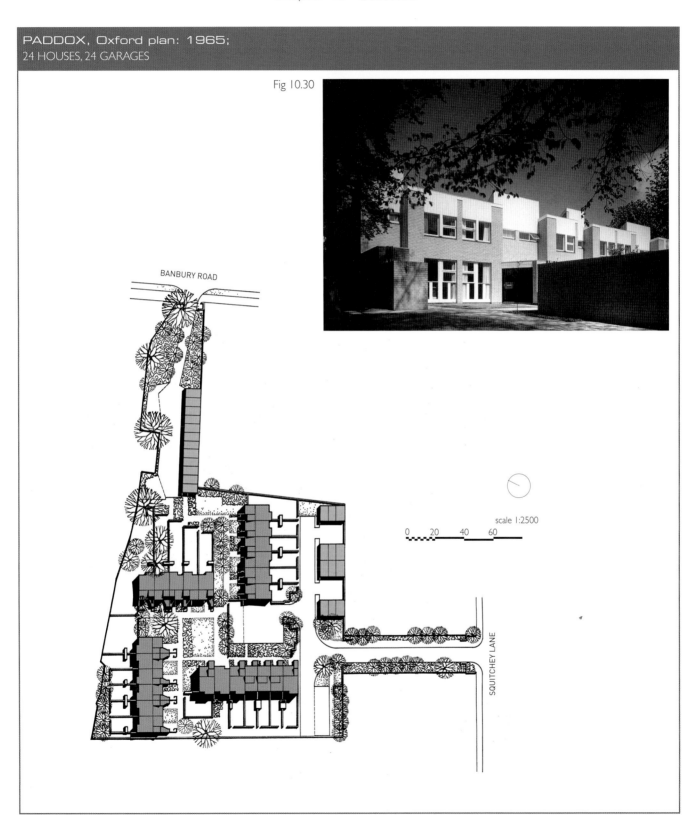

BANBURY ROAD

SQUITCHEY LANE

scale 1:2500

0   20   40   60

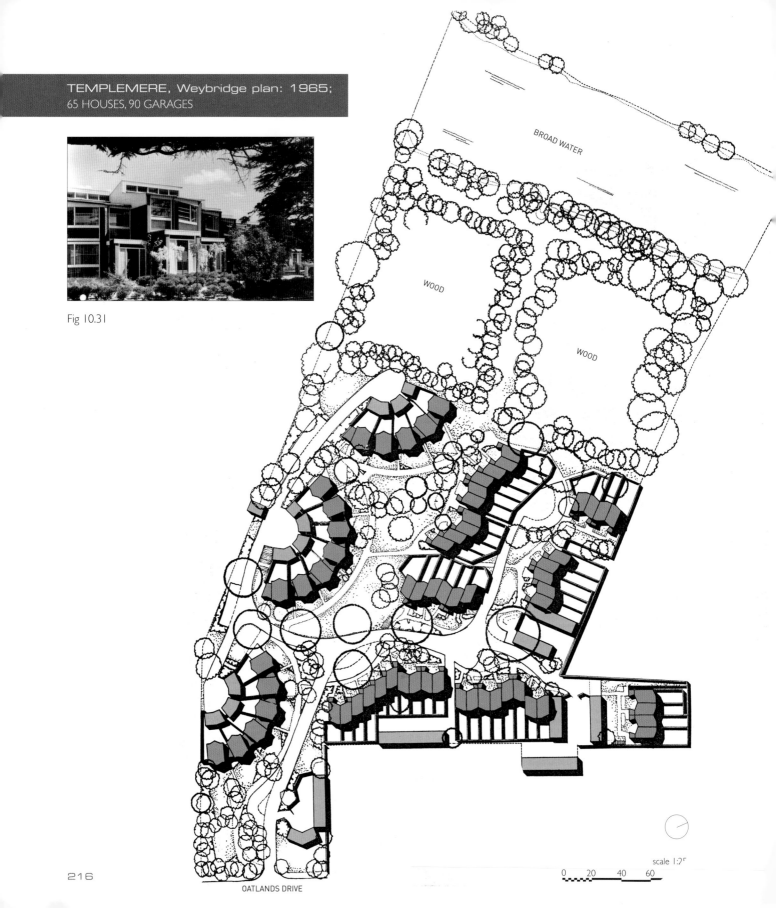

TEMPLEMERE, Weybridge plan: 1965;
65 HOUSES, 90 GARAGES

Fig 10.31

BROAD WATER

WOOD

WOOD

OATLANDS DRIVE

scale 1:2⁵

0   20   40   60

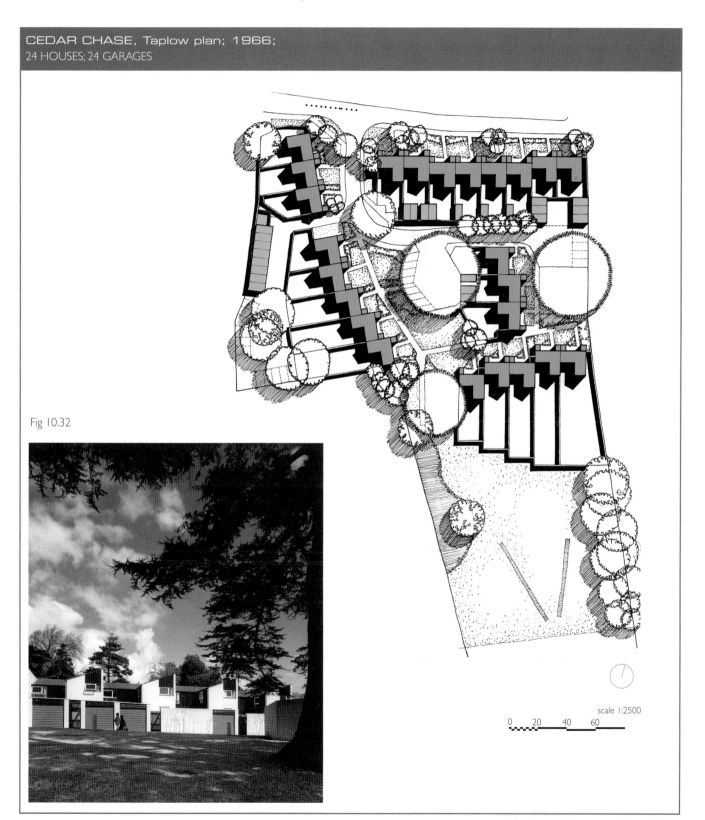

CEDAR CHASE, Taplow plan; 1966;
24 HOUSES; 24 GARAGES

Fig 10.32

scale 1:2500

0   20   40   60

HOLME CHASE, Weybridge plan: 1966;
62 DWELLINGS; 62 GARAGES

Fig 10.33

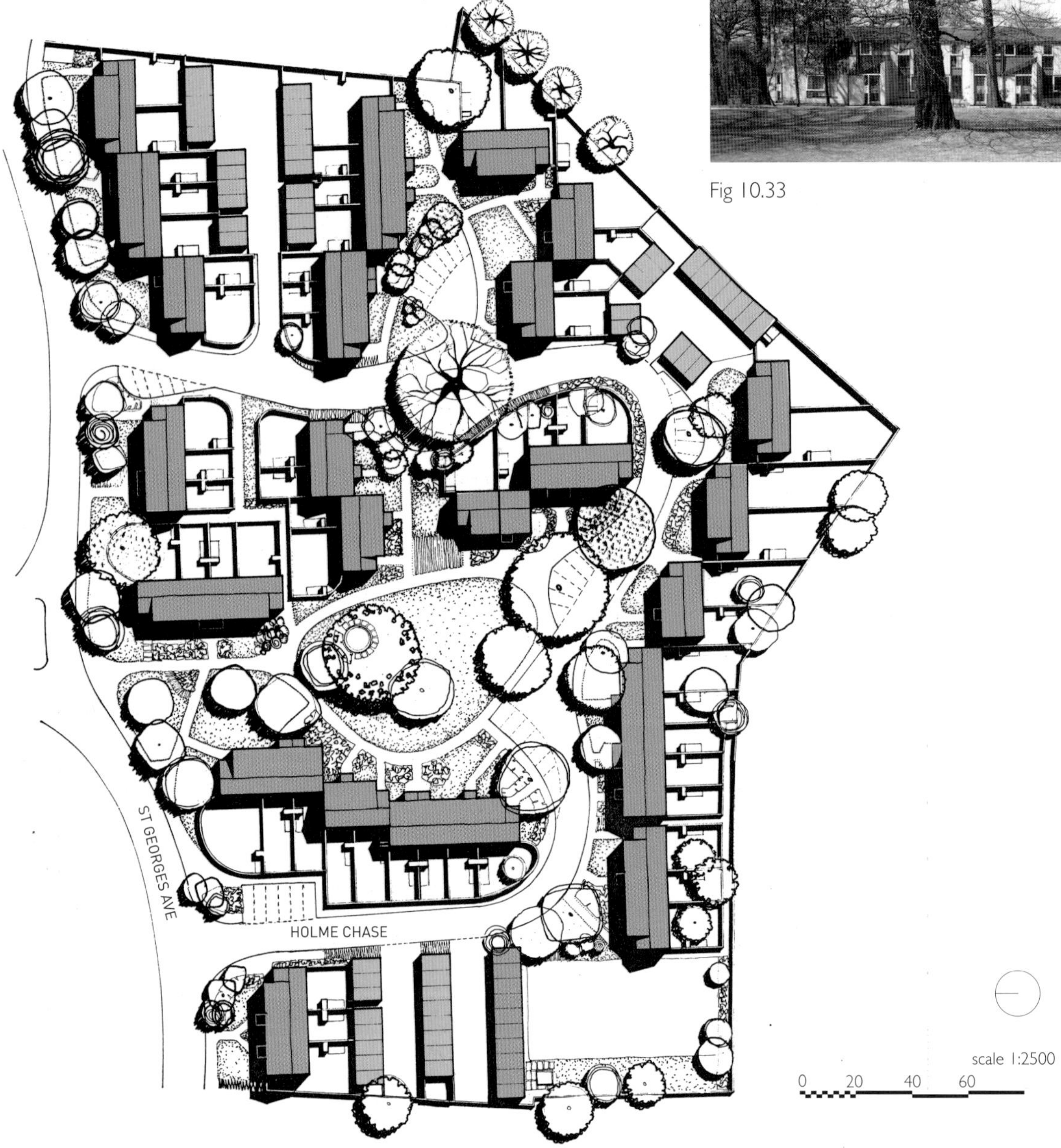

ST GEORGES AVE

HOLME CHASE

scale 1:2500

0   20   40   60

WEYMEDE, Byfleet plan: 1966;
130 HOUSES, 139 GARAGES

Fig 10.34

scale 1:2500

0   20   40   60

PARVIS ROAD

GREEN LANE

RIVER WAY

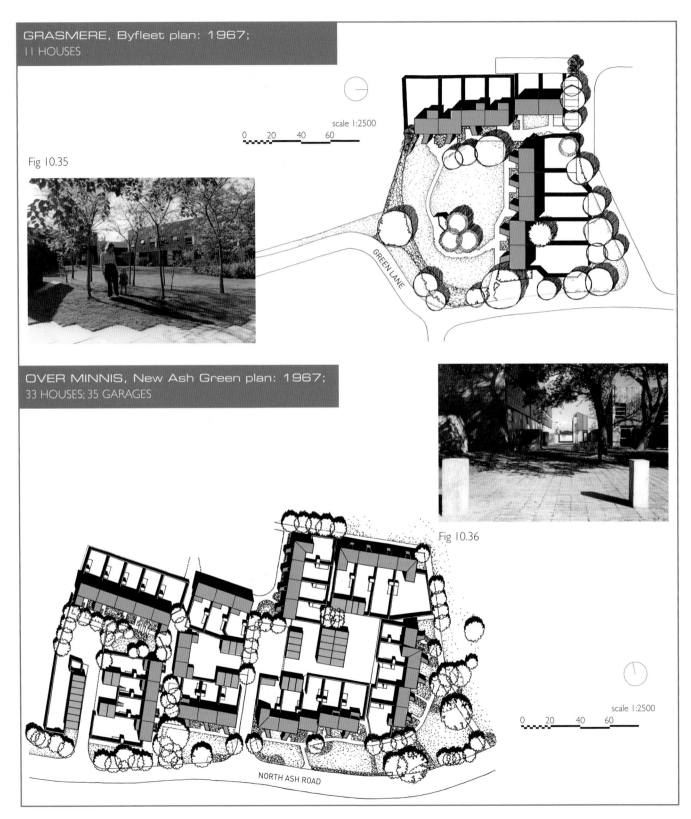

GRASMERE, Byfleet plan: 1967;
11 HOUSES

scale 1:2500

0   20   40   60

Fig 10.35

GREEN LANE

OVER MINNIS, New Ash Green plan: 1967;
33 HOUSES; 35 GARAGES

Fig 10.36

scale 1:2500

0   20   40   60

NORTH ASH ROAD

PUNCH CROFT, New Ash Green plan: 1968;
140 HOUSES; 144 GARAGES

Fig 10.37

scale 1:2500

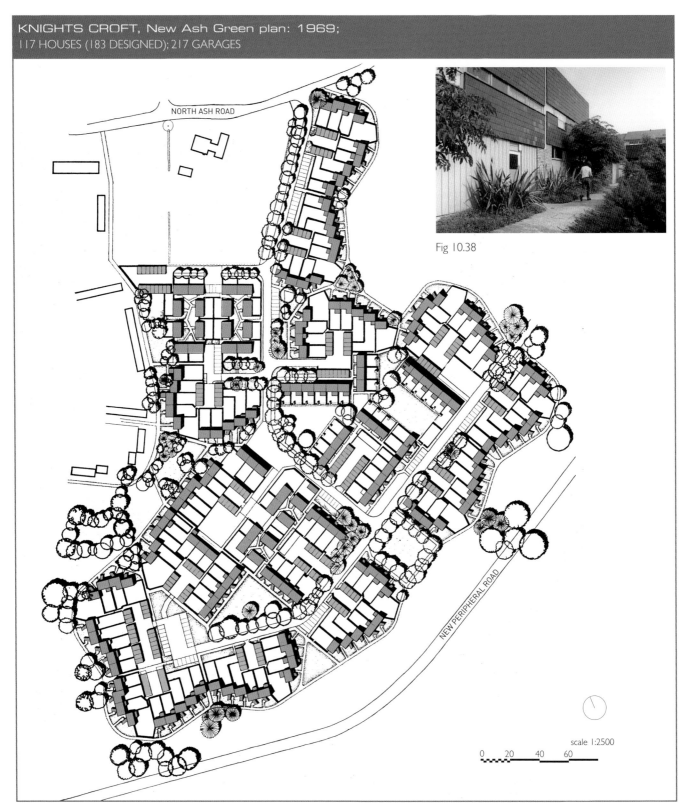

KNIGHTS CROFT, New Ash Green plan: 1969;
117 HOUSES (183 DESIGNED); 217 GARAGES

NORTH ASH ROAD

NEW PERIPHERAL ROAD

Fig 10.38

scale 1:2500

0   20   40   60

LAMBARDES, New Ash Green plan: 1969;
37 HOUSES (57 DESIGNED); 83 GARAGES

Fig 10.39

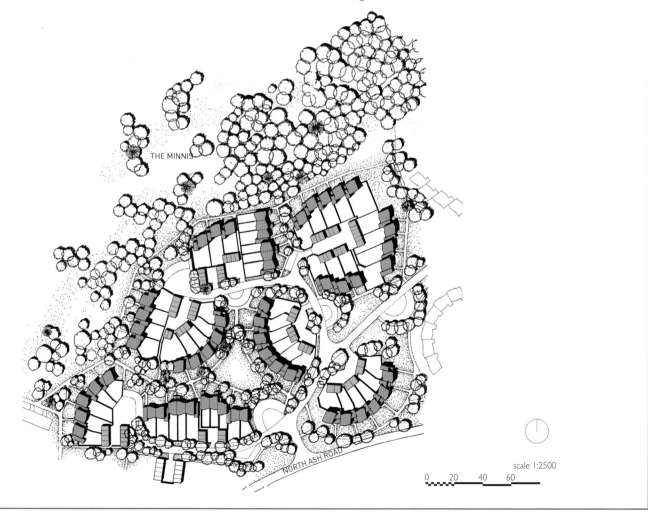

THE MINNIS

NORTH ASH ROAD

scale 1:2500

0   20   40   60

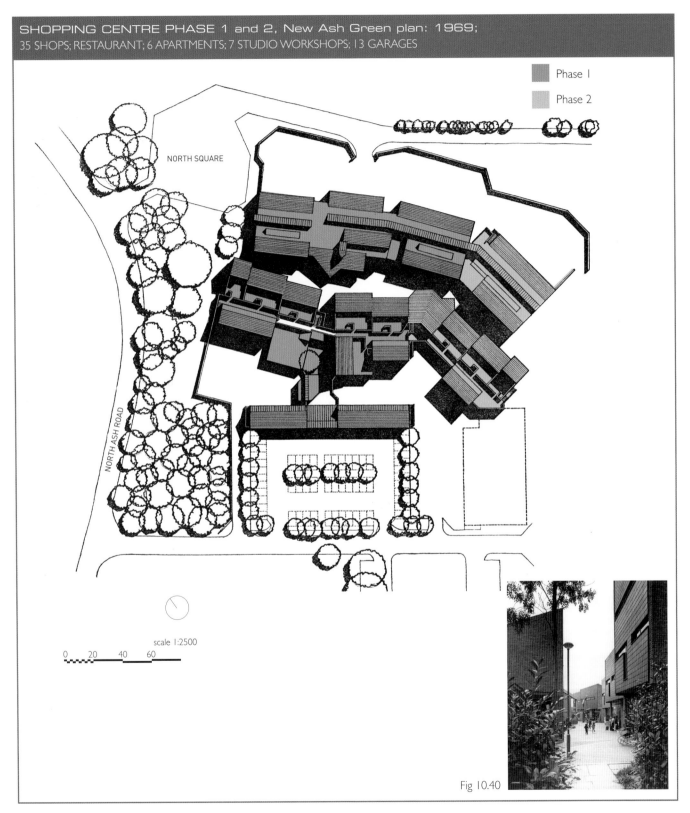

SHOPPING CENTRE PHASE 1 and 2, New Ash Green plan: 1969;
35 SHOPS; RESTAURANT; 6 APARTMENTS; 7 STUDIO WORKSHOPS; 13 GARAGES

Phase I

Phase 2

NORTH SQUARE

NORTH ASH ROAD

scale 1:2500

0   20   40   60

Fig 10.40

CORNER KEEP (CORNER GREEN PHASE 2), Blackheath plan: 1979; 10 HOUSES; 11 GARAGES

Fig 10.41

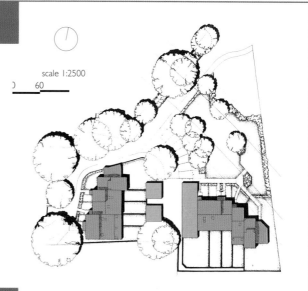

scale 1:2500

0   60

MALLARD PLACE, Twickenham plan: 1984; 45 HOUSES; 57 FLATS; 34 GARAGES

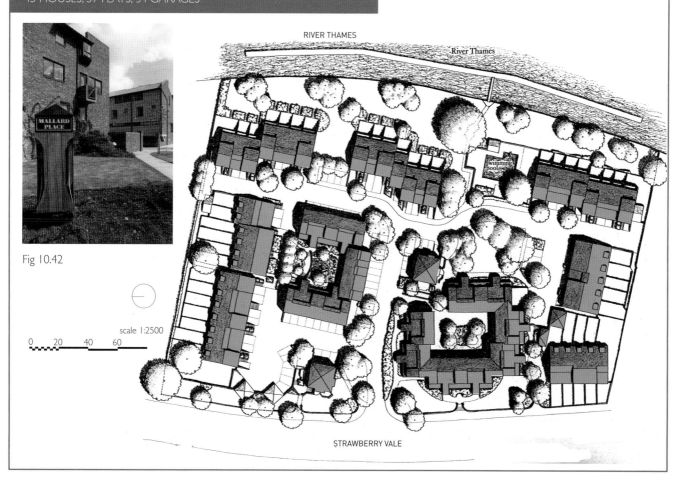

Fig 10.42

scale 1:2500

0   20   40   60

RIVER THAMES

River Thames

swimming pool

STRAWBERRY VALE

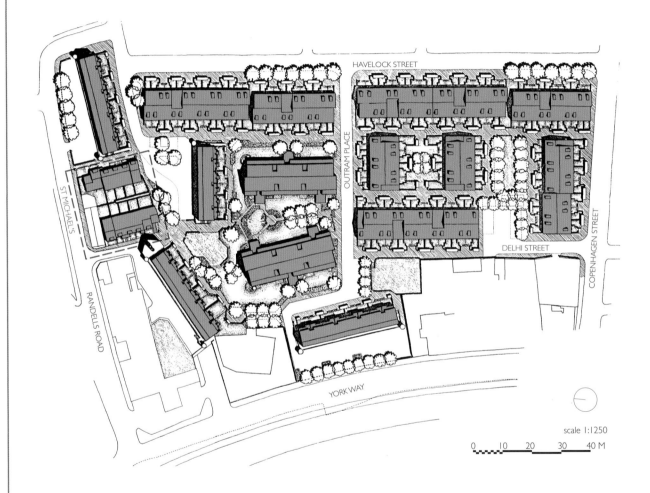

DELHI STREET ESTATE, Islington, plan: 1979 (St Michael's completed 1982)
110 HOUSES; 60 MAISONETTES; 72 FLATS (370 PERSONS PER HECTARE)

HAVELOCK STREET

OUTRAM PLACE

ST MICHAELS

RANDELLS ROAD

DELHI STREET

COPENHAGEN STREET

YORK WAY

scale 1:1250

0   10   20   30   40 M

WORLDS END, London plan: 1979 (Eric Lyons Cadbury-Brown Group Partneship)
742 FLATS, SCHOOL, CHURCH AND COMMUNITY CENTRE

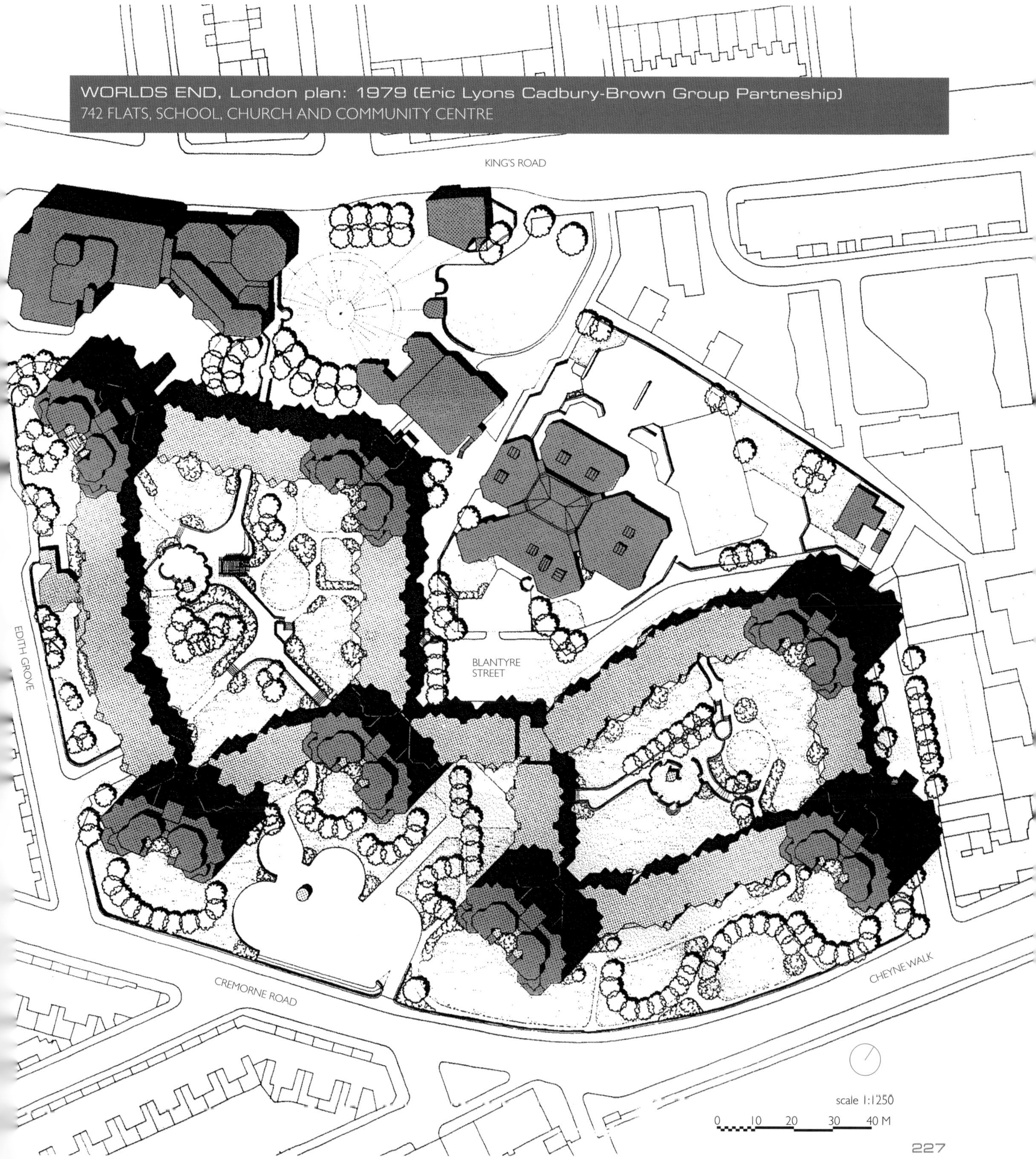
KING'S ROAD
EDITH GROVE
BLANTYRE
STREET
CREMORNE ROAD
CHEYNE WALK
scale 1:1250
0 10 20 30 40 M

House of Ideas 1957 (T3 house Foxes Dale, Blackheath)

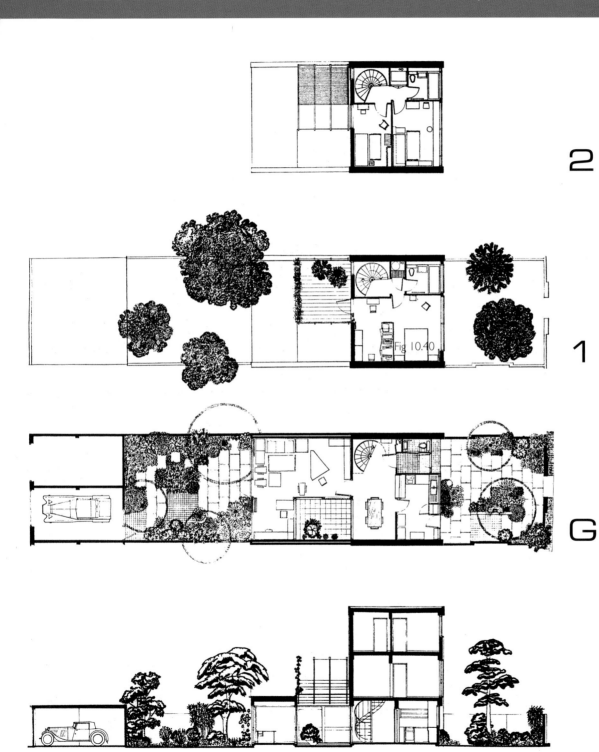

2

1

Fig 10.40

G

Fig 10.43 Photograph of number 2 Foxes Dale (the House of Ideas), one of the most spatially complex Span houses

Fig 10.44 View of the internal garden and study.

Fig 10.45 View of garden and study alcove.

T1 to T2Y house types

The progression from T1 to T2Y (at Templemere) mirrors the progression of the larger T8 form as an option for families. The T2Y becomes a 'foil' to the L1 house allowing terraces to curve and snake through the landscape.

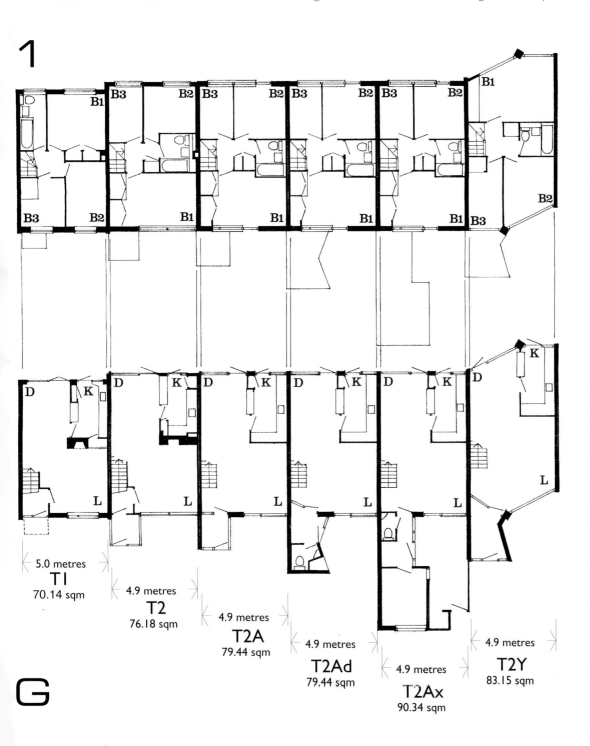

1

G

5.0 metres
T1
70.14 sqm

4.9 metres
T2
76.18 sqm

4.9 metres
T2A
79.44 sqm

4.9 metres
T2Ad
79.44 sqm

4.9 metres
T2Ax
90.34 sqm

4.9 metres
T2Y
83.15 sqm

Fig 10.46 Photograph, from garden, of the living room glazed screen of an early T2 house (The Cedars, Teddington).

Fig 10.47 View back to garden from T2 living room: note alignment of glazing bars and central pivot with the glazed screens and cabinets of the kitchen (The Cedars, Teddington).

T8 to L1 house types

A family of house forms assembled by Ivor Cunningham showing the progression of another Span 'standard', the T8, enlarged to make the T7 (at little extra constructional cost). This starts a progression of plan forms that could be 'handed' or mirrored. This provided compositional flexibility as well as sharing services connections. The logical progression from 1957 (the T8) to 1965 (the L1) is as much about understanding the impact of landscape on the house form (individually and as a terrace) as on construction.

1

G

9 metres

8 metres

11.8 metres

L1
129.5 sqm

6.1 metres	6.1 metres	6.1 metres	7 metres	7 metres
T8 81 sqm	**T7** 92.5 sqm	**T15** 100 sqm	**T16** 108 sqm	**T17** 126 sqm

scale 1:200

0 1   3   5   7   9 M

Fig 10.48 Interior of a T8 house at Fieldend. The T8 house has the kitchen at the front (Fieldend) or rear (The Plantation). As with the T2, the small size of the house is masked by the views through into other spaces.

10.49 View of study and enclosed stair. Note the posed pine beam: houses were made affordable by ng cheap materials but detailed to articulate spaces.

Fig 10.51 Porch of a T7 house at Corner Green: privacy, threshold, connection to exterior and light.

10.52 Interior
an L1 house at
nplemere, looking
he private garden
study. The
itional sliding
en allows clear
vs of landscaping
m the living room.

Southrow

Fig 10.50 Interior of one of the 10 terraced houses on the south and west sides of the Southrow quadrangle. The quality of finishes reflects the prestigious site.

Fig 10.53 Maisonette living room.

INDEX

Page numbers in italics refer to illustrations.

Prelims

pp. ii-xiv All images © Tim Crocker

Chapter One

p. xvi © Tim Crocker

p. 2, Fig 1.1 © Ivor Cunningham

p. 2, Fig 1.2 and 1.3 © Kate Lyons

p. 3, Fig 1.4 © Kate Lyons

p. 4, Fig 1.5 © *Architects Journal*

p. 5, Fig 1.6 © Kate Lyons

p. 6, Fig 1.7 © ELCM

p. 7, Fig 1.8 © Tanya House

p. 8, Fig 1.9 © Ivor Cunningham

p. 8, Fig 1.10 RIBA Library Photographs Collection

p. 9, Fig 1.11 and 1.12 © Kate Lyons

pp. 12-4, Figs 1.13 & 1.14 © Ivor Cunningham

p. 15, Fig 1.15 © Louis Hellman

p. 16, Fig 1.16 RIBA Library Photographs Collection

pp. 17-8, Figs 1.17 & 1.18 John Donat / RIBA Library Photographs Collection

p. 19, Fig 1.19 By kind permission of the trustees of Feliks Topolski. © Feliks Topolski (photo: Tim Crocker)

Chapter Two

p. 22, [Corner Green] Photo: Sam Lambert

/ RIBA Library Photographs Collection

p. 24, Fig 2.1 From: Thomas Sharp, *English Panorama*, J. M. Dent, London 1938

p. 24, Fig 2.2 RIBA Library Photographs Collection

p. 25, Fig 2.3 © Gavin Stamp

p. 25, Fig 2.4 © Alan Powers

p. 26, Fig 2.5 RIBA Library Photographs Collection

p. 27, Fig 2.6a © Taylor and Green

p. 27, Fig 2.6b © David Green

p. 28, Fig 2.7 © Emo Goldfinger

p. 28, Fig 2.8 From: Gibberd and Yorke, *The Modern Flat*. RIBA Library Photographs Collection

p. 29, Figs 2.9a-2.9c From: Trystan Edwards, *One Hundred New Towns for Britain*, 100 New Towns Association 1934

p. 30, Fig 2.10 From: Elizabeth Denby, 'All Europe House', *Architects Journal*, RIBA 1939

p. 31, Figs 2.11 & 2.12 From: Clarence Stein, *Towards new Towns for America*, Chicago Publican Administration Service 1951

p. 32, Fig 2.13 © Peter Chermayeff

p. 32, Fig 2.14 From: F.R.S.Yorke, *The Modern House in England*, The Architectural Press 1937. RIBA Library Photographs Collection

Chapter Three

p. 34 [Holm Chase] © Tim Crocker

p. 36, Fig 3.1 From: Raymond Unwin, *Town Planning in Practice*, T. Fisher Unwin, London 1909, p. 357

p. 36, Figs 3.2a & 3.2b From: Clarence Stein, *Towards New Towns for America*, Liverpool University Press 1951, p. 41

p. 37, Figs 3.3a & 3.3b From: E.A. Gutkind, *Creative Demobilisation: Volume 1 Principles of Town Planning*, Kegan Paul, Trench, Trubner, London 1943, pp. 24, 75

p. 38, Fig 3.4 From: Patrick Abercrombie, *Greater London Plan*, HMSO 1945

p. 39, Fig 3.5 From: *Architectural Design*, 30, 1960, pp. 347-8

p. 41, Fig 3.6 © Ivor Cunningham

p. 42, Fig 3.7 © Barbara Simms

p. 43, Fig 3.8 Preben Jakobsen, 25 March 1966

pp. 44-5, Figs 3.9 & 3.10 © Tim Crocker

p. 46, Fig 3.11 © Barbara Simms

p. 47, Fig 3.12 © Tim Crocker

p. 48, Figs 3.13a & 3.13b From: Brian Clouston, *Landscape Design with Plants*, Heinemann Newness, Oxford 1977, pp. 48, 50

Chapter Four

p. 52, [Castle House, Southampton] Photo:

238

p. 231, Fig 10.48 Photo: Henk Snoek

p. 231, Fig 10.49 Photo: Sam Lambert. © ELCM

p. 231, Fig 10.50 John Donat / RIBA Library
Photographs Collection

p. 231, Fig 10.51 Photo: Sam Lambert. © ELCM

p. 231, Figs 10.52 & 10. 53 John Donat / RIBA
Library Photographs Collection